PRAISE FOR INSID[

C000176542

There are fewer books that can actually c[...]
see themselves and the world around ther[...]
the tools to sustain that change. Inside M[...] [...]
of writing that simply changes you. The paradox innate to its genius – is
that, once animated by you, it can ultimately lead you to discovering that
which is not subject to change, within yourself.

Joanne Sarah Avison – Structural Integrator, Author & Lecturer,
Director of AOCY

Inside Meditation – An in-depth expose and the most comprehensive and
instructive book that demystifies meditation. It helps you to come to peace
with life and everything in it, to create lasting change from within.

Carmel Greenwood; Author of 'Letting Go & Loving Life' (Random House &
Penguin); 'Soul energy' (Random House) & 'Wake up Mum'.

Alexander leads by example. His enthusiasm for the subject is infectious. He
has thoroughly researched, implemented and experienced the processes of
meditation from both Eastern and Western perspectives. His ability to
communicate his experiences clearly and with passion is admirable. One
always leaves his presence refreshed and with a different outlook on life
situations. We are very much looking forward to his writings and continuing
this journey with his teachings.

Pashenka Gribbin & Nick Cervonaro Yoga Teachers

It has been a privilege to have been a recipient of the teachings imparted by
Alexander who in turn has continued to unveil the wisdom and knowledge
of his teachers in a most profound, yet personal way. Freely given to those
who have been true seekers, Alexander has directed each of us toward the
light within us, that is our inner essence. Through his pragmatic teaching of
the work we have, through our shared endeavours, revealed the loving
presence of the eternal, unchanging nature within. This unveiling of our
inner reality through meditation has been a process of love made visible,
facilitated by Alexander and gifted to us through Grace.

Jennifer Ellis Yoga/Meditation teacher

INSIDE
MEDITATION

IN SEARCH
OF THE
UNCHANGING
NATURE WITHIN

ALEXANDER FILMER-LORCH

Matador
9 Priory Business Park,
Wistow Road, Kibworth Beauchamp,
Leicestershire. LE8 0RX
Tel: (+44) 116 279 2299
Fax: (+44) 116 279 2277
Email: books@troubador.co.uk
Web: www.troubador.co.uk/matador

ISBN 978 1780881 997

British Library Cataloguing in Publication Data.
A catalogue record for this book is available from the British Library.

Typeset in 12pt Adobe Garamond Pro by Troubador Publishing Ltd, Leicester, UK

Matador is an imprint of Troubador Publishing Ltd

Printed and bound in the UK by TJ International, Padstow, Cornwall

Dedication

This book is dedicated to my great friend Shelagh.

She is terminally ill and is teaching me about dying and non-identification, like no book or teacher possibly ever could.

She has never become her illness, that's her simple method, and because of that she has become a living example of the essence of the universal teachings.

So this is her book, containing lots of things I've learned from her during our weekly walks with the dogs and during the treatments I was privileged to give her after these walks.

Here is what she said to me last week:

"I will always be a whisper in your ear once I am gone." Then she laughed.

I know it's true because she always keeps her promises.

My dear friend Shelagh departed peacefully two days ago on Tuesday the 13th of March 2012 and kept her promise.

Contents

Joanne Sarah Avison on Inside Meditation

There are many books *about* things. They contain ideas from the author or wonderfully woven stories of fiction and inspiration. Others might list facts and instructions, or present information visually and intellectually – *about* their subject.

There are fewer books that can actually *cause* the reader to change how they see themselves and the world around them – and fewer still that can provide the tools to sustain that change. Inside Meditation is one of those rare pieces of writing that simply *changes* you. The paradox innate to its genius – is that, once animated by you, it can ultimately lead you to discovering that which is not subject to change, within yourself.

It has been a privilege to be a close friend of Alex over many years and watch him in action, developing and expanding his unique ability to express this work. To see it encapsulated in such clear and beautiful language is like holding treasure. For a thirsty being, the gift of a fruit and the taste of a sweet juice is heaven sent. This book is an orchard of fruit trees that has an endless supply of sweet juice – if only we take the care to pick it…and taste it and – literally and symbolically – *juice it.*

Inside Meditation has life within its pages. The author has lived the life of the work himself over many years of dedication and it is the concentrated essence of that experience. It is a body of work that is presented with clarity – while it contains some of the deepest mysteries about the being of human beings. You, the reader, are invited to join in with this experience and become part of that body of work. It is not an intellectual "download" to be read and learned. It is a profoundly beautiful invitation to walk an authentic path to your Self – while you live your life. Indeed, it deepens and expands the experience of every day life itself. Eventually *that* becomes the teacher.

Inside Meditation is also a lot of fun! It is written with a lightness of heart despite the very serious nature of the work. That is what makes it so delightful to be in the classroom with Alex. There is as much laughter as there is quiet, inexorable change – accumulating gently over time. This book is like that, if you allow yourself the time to read a little here and a little there and engage in the exercises. It will not do it *for* you – it can – and *does* – provide an authentic and safely lit pathway to walk for yourself, to the point that you choose to travel.

That pathway glows with Grace – and this book is a grace field that will expand with you as you work with it. The true magic lies in the questions it invites you to ask, the observations it encourages you to make and the experiences it invites you to accumulate. The rest just happens as it does.

My profound gratitude to you Alex for the treasure your work has been in my life – and for the difference it has made to me. That means the difference it has made directly and indirectly to all those I have worked with. In Native American wisdom, the Spider is the bringer of writing, of words expressed on a page, like a web woven in an exquisite matrix. May the Grace and elegance with which you have woven these threads inspire many people to see and treasure the jewels at every connection – and share them in the same spirit.

Thank you, with love,

Joanne Sarah

Foreword

Who has the time to meditate? Across the globe our conventional boundaries are dissolving and economies are in flux. Virtual organisations and new technologies mean that our certainty about how everything in life works dissolves too. The world is no longer linear and predictable and this gives rise to ambiguity and anxiety.

There are at least two natural human reactions to such spectacular uncertainty. One is to seek absolute assurance. The other is to search for meaning in order to cope in a world of ever-increasing complexity. Alexander Filmer-Lorch's book is a beautifully timed publication. He teaches us how to find that still point in the centre of ourselves so that we can deal with whatever life throws at us.

Alexander is a virtuoso of movement. A child born with physical abnormalities, he turned these to advantage, dancing with a major European ballet company by the time he was seventeen. He went on to develop innovative syntheses of schools of yoga, Pilates, cranio-sacral and somato-emotional release. In my first encounter with him I physically expanded – my body rediscovered movements on his Gyrotonic machine that I had not been able to do for some 20 years. I had had an amateur training in contemporary dance, Graham technique, and in minutes Alexander had me, effortlessly, back into a level of movement my body had long forgotten. I loathe gym machines but this was working dynamically in all three dimensions with a master practitioner who knew exactly how to unlock me. This was joyful flight!

Alexander is also a sage of the dynamic between body and mind. Now he has written a manual in which he shares his thirty years of deep study and practice of integrating 'self' on all planes. Reader beware – this book is not for complete beginners – there is much literature already available for the novice. However, if you are serious about deepening your awareness and all aspects of your life, then you will find an immensely practical resource for a lifelong journey. You will find many inter-linked lessons for finding 'the unchanging nature within'.

All of Alexander's learning has taken place, and continues to do so, in the crucible of his own heart, mind, body and spirit. Despite the many schools he has learnt from, he is no eclectic practitioner – Alexander *integrates* his learning. This means he does not just pull out one theorem, exercise or another as the mood or situation suits. He has a deep emotional, intellectual and physical understanding of the principles from many schools of thought and practice. By exquisite discernment, he brings together inter-relating aspects into powerful new forms. He has achieved this with his version of dynamic myo-fascial flow yoga, working with the body and mind in refined attunement, taking the benefits to new levels – using methods, which suit the western body. I have witnessed the tremendous regard that yoga teachers have for Alexander.

As a corporate psychologist, a key clinical interest of mine is: how do some people learn to thrive, not only survive, in extreme situations? I work with leaders who need to find ways of transforming organisations and people despite greatly reduced resources in ever more turbulent times. As a professional mediator, I observe that those people who are able to tolerate multiple realities are those who are more likely to find creative solutions. I cannot help but notice that those who have a strong, integrated sense of self have a great advantage. The big question is: how does that strength come about?

The research that has come out of the Mind and Life Institute[1] arose from the combined efforts of an international community of neuroscientists together with advanced practitioners of Tibetan Buddhist meditation. Their findings reveal that the East has much to teach the West in advancing our knowledge of neuroplasticity and inner balance. It is crucial that we heed these ideas if we are serious about bringing about peace in turbulent times. So many people clamour for a more humane world[2]. A fundamental and recurring theme is that we need to let go of certitude, surrender to ambiguity and suspend our overly critical minds. Only then will we see the patterns emerge that will guide us to each next step.

Like those scientists from the Mind and Life Institute, and psychologists such as Professor Marvin Levine[3], Alexander interprets ancient wisdom for contemporary Westerners facing new challenges. He has been putting this wisdom into practice in his daily life for thirty years. This cross-cultural integration benefits all groups. It is precisely the blend of modern science with foreign knowledge paradigms that creates the potential for new forms of knowledge. This is new knowledge that goes far beyond the sum of the parts of these unusual bedfellows. It takes the lifetime dedication of a practitioner like Alexander to gift us with practical, but deep, teachings.

The point of meditation is not to escape reality or become a superb meditator – but to lead a fully conscious and rich life - one lived with self-awareness, objectivity, equanimity and compassion. A life that offers something back to humanity. Alexander's approach focuses on just that. He does this with unquenchable curiosity, lightness and infectious humour. My hope is that you become infected with the desire to live a more conscious, more kindly, more fully lived life.

Valerie James
London, England 2012

1. Introduction

Life wrote this book and I just happened to be there.

Unfortunately I wasn't there all the time, which sounds like a paradox. If only I'd known what life had in store for me, I would have been much more appreciative, humble and thankful during the periods of struggle, friction and resistance. But that's with hindsight and at the time I simply didn't know any better.

MEDITATION is such a big word, full of pre-conceived ideas and daunting for so many people I encounter.

Some of the most common responses I get when giving talks or lectures about meditation are:

"Oh I can't meditate."

"Isn't that about blanking my mind and stopping my thoughts?"

"I am actually thinking all the time so I will never be able to stop my thoughts in the first place."

"Isn't that where people do that OM thing?"

"I have no time for meditation, because my life is too busy."

This demonstrates just how little is known and understood about the many aspects that comprise the vast field of meditation and philosophy.

For most people, meditation has never been a natural part of our modern culture, upbringing or conditioning, where the development of intellect, knowledge, formative thinking and academic understanding is encouraged and believed to be an essential requirement to succeed in life.

Very little is known about the science of meditation, which generously offers very powerful tools and specific techniques, that enable us to respond differently to life's events, in order to help us grow into our full potential; to develop a true sense of self, as well as to enable us to look and understand things from a greater perspective and, ultimately, to find our very own meaning in life, as a compassionate and balanced person.

This book is not a theoretical book and it will challenge you on all levels.

It is not based on any belief system. Nor does it claim to show you another path or shortcut to enlightenment.

In fact, if you are casually reading this book, or just looking to accumulate additional theoretical knowledge, it does not promise you anything at all. Rest assured, you have already acquired enough theoretical knowledge in your life.

My teachers have always stressed this point: **The path of meditation is about action; becoming active, practical and using one's common sense**.

So this book is an attempt to inspire and encourage you to *put things into action*.

If you do choose to implement and practice the different techniques and exercises described in this book, *and put them into action*, you might be surprised by exactly what the path of meditation has to offer you.

You might start to think and feel differently; perceive differently and discover possibilities and a wealth of potentialities within yourself, and in your life, that you hadn't seen or recognised before.

The only prerequisite you need to study and practice the path of meditation, is a strong, deep longing and desire to change and evolve. Everything else will fall into place and the 'how's & why's' will be answered along the way.

You will find a brief autobiography about my personal journey and quest for the unchanging nature within, at the end of the book. If you want to know what attracted me to this work and how it became an integral part of my life, please don't hesitate to go straight to chapter 17 My Own Journey.

How to use this book

Inside Meditation is written for all those people who have a sincere interest in meditation and philosophy.

The following comments are intended to guide you towards a deeper understanding when reading this book. Some of them were direct instructions from my teachers. Others came through various 'A-ha' moments whilst studying books on philosophy and psychology, as well as hours of daily self-practice. But most of them evolved throughout thousands of sessions with clients, teaching classes, leading workshops and teacher trainings, giving lectures and facilitating people through their own inner development.

Some of the techniques and exercises in this book may become a long-term part of your life. Sometimes, this is what's required to transform theoretical knowledge into your very own personal experience.

At first the process of meditation and self-study is slow, especially when your objective is to manifest something more permanent. However, once you regularly put the theory into practice, results can be seen relatively quickly.

Applying the techniques in this book and observing the results for yourself, is the only way to prove and discover that whatever is said or advised theoretically is true and not just based on hearsay.

All theories need to be proven. If we take them for granted, or think that others will do the practical work for us, then we live in imagination and all that we study and read will fall into the department of *belief.*

When reading this book you will come across Great Ideas, theories and exercises that are unfamiliar or entirely new to you.

It is important that you:

- Don't try to explain or interpret these new ideas and knowledge from the perspective of your old knowledge[4].
- Don't blindly believe or take for granted that whatever you read is true.
- Don't judge new ideas or techniques.

3

- Keep an open mind. Instead of dismissing an idea or concept, work to put the theory into practice and this way you can base your judgement on sound personal experience.
- Don't expect instant results.
- Avoid judging yourself and others along the way.
- Leave plenty of space for questions, which might not be answered instantly. These answers will come when you are ready to understand.
- Be gentle with yourself. It's not the quantity of practice or a rigid discipline that leads to results.
- Some of the themes or techniques in this book might not make any sense to you in the beginning. Come back to them at a later point, they will become full of meaning when you are ready for their knowledge.
- Keep a diary of all your observations, discoveries and experiences along your journey. This will become very useful much later in life and are written proof of how far you have already come.
- It is vital to keep your inner experiences to yourself. Only share them with your teacher or facilitator. Be aware that a certain kind of knowledge has to be told, we can't invent it out of our own limited understanding. It usually is passed on and never should be considered one's own possession.
- Don't compare your process with that of others or let yourself be put off by their wonderful and uplifting experiences during meditation. In meditation and self-study we are not interested in other people's achievements. This kind of practice can only be done by you.
- And most importantly, don't take yourself too seriously and enjoy.

The work, or the process, is divided into **nine stages**.

It begins with an understanding of the different brain functions, our intellect and the physical body, and then leads into the emotional and energetic. In addition you must explore the functions of mind and thought, down to more refined ways of perception and levels of consciousness, which illuminates what lies beyond our human mind and uninterrupted thought patterns.

This book focuses on the most important and accessible aspects of meditation and philosophy, as well as self-study and the underlying psychology of meditation. Only you can make the exercises and ideas come to life, so please be aware that any book can only take you that far.

I actively encourage you to start meditating right now.

There is no need to first read the whole book before starting to practise mediation. In fact, regular meditation practice will help to assimilate the new ideas.

My advice is to start practising the *Rooting Meditation*, which is described in the section Asanas For The Finer Body within Chapter 15 called The Art of Meditation.

Inside Meditation intends to ignite your curiosity and interest to practice regularly, until meditation becomes an inseparable part of your life - enriching it with happiness, joy and contentment.

2. The Origins of Meditation

If one starts to inquire into the origins of meditation one soon discovers that there is very little documented knowledge or research available as to how, when and where meditation originated.

According to findings in history and various sources of literature, meditation dates back to more than 5,500 years ago, to around the same time as the invention of writing.

The earliest evidence of prehistoric religion dates back to the late Neolithic Age in the early Harappan period (5,500-2,600 BCE). Several seals discovered at Indus Valley Civilization sites dating to the mid-third millennium BC, depict figures in positions resembling a common yoga or meditation poses, showing, 'a form of ritual discipline, suggesting a precursor of yoga', according to archaeologist Gregory Possehl.[5]

A connection between the Indus Valley seals, and later yoga and meditation practices, is much speculated upon by many scholars, although there is no conclusive evidence.[6] More specifically, scholars and archaeologists have remarked on the close similarities between the yogic and meditative postures depicted in the seals with those of various Tirthankaras (the kayotsarga posture of Rsabha and the mulabandhasana of Mahavira), along with seals depicting meditative figures flanked by upright serpents bearing similarities to the iconography of Parsva. This evidence suggests a link between Indus Valley Civilisation and Jainism, and also show the contribution of Jainism to various yogic practices.[7]

Historians agree that the evolution of meditation gave rise to philosophy, psychology and all major religions. Descriptions of meditation practice can be found in Hinduism, Buddhism, Mayan Culture, Taoism, Islam and Christianity.

When looking at the wider picture, the ability to express concepts in words, requires the ability to put these concepts into a greater perspective based on a more refined awareness of their relationship to the whole. This ability seems to be directly related to the biological evolution and development of the way our brain functions. It is believed that the development of the voice box (allowing sounds) and the re-organization of the brain structure (without altering in size), facilitated the ability to develop language.

It is these changes that distinguish the Neanderthal from the Cro-Magnon man.

'The Cro-Magnon Man was able to produce a variety of tools, weapons and pieces of art 50,000 years ago, which led to the invention of watercrafts and to colonisation in Australia and New Guinea and ultimately the whole world.

Highly developed burial sites had been found dating back 40,000 years, which is evidence that our Cro-Magnon ancestors had stepped away from what was necessary for immediate survival. They treated the dead with respect, which shows that they had developed a greater perspective on themselves, their families and enemies, which evolved into an interactive mechanism in our brains and indicated the beginning of modern consciousness.'[8]

Terminology

The English word *meditation* is derived from the Latin *meditatio*, from a verb *meditari* – meaning, 'to think, contemplate, devise, ponder, meditate'.[9]

- In the Old Testament hāgâ (Hebrew: הגה), means to sigh or murmur, but also to meditate. When the Hebrew Bible was translated into Greek, hāgâ became the Greek *melete*. There is a hidden pointer in both to sigh or murmur, which also means to meditate in the sense, that in this case to murmur means to repeat a mantra, a technique which will generate a state of meditation, as well as to sigh points towards the empty pause of the breath in which all thought stops and a moment of meditation can be experienced.
- The Latin Bible then translated hāgâ/melete into *meditatio*.[10] The use of the term *meditatio* as part of a formal, stepwise process of meditation goes back to the 12th century monk Guigo II.[11]

Apart from its historical usage, the term *meditation* was introduced as a translation for Eastern spiritual practices, referred to as *dhyāna* in Buddhism and in Hinduism, which comes from the Sanskrit root *dhyai*, meaning to contemplate or meditate.[12]

The word meditation in English may also refer to practices from Islamic Sufism,[13] or other traditions such as Jewish Kabbalah and Christian Hesychasm.[14]

Scholars have noted that the term meditation as it has entered contemporary usage is parallel to the term 'contemplation' in Christianity.[15]

History

Data suggest that even at prehistoric times older civilizations used repetitive, rhythmic chants to appease the gods.[16] Some authors have even hypothesised that the emergence of the capacity for focused attention, an element of many methods of meditation,[17] may have contributed to the final phases of human biological evolution.[18]

- References to meditation with Rishabha in Jainism go back to the Acaranga Sutra dating to 500 BC.[19]
- Around 500-600BC Taoists in China and Buddhists in India began to develop meditative practices.[20]
- In the west, by 20BCE Philo of Alexandria had written about some form of 'spiritual exercises' involving attention (prosoche) and concentration[21] and by the 3rd century Plotinus had developed meditative techniques.
- The Pāli Canon, which dates to the 1st century BCE, considers Indian Buddhist meditation as a step towards salvation.[22] By the time Buddhism was spreading in China, the Vimalakirti Sutra, which dates to 100CE, included a number of passages on meditation, clearly pointing to Zen.[23]
- The Silk Road transmission of Buddhism introduced meditation to other oriental countries, and in 653 the first meditation hall was opened in Japan.[24] Returning from China around 1227, Dōgen wrote the instructions for Zazen.[25]
- The Islamic practice of Dhikr has involved the repetition of the 99 Names of God since the 8th or 9th century.[26]
- By the 12th century, the practice of Sufism included specific meditative techniques and its followers practiced breath control and the repetition of holy words known as mantras.[27] Interactions with Indians or the Sufis may have influenced the Eastern Christian meditation approach to hesychasm, although this cannot be proved.[28]

- Between the 10th and 14th centuries, hesychasm was developed, particularly on Mount Athos in Greece, and involves the repetition of the Jesus prayer, which is a technique that directs the focus of the mind into a meditative state.[29]
- Western Christian meditation contrasts with most other approaches in that it does not involve the repetition of any phrase or action and requires no specific posture. Western Christian meditation progressed from the 6th century practice of Bible reading among Benedictine monks called Lectio Divina (divine reading).
- Its four formal steps as a 'ladder' were defined by the monk Guigo II in the 12th century with the Latin terms *lectio, meditatio, oratio*, and *contemplatio* (i.e. read, ponder, pray, contemplate). Western Christian meditation was further developed by saints such as; Ignatius of Loyola and Teresa of Avila in the 16th century.[30]

By the 18th century, the study of Buddhism in the West became a topic for intellectuals. The philosopher Schopenhauer discussed it,[31] and Voltaire asked for toleration towards Buddhists.[32] The first English translation of the *Tibetan Book of the Dead* was published in 1927.[33]

- Secular forms of meditation were introduced in India in the 1950s, as a Westernised form of Hindu meditative techniques but didn't arrive in the United States and Europe until the 1960s. Rather than focusing on spiritual growth, secular meditation emphasizes stress reduction, relaxation and self- improvement.[34]
- Both spiritual and secular forms of meditation have been subjects of scientific analysis.
- Research on meditation began in 1931, with scientific research increasing dramatically during the 1970s and 1980s. Since the beginning of the 1970s more than a thousand studies of meditation in English language have been reported.[35]

The External and the Internal World

Ever since humankind have developed the ability to place their lives in context to a bigger whole, an internal drive and longing to explore and inquire has given rise to a number of universal and unanswered questions, including:

- Why are we here?
- What is the purpose of this life?
- What animates this body?
- Is there another existence after death?
- What created this whole universe?
- What is life's purpose and is there such a thing as a creator who created this universe?

Despite this questions, man's initial quests where focused on the external, rather than the internal, world. People's research of the external world evolved into sciences with the very early scientists discovering the Laws of Nature; developing machines and concluding that everything is made up of five elements.

In ancient times philosophy, psychology, alchemy and cosmology were considered to be four different aspects of the internal and external universe, encompassing one unity.

The development of religious and philosophical structures led to an examination of the internal world and the mind. As the research evolved, more refined levels and frequencies, belonging to higher faculties were discovered, though often lying dormant. A variety of pranayama techniques were developed with the sole propose of defining what was to become known as consciousness.

In the meantime, scientists came to the conclusion that the world is comprised of 108 elements, each element being made of atoms, each with a different attribute attached to it. Further research proved that the atoms were not the underlying basis of everything; that there existed another building material, which they named electron. With more refined devices they discovered that the electron had two properties: it is both moving and not moving and it acts like a particle and like a wave. This gave rise to a new definition —'the quantum', which means dual.

After years of more research, they discovered that on a very subtle level the electron is nothing more than an infinitesimal formless energy particle and that it is this particular energy, which can transform itself into an electron and subsequently into matter.

While the first group of people progressed in researching the external world, the second group, through focusing their attention inwards, had refined their techniques to such an extent, that they discovered a subtle, all encompassing, frequency known as the **Universal Pulse of Consciousness**, which is omnipresent throughout the whole universe and infinitely present in all there is.

Thus in time, Western science may well come to the same conclusion that the underlying building material is not an infinitesimal energy particle but the pure, ever expanding universal pulse of consciousness.

3. Scientific Research on Meditation

Since the beginning of the 1970s more than a thousand studies have been carried out on meditation. However, much of this work is fragmented and uncoordinated. The research was taken more seriously after collaborations took place in 1992 between Richard Davidson, a neuroscientist from the W.M Keck laboratory for Functional Brain Imaging Behaviour at the University of Wisconsin, and the Dalai Lama.

During a lecture at the annual meeting of the Society for Neuroscience in Washington DC in the autumn of 2005, the Dalai Lama shared his personal experience with the audience of scientists, that meditation was very hard work for him (he meditates for four hours every morning). He suggested that if the scientists could find a way to develop a device which could be connected to the brain and could provide him with the same outcome as he gets from his meditation, he would definitely become a volunteer!

After learning about Davidson's innovative research into the neuroscience of emotions, the Dalai Lama became very interested and ultimately sent eight of his most experienced meditators to Davidson's laboratory, so that the research could explore the workings of his monks' meditating minds.

'The Buddhist practitioners in the experiment had undergone training in the Tibetan Nyingmapa and Kagyupa traditions of meditation, for an estimated 10,000 to 50,000 hours, over time periods of 15 to 40 years. As a control, ten student volunteers with no previous meditation experience were also tested after one week of basic meditation training.

The monks and volunteers were fitted with a net of 256 electrical sensors and asked to meditate for short periods. Thinking and other mental activity are known to produce slight, but detectable, bursts of electrical activity as large groupings of neurons send messages to each other, and that's what the sensors picked up. Davidson was especially interested in measuring gamma waves, some of the highest-frequency

13

and most important electrical brain impulses that can be generated within the brain'.[36]

Before we look into the encouraging results of Davidson's experiments we need to gain a greater understanding of brain functions; their different frequencies as well as the way the brain perceives and translates external impressions.

Meditation And The Human Brain

The brain is conventionally divided into three parts: the fore brain, the mid brain and the hindbrain. The brain forms the central part of our nervous system, which is the most complicated system in the body.

The bulk of the brain, called cerebrum, is divided into two hemispheres, the right brain and the left-brain hemispheres. Both hemispheres are symmetrical and each of the hemispheres interacts with one half of the body.

The Function of The Left-Brain Hemisphere:

- The left-brain hemisphere controls the right side of the body and is the seat of our personality. Linear reasoning, language and grammar, precision and arithmetic skills belong to the left-brain function. Our left-brain thinking is logical, sequential and rational. From the perspective of Far-Eastern psychology, we can say that the left-brain hemisphere symbolises the quality of *attention* - an active force enabling us to give greater attention to detail and to zoom in.

The Function of The Right-Brain Hemisphere:

- The right-brain hemisphere controls the left side of the body and is the seat of our intelligence. Processing visual and audio logical stimuli, facial perception and artistic ability belong to the right brain function. Right brain thinking is random and intuitive, holistic, synthesizing and looks at the whole. From the perspective of Far Eastern psychology, the right-brain hemisphere symbolises the quality of *awareness* - a passive force enabling us to put things into a broader perspective and ultimately into relation to the whole.

A Brief Anatomy of The Brain

In the same way that our body needs regular exercise to stay healthy and strong, the brain also needs specific training and exercises to be able to work to its full potential. We often underestimate the impact and benefits that we can gain from giving the brain some 'time out' on a regular basis. These periods of rest allow the brain to synchronize, assimilate and integrate life's uninterrupted sensory impressions, to be able to stay healthy throughout our entire lifetime.

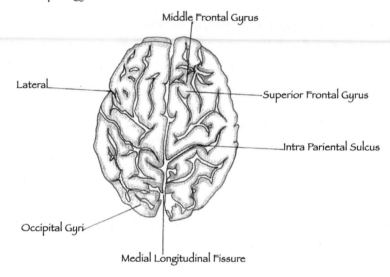

Illustration: Annabelle Hartley

Understanding the design and complexity of this beautiful instrument we all take for granted, gives us vital insight into precisely how this structure functions. It allows us to understand that the slightest imbalance in brain function will impact on the homeostasis, or equilibrium, in our body.

For a more detailed understanding of the Anatomy of the Brain, please refer to Appendix A.

Our Five Senses

Each of our five senses (*hearing, sight, touch, smell, and taste*) is made of a complex structure of neurons, which stimulates a specific area in our brain. This impulse is then interrupted by the brain, becoming a conscious signal in the process.

For the sense of sight the following process occurs. The entire field of our vision is made up of, and divided into, billions of little pixels, which are filled with vibrating atoms and molecules. Our retinas in the back of our eyes are able to detect the movement of the atomic particles. The atoms vibrate at different frequencies and consequently different wavelengths of energy are emitted, which are translated into different colours, edges, shapes and motion by the visual cortex at the base of the back of our skull. This complex process enables us to grasp and see three-dimensional shapes, forms and spaces, instead of vibrating atoms, frequencies and pulsations, which are the underlying reality of all there is to see.

The sense of sound is also achieved via a similar biological process. Sound is an energy, which travels at different wavelengths. It is produced by colliding atomic particles travelling in space, that create different energy patterns. The tympanic membrane in our ear is bombarded by countless waves of sound and the hair cells of our hearing faculty called Organ of Corti, translates these energy vibrations into a neural code. From there, the information travels to the auditory cortex located at the temporal area of our brain, enabling us to hear sound, understand words, listen to music and the sound of nature, instead of perceiving the sound of billions of colliding atoms, which is the underlying reality of all there is to hear.

The closest we can come to sense and experience atomic or molecular sensations, is via our sense of taste and smell. Our taste/smell receptors are very sensitive to different electromagnetic particles and can distinguish them via a complex cortex of cells, which link to the reptilian brain.

Our skin, called the epidermis, is the second largest sensory organ after the fascial matrix, which is the most intricate and most complex of all organs. The epidermis is filled with a variety of different sense receptors, each of which are individually designed to experience pain, touch, temperature, vibration, light and pressure.

The functions of our five senses determine the way to which we respond and perceive the world. Any imbalance in one or the other sensory organ will restrict the way we perceive and are able to live in the world or interact with people.[37]

To biologically evolve means 'to develop by evolutionary process from a primitive to a more highly organized form.'[38]

Our human brain is in a process of constant evolution. The brain today looks different to the brain of our ancestors. However, in regards to a person's individual brain major change is not something that occurs. Unlike most of the cells in the body, which die and are replaced within weeks or months, neurons, are stable and remain in place. This means that the majority of neurons in our brain today are as old as we are. This longevity of the neurons, partially accounts for why we feel pretty much the same on the inside at the age of 10 as we do at the age of 30 or 77. The cells in our brain are the same but over time their connections change based upon their/our experience.[39]

The Different Brainwaves

Our brain is made up of billions of brain cells called neurons, which use impulses to communicate with each other. The combination of billions of neurons, all sending signals at once, produces an enormous amount of activity in the brain, which is commonly called a Brainwave Pattern.

Our brain regulates its activities by emitting tiny electrochemical impulses of varied frequencies. These frequencies can be measured by a clinical device called Electroencephalogram or EEG.[40]

The EEG is typically described in terms of (1) rhythmic activity and (2) transients.

The rhythmic activity is divided into bands by frequency. To some degree, these frequency bands are a matter of nomenclature (i.e., any rhythmic activity between 6–12 Hz can be described as "alpha"), but these designations arose, because rhythmic activity within a certain frequency range was noted to have a certain distribution over the scalp or a certain biological significance.

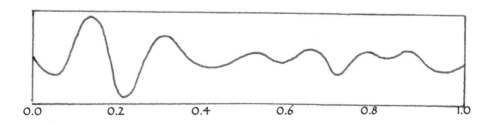

One Second of EEG signal

Illustration: Annabelle Hartley

Most of the cerebral signal observed in the scalp EEG falls in the range of 1–20 Hz.

There are five main brainwaves called, beta, alpha, theta, delta and gamma.

- **Beta waves** have a low amplitude but are the fastest of the main four brain waves. We emit beta waves when the brain is aroused and engaged in mental activities. For example, when we are in conversation with another person, we would be in a beta state. If we were teaching, speaking, or are engaged with our work, these would all be beta states. Typically beta waves will range in frequency from 13 to 30 cycles a second.

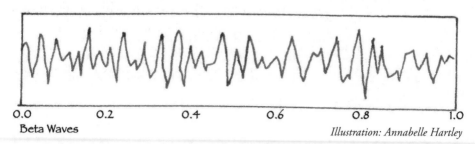

Beta Waves

Illustration: Annabelle Hartley

- **Alpha waves** are next in order of frequency. They are much slower than the beta waves and have higher amplitude. Alpha waves represent non-arousal and calmness. When someone takes time out to rest or relax, they are typically in an alpha state. It is when we calm our mind and feel peaceful. Alpha waves can range in frequency from 8 to 13 cycles a second.

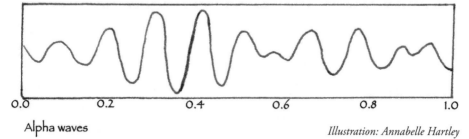

Alpha waves

Illustration: Annabelle Hartley

- **Theta waves** are even slower than alpha waves and have higher amplitude. Theta waves can be difficult to accomplish, because they require a complete break from our conscious reality. Most of us have experienced times when we simply blank out from the world, where we are daydreaming or perhaps driving and suddenly realize we can't remember the last ten minutes of the drive. Theta waves are often induced by things of a repetitious nature, for example when our actions become so automatic that our mind disengages. The frequency range of theta waves is typically between 4 and 7 cycles per second.

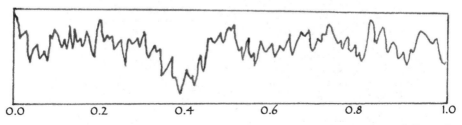

Theta Waves   *Illustration: Annabelle Hartley*

- **Delta waves** occur when we are in deep dreamless sleep. Our brain frequency in this state is very slow and of the greatest amplitude. The frequency range is usually somewhere between 1.5 to 4 cycles per second, which it is about as slow as one can get without causing damage to our brains.

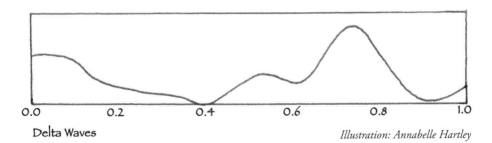

Delta Waves   *Illustration: Annabelle Hartley*

- **Gamma waves** are often not distinguished as a unique class of brain wave by some researchers. It's worth noting that until recently, gamma waves were not researched to the same extent as the other four brain waves. Today they have gained more popularity and are known to be associated with perception and consciousness. Gamma waves can be between 30 and 100 Hz per second but most often correspond to frequencies of 40 Hz or higher. It has been shown that gamma waves are typically present during the process of awakening, as well as during active rapid eye movement in (REM) sleep, as well as in a state of deep meditation.

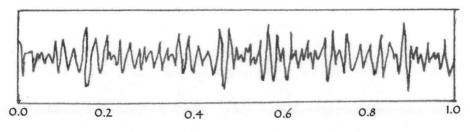

0.0   0.2   0.4   0.6   0.8   1.0

Gamma Waves   *Illustration: Annabelle Hartley*

Summing up the different brainwave frequencies:

- During the day, we are usually in a beta state.
- When we go to bed, and possibly read a book for a while, we will likely be in a low beta state.
- Once we turn the lights off and close our eyes, our brainwaves will begin to descend from beta, to alpha and eventually to theta.
- Once we fall deep asleep, we will experience the delta waves.
- Gamma waves are present when we are awakening from sleep, as well as during REM sleep. In addition, meditation and the state of absence of thought and mind activity will simulate gamma waves.

What The Scientists Discovered

The results from several research programmes on meditation, which are described on the following pages, prove what mystics have known for hundreds of years and what long-term practitioners experience on a daily basis in their meditation practice.

The single most important finding from the scientifically valid research is that:

Meditative practice changes the brain.

Brain research is producing definitive evidence that meditation can change the way our brain works and enables people to experience different and more refined levels of consciousness.

It was formerly believed that those transformed states of consciousness, could not be measured and objectively evaluated. However, research at the University of Wisconsin has translated those mental states into scientific language by testing brain synchrony, high-frequency gamma waves and coordination. Whilst working with the Tibetan monks, gifted by the Dalai Lama, researchers were able to accurately detect an area in the brain (behind the left frontal bone called left frontal cortex), where brain activity during meditation was most intense.

Richard Davidson[41] found that long-time meditators showed brain activation on a scale never previously recorded. It was also discovered that the patterns of brain activity produced by regular mental practice was similar to that seen produced by sustained practice of sports such as golf or tennis.

This clearly demonstrated that the brain is capable of being trained and physically modified in ways few people can possibly imagine.

Scientists formerly believed that brain cells and nerves were fixed at an earlier stage in life and could not change in adulthood. This was disproved through brain research and is now replaced by the concept of on-going brain development and neuroplasticity. Davidson feels that meditation study[42] is taking this concept of neuroplasticity a step further by showing that meditation can itself change the inner workings and circuitry of the brain.

The meditative practice experienced by the Tibetan monks, and volunteer control group, was not focussed on a particular object, image or the breath, but instead, worked to cultivate a transformed state of being.

Davidson's results showed that the trained minds of the monks were activated in significantly different ways than the minds of the volunteers. But most importantly, the electrodes picked up far greater activation of fast moving and unusually powerful gamma waves in the monks. The results also showed that the movement of the waves through the brains of the monks was far more organized and coordinated than the movement of the waves in the volunteers.

Some of the monks produced gamma wave activity far more powerful than previously reported in any healthy person. The monks who had spent the most time in meditation throughout the years showed the highest level of gamma wave activity. Davidson indicated that this 'dose response', in which higher levels of activity have greater effect than lower levels, is significant in assessing cause and effect.

In previous studies, mental activities such as focus, memory, learning and consciousness were associated with the kind of enhanced neural coordination found in the monks. The intense gamma waves found in the monks, have also been associated with knitting together disparate brain circuits and are also connected to higher mental activity and heightened awareness.

Davidson's research is consistent with his earlier work that pinpointed the left prefrontal cortex as the brain region associated with happiness and positive thoughts and emotions. Using functional magnetic resonance imagining (fMRI) on the meditating monks, Davidson found that their brain activity, as measured by the EEG, was especially high in this area.

He concluded that meditation not only changes the workings of the brain in the short term, but also quite possibly produces permanent changes.

Appendix B contains an abstract of a scientific research paper on the impact of regular meditation practice.

The Benefits of Meditation

Compassionate Meditation Can Reduce Stress And Anxiety

Another study by Richard Davidson[43] discovered that by cultivating compassion and kindness through meditation, brain regions are affected, that, in turn, make you more empathetic to other peoples mental and emotional states.

The research showed that long-term meditators exhibited significant activity in the brain's insula, which is an area known to be important in detecting emotions and monitoring responses such as heart rate and blood pressure. In addition, the temporal parietal juncture area of the right brain, associated with processing empathy became very active. These two areas of the brain studied with an fMRI, underwent significant activation in the test subjects.

The research led to the conclusion that a person's capacity to cultivate compassion, which involves regulating thoughts and emotions, may be useful in preventing depression. Self-compassion, which is the necessary first step in developing compassion for others, can be developed through meditation.[44]

A second study concluded that meditation improved an individual's response to stress. Practicing meditation showed reductions in inflammation and distress, in response to stressors. It reflects several studies, which also showed that meditation is an effective method for controlling high blood pressure.

Both studies demonstrate that practicing meditation regularly can be beneficial both to the individual and in relationships with others.[45]

Meditation practice delivers benefits that go all the way down to the chromosomal level.

Tonya Jacobs,[46] has reported that meditators show improved psychological well being, and that these improvements lead to biochemical changes associated with resistance to aging at the cellular level. Specifically, an analysis of meditators' white blood cells showed a 30% increase in an enzyme called telomerase, a chemical essential to the long-term health of the body's chromosomes and cells.

The scientists emphasize that meditation does not lead directly to cellular health and longevity. *Instead, the practice appears to give people an increased sense of meaning and purpose in life, which in turn leads to an increased sense of control over their lives and to less negative emotion.*

This cascade of emotional and psychological changes is what regulates the levels of telomerase, the anti-aging enzyme.

Positivity appears to be the link between meditative practice and a variety of health benefits.

In a study[47] UC Davis psychological scientist Baljinder Sahdra reported that meditation leads to a decrease in impulsive reactions. This is important since impulsivity has been tied to an array of health problems, including addictions and other risky behaviour.

It's well known that stress, and distress, lead to poor health, including a decline of telomerase and its healing properties.

What hasn't been known, and what these studies are beginning to document, is the exact order of psychological and physiological events in this chain and, what's more, that this chain of events can be reversed.[48]

Meditation Produces Alterations in Brain And Immune Function.

Negative psychosocial influences on immunity have now been well established.[49]Recent research indicates that relaxation and stress management procedures increase T-cy- totoxic/suppressor (CD3 CD) lymphocytes in individuals.[50]

Another study performed by Richard Davison explored the effects of meditation on brain and immune function. Twenty-five healthy subjects were tested in an eight-week meditation programme. Their electrical brain activity was measured directly after the training programme and a second time four months later. At the end of the eight weeks the people taking part in the study were vaccinated with an influenza vaccine.

Researchers found significant increases in antibody reaction to the vaccine in the meditators, as compared with the non-meditators. These findings led to the conclusion that even a short training programme in meditation produces a demonstrable effect on brain and immune function and that meditation is changing our brain and immune function in a very positive way.[51]

The Impact And Benefits of Alpha Brain Waves

When we diminish our brain rhythm to alpha, we put ourselves in the ideal condition to learn new information. We are able to keep facts and store data or perform elaborate tasks like learning languages and analysing complex situations.

Both relaxation exercises, and activities that induce a sense of calm, can produce this alpha state.

Research studies have shown that attentive relaxation or deep relaxation techniques produce significant increase in the levels of beta-endorphin, norepinephrine and dopamine, which are linked to feelings of enlarged mental clarity, and that this effect can last for hours and sometimes even days.

The alpha state is an ideal state for synthetic thought and creativity. It is easy for the right-brain hemisphere to create images, or to visualize ideas and concepts or to make associations.

The Impact And Benefits of Theta Brain Waves

The discovery of Great Ideas and inspirations is often linked with the production of theta waves. Theta waves induce a shift in consciousness that draws us into a deeper state of meditation. The abundant healing properties of theta waves means that they are able to impact on all levels.

They enable us to blank the world and detach from the physical in meditation and they connect us with our sixth sense, our intuition.

It is important to understand that theta-brainwaves are not inducing higher states of consciousness. This is indicated by the fact that they are easily produced while we execute habitual patterns and tasks during the day, shifting us into states of daydreaming or imagination. From a self-study point of view theta waves belong to a lower level of consciousness, which obscures our ability to self-observe.

The Impact And Benefits of High Frequency Gamma Brain Waves

Our brains normally produce only short bursts of gamma waves. These gamma waves are associated with perception and consciousness and are mostly produced during the process of waking up in the morning or in REM sleep. However, deep states of objectless meditation will also stimulate gamma waves.

No other brain wave can alter and synchronize brain wave activity to the same extent as the high frequency gamma waves, which lead to possible lasting changes in the brain. The gamma waves produce positive alterations in our immune functions leading to biochemical changes on the chromosome and cellular levels. They can also help to regulate our thoughts and emotions reducing high blood pressure, anxiety and stress.

Conclusion

Scientific research demonstrates that long-term meditation practice, not only enables us to evolve within and experience different states of consciousness, but also has a positive, and lasting, impact on our health and wellbeing.

Long-term meditation is the tool to continuously evolve our own brain and to develop more compassion and relatedness towards ourselves, as well as to others.

Scientists have identified three types of meditation practice.

- **Deep Relaxation Techniques**: These take us into the alpha state in which we enhance our learning abilities, store data and gain mental clarity and a sense of calm.
- **Object Meditation/Focused Attention Meditation**: This is the focus on the breath, a mantra or an image. During object meditation changes in the networks of the brain were seen that are known to improve attention. Object meditation takes us into the theta state which impacts on our self-healing properties and draws us into a deeper state of meditation.
- **Objectless Meditation/Open Monitor Meditation**: This mediation type doesn't focus on a specific object, but rather cultivates a state of being. This advanced state of meditation produces sustained high frequency gamma activity in the left cortex of the frontal lobe, which ultimately leads to permanent changes of brain function in long-term meditators.

4. The Benefits And Limitations of Philosophical Books

Almost since the first written word, scholars, mystics, yogis, philosophers and scientists have made their knowledge available to us through their books and other publications. These types of books were originally designed to transmit a certain kind of knowledge, or Great Ideas, that was not produced by mind created life.

Books, which are intended to transmit this knowledge, can be divided into several categories:

- **Highly academic or conceptual books,** which are mainly based on theory and address our intellect and formative thinking as well as our analytical mind and more pragmatic understanding. These include books on anatomy or physics and maths, as well as books on medicine, law or biology. Lawyers, medical students and all academically conditioned people who respond more intellectually to their surroundings, are usually drawn towards this first kind of book.
- **Entirely practical books**, which usually teach and describe a special protocol or discipline, such as a specific yoga programme.
- **Books that touch us on an emotional level** such as a biography describing someone's journey and life experience. Nurses and social workers, as well as artists and anybody who responds through feelings and emotions to their surroundings, are usually inspired by this third kind of book.

The majority of books fall into these first three categories. They are written to inspire and teach. Though individually they have little power, if our mind gets enough food and excitement out of this particular literature the impressions and imprints they produce within, accumulate and start touching us on a deeper level.

The next four categories of books require a more serious engagement from the reader and take much more time to be absorbed and assimilated, due to the density of the knowledge they contain. Very often, these books follow us throughout a longer period in our life and we are drawn back to them repeatedly.

- **Books, which are a combination of the first three categories** and have an impact on us on a much deeper level of understanding. They awaken in us new possibilities or different ways of thinking, as well as encouraging us to explore Great Ideas.
- **Books, which are connected to a higher source of consciousness and enrich our life with greater meaning.** The knowledge transmitted in these books is based on sound long-term experience. These books are full of hints and pointers that direct us towards a greater perspective. They are written in a neutral language and always emphasise people's potential for inner development and ability to evolve. The perception of the content of these kinds of books is constantly changing in accordance to the state of consciousness of the readers.
- **Books, which transmit their knowledge through poems, parables or stories.** These types of books usually require the reader to undergo special preparation and training before they are able to obtain an objective understanding. The reader is required to read 'between the lines' in order to access a deeper knowledge and hidden meaning. These books carry an energy that awakens a special kind of finer emotions, as well as leaving the reader in a state of awe.
- **The last category of books can't be discussed since they may no longer be around or simply don't attract anyone's attention.** In essence they are hidden. This may be due to the fact that the secret hides itself. Personally, I have never come across a book falling into this last category, but have not given up on the possibility of encountering one.

The understanding that there is an almost infinite amount of knowledge contained in books, answering practically every question we have, gives rise to the question - *Where are the limitations of books to be found?*

The answer is simple.

The limitations of books can be found in the readers themselves. People are rarely in a neutral state of mind that allows these precious books to be observed through clear and objective lenses. Readers are usually wearing their own individual subjective lenses, which prevent them from assimilating the transmission of knowledge or being open to new or Great Ideas. Some knowledge does not even enter, because it is unconsciously blanked out or filtered. Sometimes only a part of the knowledge enters and instantly transforms into half-knowledge, which in turn contains only half of the truth.

In time, a certain amount of accumulated half-knowledge turns into a personal concept based on the individual's interpretation and most often into something entirely different - far removed from the original idea and the source from where the knowledge originated.

People are used to explaining new ideas with what they already know, which leads to misunderstanding and misinterpretation.

This is because people can only absorb knowledge from the level of consciousness or state of mind they are in at a particular moment in time. This explains why, if a person reads the very same book a couple of years later, they experience different 'A-ha' moments and are usually hit by the question, "Why haven't I seen or understood this before."

However, no matter how profoundly a book impacts on us and regardless of how much knowledge it is able to transmit, if it does not make us question and think differently; if it does not penetrate through our old ideas and ways of being and kick start a process to put its message into action, it will only remain a humble and passive device.

5. The Meaning of Scale

The term scale is mainly applied to systems containing the capacity to expand, yet very little is known about the internal psychological scale or the cosmological universal scale.

The moment one contemplates on the meaning of scale and the possibilities the meaning of scale provides, one realizes that everything we see or experience has an almost infinite degree of scale attached to it, hence all we can observe externally or internally can be perceived from different perspectives along the line, or within the different dimensions of scale.

Many systems, ideas, concepts or events can't be grasped, understood or experienced to their full extent, without keeping the idea of scale in mind. Practically applying the idea of scale to the relevant things in life expands our limited way of thinking and has a transformative impact on perception, hence it leads to greater freedom in the way we respond.

Scale is a vibration, which is under the influence of increasing or decreasing laws, depending on whether we are ascending or descending within its field or range of possible expansion.

The higher its frequency the less limiting our take on things becomes and the less identified we will become.

The lower its frequency, the more limiting our view on things will be and the more identified we will become.

There are different dimensions to scale and we are most familiar with the scale of cartography, which is a two dimensional or linear scale. Cartography portrays the ratio between two points on a map to the real distance between the two corresponding points. Scale can be expressed numerically like 1:100,000 or verbally like one centimetre on the map equals one kilometre on the earth. A map on a large scale shows much more detail than a map on a small scale.

Another very familiar scale is the musical scale or octave in which ascending and descending notes are arranged by the composer in a specific scheme of intervals to create a piece of music.

In medicine the idea of scale is used to measure mental and physical developments using a graded series of tests.

Scale in maths is the notation of a given number system. A ruler or other measuring device represents the idea of scale as well as a weighing device.

The scale of architecture takes us into three dimensions and features the relationship between different dimensions of organized space and structures in their relationship to the viewer. The scale and size of buildings, not only impresses the viewer, but also creates different moods, which are the result of the total interaction of dimensions in space, underlying every element of the composition. A variety of artistic effects can be achieved by creating a perfect balance between the geometry, height and textures and the way natural light enters the building. A relatively small architectural structure viewed from the outside, can give a much larger impression and sense of spaciousness once one enters the building, depending on the structural layout and use of space.

Grand scale structures like ancient temples and cathedrals often symbolize the power and social position of the person ordering its construction. Some of them intend to make us feel insignificant where others are supposed to create an image or feeling, which is understood not only by contemporaries but also by future societies and cultures.

A completely different kind of scale is the scale of events in everyday life.

Our life from birth to death is nothing more than a succession of events. Each day is a structure of events that are crowded in on many different scales.

It is personal events that attract most of our attention, and these can be divided into external and internal events, which take place simultaneously. Our attention is constantly drawn back and forth between internal and external events, depending on the intensity of their gravitational pull of importance or priority.

As we move along the scale we come to family events, that see us usually discussing the internal and external events effecting individual family members.

Then there is a larger circle of events gyrating around our personal and family events, which relate to our profession, friends and community. Those are, in turn, surrounded by our local events, which we usually come across by reading our local newspaper or watching a local T.V. channel, though we are not necessarily personally or actively involved in them.

The local events link to our national events, which form part of the world events and all of them take place simultaneously on different scales.

These examples of scale illustrate the point well, but the most impressive and transformative example of scale is the night sky. The impact of the infinite scale of our sky at night reflecting billions of stars, planets and galaxies, can lead to a different sense of scale in both thoughts and ideas.

The expansive nature of the night sky may make us aware of our own insignificance in relation to the whole and in the process connect us with the omnipresence of a far greater presence, which governs and determines all there is - manifesting through myriads of seemingly incidental scales of universal events, which are ultimately forming the events of our own personal life. This different scale of thought, which usually appears when we are touched on a deeper level, awakens our higher emotions and this is the beginning of meditation.

Please take a moment to reflect on the meaning of the last paragraph.

Exercise 1: Defining Scale

- *Observe the succession of events during the following days. Attempt to define the different scales on which they take place in your own life. For example, observe a specific event you experience at work and how you automatically alternate between the external event and the internal event within you. Remember both usually take place simultaneously.*

- *Try to view events from the perspective of other people in your company, team or family. Notice how events impact on the company/team/family as a whole.*

- *Apply this technique of observation to other events you are experiencing in your life, such as going for lunch, meeting up with friends and family, working out at the gym, or preparing dinner. Make notes about the impact of your observations.*

6. The Separation of Theory And Practice

The economic developments of the last century have led to a movement towards increased specialisation within the work force. There is an accelerating trend for increasing compartmentalisation within each profession.

Forty years ago, a General Practitioner doctor had to be skilled and knowledgeable in his field on multiple levels and in numerous areas. Today it would take him or her a lifetime of studies to cover as broad a field of knowledge and the same goes for other professions. Nowadays, surgeons acquire surgical and procedural skills in human dissection virtually via a computer screen. Nurses now have to acquire a degree in nursing. Both outcomes result in an accumulation of enormous amounts of theoretical knowledge.

This development has led to an increased division between theory and practice. This has isolated the world of specialists and theorists from the actual events of life and real people. What seems to work in theory does not necessarily work in real life situations.

We can all remember the time when we actually started working; full of illusions of how much we knew and how it had to be done and applied, before ultimately realising that the real learning process had only just started. So we accepted and embraced life and its events as our teacher. Sometimes it can take decades before we succeeded in transforming all the theories and knowledge we had acquired during our studies to be applicable, workable and most importantly accessible to other people.

It seems to be unavoidable that in whatever we do, our professional life starts by being an apprentice. By repeatedly practicing and applying what we have learned theoretically we become a junior. Through our own effort and the help and guidance of more experienced people around us, we evolve into becoming a senior. Finally, and after many years, we evolve into a master of our profession. It is usually these later people, who are the most highly respected and taken the most seriously, when advice or guidance is sought, regardless of how many certificates, qualifications or degrees the juniors and even seniors have on display in their offices.

Why is this relevant to meditation?

The answer to that is very simple. We are usually drawn towards the idea of meditation at a later stage in our life, once we have gone through decades of accumulated knowledge and life experiences. We might have already acquired all the theoretical knowledge regarding the process of meditation and the philosophy behind it. By that time our head is filled to capacity with concepts, theories, past memories and countless different ideas about all aspects of our life.

All this information can seem to be in conflict with itself leading to friction and even more stress on top of our already stressful life, yet our mind has started to tire and is searching for a way out. In a lot of cases people end up completely burned out or suffer a serious illness such as a heart attack.

Meditation gradually starts to undo and unwind all the highly charged imprints that the accumulation of all the ideas, concepts and theories have left behind in our mind. It slows down the speed of our uninterrupted habitual thought patterns and creates more space between the gaps of our thoughts. It utilises the unbalanced charge of thoughts and emotions, concepts and ideas, to make our perception more spacious. It helps rid ourselves of that which is no longer required in the workings of our mind.

A regular meditation practice might lead to a complete reversal, *an undoing*, of the psychological patterns and habits that have been created throughout our life, and draw us back to the pure state of being we were born with at the beginning of our life. This does not imply that we have lost all of our precious accumulated knowledge. Far from it, as we benefit from both ends of the scale as well as everything in between.

7. Do We Need A Teacher?

From birth we are surrounded by a variety of teachers. The first teachers are our parents who teach us how to speak, eat and behave. They teach us certain boundaries, social ethics and the way we should interact with others. At school we are taught by a succession of teachers across a variety of subjects. Later, we are strongly influenced by what we are taught from our professors, our managers and senior colleagues.

In our private lives we might take lessons in dance, pilates, yoga and sports. Everything we learn, we usually learn from someone who is highly accomplished and trained in the particular subject to which we are attracted and who want to further their mastery and become even more familiar with their field of expertise.

When it comes to meditation, the need for a teacher depends entirely on your personal objective. If your objective is to learn and practice deep relaxation, than a book or listening to a CD will probably do the job. The moment your objective is to work with more refined and advanced breathing and meditation techniques, a book or CD might only take you to a certain level of understanding. Your practice might give rise to certain questions, which may not be addressed by what you find, described in a book.

You will definitely require a teacher if your objective includes *self-study, work on consciousness, the cosmological side of meditation or the whole field of the psychological teaching.*

Why?

The first reason is that certain things can only be transmitted by word of mouth. As an example, a golf teacher can only impart his most secret skills or tips once he has seen your golf swing and observed the habits you have acquired through your golf practice.

The second reason is that it requires a lot of effort and practice to establish a neutral or objective state of mind. We are usually too close to ourselves, or we are standing in our own way, to be able to relate things to a greater perspective

Additionally, without the support and facilitation of a teacher, the attraction and gravitational pull of our meditation practice in itself, might not be strong enough to sustain the initial interest and fascination of our mind over a longer period of time. Soon the mind will become distracted by other more powerful attractions and temptations in life, the mind will then happily allow you to sacrifice the idea of meditation in order to replace it with something more satisfying. That's part of the nature of our mind.

The third reason is, that simply being in the presence of an accomplished person who is settled and completely at ease in what he or she is teaching - whether its sports, carpentry or yoga - can have a powerful influence on how we absorb and practically apply what we are being taught. To these teachers, no question seems unanswerable due to their profound experience and knowledge in their chosen field, which has been accumulated through years of hard work and effort. They know how to speak to many different kinds of people, whilst at the same time, always finding a way to make things work for each individual. They have witnessed the difficulties people are struggling with in certain areas many times before and it does not take long for them to come up with a solution or a different approach, which usually solves the problem.

How does the work of a meditation teacher take place?

This depends on one's own objective and individual needs as well as whether one decides to attend a meditation class or chooses to be taught on a one-to-one basis. Most people choose to learn meditation as an alternative method to stress management, to help balance their stress levels during the day. All modern stress management methods are based on ideas of ancient meditation and psychology. As laid out in the Modern Science and Meditation Chapter, scientific research supports the fact that specific meditation techniques can have a powerful impact on our stress levels and adrenal glands.

Others want to meditate in order to come to terms with upsetting experiences from their past, dealing with conflict or grief. Many people choose to learn meditation to help balance their mood swings, control their emotions or simply because they want a break from the busy chatter in their head.

An accomplished meditation teacher is trained to be able to address and work with an individual's needs and requirements. They are also able to do this in a neutral, patient and non-invasive way; without any trace of judgement, prejudice or personal opinion. A teacher will be un-fazed by the unknown and their overarching incentive and objective is to facilitate change in a safe and transformative way. Yet they can only instruct and guide a person up to the level of experience or state of being they themselves have established within, via the help of their own teachers or facilitators.

Illustration: Erika Shapiro

8. The Process – Stage I:
Understanding The External World

In order to fully grasp the power of meditation, the process or idea of meditation has to be put into context with ourselves as the *subject* and everything or everybody else as the *object*. This can be thought of as our sense of ''I' or 'me' (internal world), in relation to 'them' (external world).

Most people struggle with the great divide between their internal and their external experiences, which frequently seem to oppose each other, creating a variety of different frictions and contradictions. The main objective of meditation is to manifest balance internally and externally so that the external world is nourished by the internal world and vice versa.

It has to work both ways, otherwise a lasting harmony and centeredness can't be sustained. We have a deeply engrained concept of duality, that is the notion of me as the 'subject' and everything else as the 'object'. Whilst this belief holds the upper hand, then the sense of friction will remain.

This on-going friction (struggle between internal and external) influences the way we act in life, in the process consuming large amounts of physical and mental energies and ultimately creating stress in the body and agitation in the mind.

On the other hand, this friction ultimately brings us to a certain turning point in our life where we start asking different questions and search out possible solutions that would enable us to channel our energies and create a balance between our internal and external world of experiences.

This turning point in life very often brings up the question - "But where and how to begin?"

Where And How to Begin?

The clear realisation that things can't stay as they are, gives rise to many new possibilities. Something that until this point has remained dormant within yourself, yet very alive, begins to gain momentum.

That dormant part deep within you carries the ability to think differently, to feel differently and to move differently. It was buried and enveloped by the deeply engrained habits and conditioning you acquired up to this point in your life.

But how can we possibly bring that other part back up to the surface?

Nothing more is required than to start exactly where you are and how you are. As long as you stay in touch with a strong sounding conviction that a different way and outlook on your life is possible, and as long as your longing to change and evolve within keeps burning – things will simply just happen.

But why will things happen now when they haven't happened before?

Due to your realisation that things can no longer stay as they are, you have suddenly shifted onto another level of consciousness and have distanced yourself from the way you have lived your life internally and externally.

For a glimpse of a moment you have ceased to be 'It'. And the only thing you feel within that moment from the bottom of your heart is: that things have to change, and that it is only you who can change them and nobody else or life itself can change them.

Putting this into a universal or neutral language, this process is called **dis-identification** caused by a positive shock, which connects one with a far greater scale, which could be called, 'the scale of our possible inner evolution'.

The scale of our possible inner evolution enables us to see things in our personal life through a different, or more objective, lens. This allows us to formulate a new objective, which ultimately will manifest as a lasting balance between our internal and external worlds.

However, before this can happen we have to find the correct circumstances. This may mean discovering different methods to which we can relate, and we may have to learn a few new practical skills.

Yet one shouldn't underestimate that in itself, the intensity of the need and desire to change and evolve within, can and will provide the necessary energy and will action, to attract the right circumstances and influences into our daily life, to turn the strong sounding intent of our new objective into a living reality.

Exercise 2: Applying Scale to Friction And Contradiction

The following exercise takes no more than five minutes:

- *Pause for a minute and reflect on possible internal and external frictions and contradictions acting on you in this particular time of your life. You will be very familiar with them because you have met them many times in the past. They usually don't allow you to fall asleep at night and follow you throughout the day.*

- *Become aware of how much energy they take from you and how much time you spend with them during the day.*

- *Close your eyes for a moment and connect with the feeling of how tired you have become of them, without any intent to oppose or resist them.*

- *Be absolutely honest about the extent of your inability to be able to change them and rank them on a scale from 0 to 5.*

- *Then connect with that part within you which longs and desires to rise above your frictions and contradictions, and stay absorbed in it for a couple of minutes.*

- *Practice this exercise for five minutes daily for seven days, without trying to change things or take any action.*

- *After a week re-evaluate the scale of your inability to change them and be aware of what has shifted along the scale from 0 to 5.*

Food For The Intellect

We are all comprised of three main gross bodies. One is the *Intellectual body*, the second is the *Physical body* and the third is the *Emotional body*. Each of these bodies requires very specific food, so that they can function to their fullest capacity and potential.

Besides these three bodies, there are three further functions active within us, and a further three higher faculties, which lie dormant and are waiting to evolve. But let's look at our intellect first, before we explore the other bodies, functions and faculties at a later stage in this book.

To avoid any misunderstanding we have to know how the word 'intellect' is defined and understood by us today.

From a historical point of view the term 'intellect' comes from the Greek philosophical term 'nous', which was translated into Latin as 'intellectus' comprehension or perception, derived from the verb 'intellegere' to understand or perceive, and into French (and then English) as 'intelligence'.

In Western psychology the term Intellect relates to the capacity for understanding, thinking and reasoning as distinct from feeling or wishing.

Besides the definitions of the Intellect described above, it is very interesting to note that 1,200 years ago the term 'heart' had been understood and was used as the seat of our intellect and feelings.

Now, to remind you of what was mentioned in the introduction:

'For most people, meditation has never been a natural part of our modern culture, upbringing or conditioning, where the development of intellect, knowledge, formative thinking and academic understanding is encouraged and believed to be an essential requirement to succeed in life.'

According to this development our intellectual mind has reached a level of gravitas and status in our ordinary life, which makes it appear to be far more superior than any of the other bodies or faculties.

What was known as 'Mind over Matter' in the previous sixty years has turned into 'Development of Intellectual Mind over everything else' today,

45

subconsciously manifesting as the new Mantra of this Millennium.

Nevertheless this describes only one side of the coin.

For example, because we are only giving attention to, and are attracted by, the illuminated side of the moon due to its beauty and constellation to the earth and the sun, we hardly ever consider that there is a whole other side to the moon, which is hidden and enveloped in darkness.

Similarly the other side of the coin regarding the intellectual mind will reflect a completely different potential, once it comes into the field of light of our awareness and starts attracting our attention. Unfortunately human beings have acquired a deeply engrained attraction to glimmer and gold, which is a representation of power and status, and the new mantra 'Development of Intellect and Mind over everything else', seems to promise exactly that, thereby putting on hold the possibility to further evolve within.

So what is there to gain from the less obvious and shiny side of the coin?

This side of our Intellectual Mind requires food, which is not supplied by the more attractive glamorous side of life. It is starved by the lack of specific influences to nourish it such as through *new ideas and different ways of thinking.* At the same time it has to re-establish its connection to the other bodies', functions and faculties within.

As long as this part of the Intellectual Mind is not nourished and satisfied through studying and true understanding of the science of meditation, and the psychological and philosophical aspects of it, the opposing (shiny) side of it won't let you sit in meditation for more than five minutes.

That's why this section of the book intends to satisfy the Intellectual Mind and give it enough food to digest, different techniques and exercises to practice and many new ideas and different ways of thinking, by offering it chunks of dense knowledge it can chew on, which will keep it busy for a sufficient amount of time. By then you will be fully established in your meditation practice and will have made meditation a part of your life. In time, with a bit of your own effort and some help and encouragement along the way, you will find that most of your internal and external frictions will have ceased to exist.

Exercise 3: Food For The Intellect

A question for the Intellectual Mind:

- *What is your understanding of the philosophical term 'Non-self' and its connection to 'I-thought'?*

- *What happened in your Mind the very moment you read the question? Write that experience down first, then go back and answer the question.*

The Paradox Of Belief

There are a lot of connotations attached to meditation. Many people hesitate or object to the idea of meditation because they still *believe* that meditation is based on a belief system, or that they have to follow a religious movement or become part of a sect.

In our ordinary life belief is something we acquire from others during our upbringing. Depending on which culture we are born into, our belief will manifest and express itself through different forms, concepts, rituals and systems. There are many different levels of belief, but all of them have one thing in common – belief can be shaken and can change at any given moment. This is due to the fact that there is nothing permanent within us; hence whatever my belief is today might change into a different belief tomorrow.

On the one side of the scale, after a long time of internal and external reaffirmation, belief can become habitual and even mechanical.

Several psychological mechanisms and unconscious response systems manifest themselves during our upbringing and form part of our psychological and mental makeup. The most obvious manifestations are fear, authority, absence of sense of self, imagination and identification. They keep our different forms of belief in place. There are many other manifestations, which I will leave to you to discover and differentiate yourself.

According to our dictionaries the definition of belief can be divided into five main categories:

1   The feeling of being certain that something exists or is true.[52]
2   An acceptance that a statement is true or that something exists.[53]
3   A state or habit of mind in which trust or confidence is placed in some person or thing.[54]
4   A belief is an opinion or something that a person holds to be true.[55]
5   Assumptions and convictions that are held to be true, by an individual or a group, regarding concepts, events, people, and things.[56]

All those different definitions are based on the assumption of something that exists or is believed to be true, without any *verification or first-hand experience*.

In addition to all the different religious and political beliefs, we can assume that there are as many belief systems as there are people.

Atheism, or no belief, is in fact a belief in itself, and many people hold on to their belief out of habit or because everybody else in their environment follows that particular belief. Giving up their belief would turn them into outsiders within their own community and they would become prone to criticism or even be expelled from social events or their community.

Many people take on a belief system because it is the easy way out and takes less effort than engaging with the subject more consciously. Others have to keep up their belief to avoid being faced with their own reality or truth.

"I believe…" is a phrase we hear multiple times a day. Most of the time this phrase could be replaced with, "I don't agree with you or them."

In time, the accumulation of 'I belief' we hold form our own personal philosophy, which differentiates us from others and nourishes the 'little I'.[57]

Depending on the level of objectivity and neutral state of mind a person has aspired to during their life, the more the 'I beliefs' are based on actual truth and have therefore transformed into real knowledge, the higher the possibilities that 'little I' or 'little ME' has transformed into 'real I'.[58] The personal philosophy has transformed into a true philosophy in which everything is based on actual first-hand experience.

A whole psychological system was developed during the last hundred years, which focuses only on the creation of new beliefs. This system is mainly used and very efficiently applied by large corporations, the media, political parties and their leverage of communication through our increasingly globalised world. This psychology knows what is required to offer us a massive range of beliefs and philosophies, which are tailored for the market place via the power of repetitive affirmation and attention catching.

This is possible by applying specific techniques such as powerful visual images, music, scent, light and convincing or scientific catch phrases, which stimulate our emotional responses and desires.

Nowadays, most of the things we wear, eat, read, think and believe are influenced and can be traced back to this new and artificial kind of psychology.

Most of our sense of self, our identity and what we are supposed to be, how to behave and believe to be, are influenced and derived from this kind of psychology.

All these psychological techniques have one thing in common; *they create the illusion and promise us something, which we believe is lacking in our external life or internal world.*

The reason why we are so attracted to these types of external stimulations is due to an in-balance between our Essence and Personality.[59]

Religious belief is a very sensitive subject because it is deeply engrained in our mental makeup and was handed down to us through many generations. The only thing, which can be said about religious belief here, is that all the founders of world religions are no longer alive and their teachings and experiences were written down on paper long after they died. This means that their teachings were translated and interpreted many times down the line and most of the scholars and priests added their own personal understanding or interpretations. So it is down to oneself to discover and experience the truth behind one's acquired religious belief.

Regarding the matter of belief it is vital that every belief or 'I belief' is connected with 'true conscience';[60] otherwise things can become unbalanced, ultimately becoming counterproductive to our own wellbeing and that of others.

If there is absolutely no conscience connected to belief or 'I beliefs', there is a very high chance that individuals commit deeds and acts which don't comply with social ethics or the law.

For example, if someone's 'I belief' is to steal or even murder somebody, it is an indication that no conscience is active in that person. Only people without true conscience or who suffer from a mental illness are capable of executing these kinds of criminal acts.

The problem we face is, that on most occasions we don't really know if that what we believe, or what the 'I beliefs' are saying, is necessarily representing the truth.

This means that to test these beliefs we must start digging to gain first-hand knowledge that will identify which of our beliefs are actually true.

Like most manifestations there is a paradox to belief – the other side of the scale of belief shows, that without belief or without believing in something, nothing could be done and manifest or change. If scientists, artists, philosophers, entrepreneurs, politicians and physicists did not believe in their ideas or inspirations, nothing would move forward or evolve externally and internally.

The paradox is, that a strong belief is the only thing we can rely on when we are faced with the unknown. Yet within the unknown we don't know if our belief will turn out to be true. In the unknown we don't know if all the effort we put into our objective is a waste of time. This means, that when faced with the unknown our belief becomes vibrant and full of life touching us on a deeper level, in the process providing the necessary energy and will action required, to help the effort to succeed.

If we suddenly become very ill or a loved one has died, our belief can give us the strength to heal or cope with the grief.

I would not be able to keep writing this book if a strong sounding feeling within me did not believe that it can benefit other people.

I know from years of experience that this neutral school of thought and science of meditation has benefited and helped many of my clients and students. What I don't know is that by using a completely different medium, in form of a book, it will work in the same way. So, I am faced with the unknown and without my belief in the work itself I would not be able to see it through to the end. If there wasn't be a strong connection to belief and meaning, then why even bother to start writing.

To discover if our beliefs are still vibrant and full of life, rather than having turned into habits and become mechanical, we would have to apply the scale of meaning to them.

If one finds that the meaning that gives life to our beliefs has diminished or even disappeared, it's not worth keeping them. They only occupy precious space within the structure of our mind, which could be replaced with something more meaningful.

If we hold on to them for too long, all of our mechanical beliefs crystallize, leaving us inflexible towards changes in life and the way we deal with others. Crystallized beliefs are not conducive to our personal development and have to be dissolved through conscious effort.

After having explored the other side of the scale of belief we can come to the conclusion that without belief nothing would ever happen, and that without belief we would not be able to get through times in which we are faced with the unknown or have to deal with illness, pain and loss.

Now let's add another dimension to the whole scale of belief.

As previously mentioned, most of the ideas we hold and formulate are acquired by a huge accumulation of external influences that reach us through life, different concepts of belief or religion, people around us and other mediums. These ultimately form our individual 'I believe' and belief systems. And as long as the mind, our intellect and emotions are kept active via external stimulus caused by life's events, as well as internal stimulus caused by thoughts and feelings, we will constantly re-invent and update our individual philosophy due to the ever changing nature of life.

We only possess our individual philosophies and 'I beliefs' as long as our mind and thoughts are active and stimulated by events. At night when we fall asleep they disappear and are replaced by dreams or deep sleep, only to re-appear in the morning when we awaken to external stimulus.

But something entirely different takes place when mind and thought activity becomes still and motionless through the process of meditation

Meditation is an act of willing to undo – not doing.

Within that process our individual philosophies and 'I beliefs' become very spacious and less charged, and once mind and thoughts are motionless they transcend - because that what thinks has vanished.

Please note, this is a moment in which you have to be careful, because you might make the logic of this idea (and many other ideas you might find described in this book) part of your individual beliefs before you have even considered practicing meditation and apply the exercises to verify for yourself if what is said above is to be true.

Exercise 4: Work on 'I-believes'

- *Define your belief or your individual philosophy and religion. Become aware of how much of what it teaches do you apply regularly and actively in life and what aspects of its teaching do you ignore.*

- *How much within your religious belief is replaced by your 'I belief'?*

- *What are your strongest 'I beliefs'?*

- *How often do you integrate what you hear from others, media or advertising, into your own beliefs without personally researching if this is true?*

- *Observe to what extent your belief and 'I belief' has turned into a habit or has become mechanical.*

- *Connect with the time in the past when those beliefs were still vibrant and alive. What has changed? Validate if they are of any value to you today by ranking them on a scale from 0 to 5.*

A Matter Of Evolution

Every philosophy, ancient teaching and every world religion contain specific teachings that emphasize and point towards the necessity and importance of change and transformation. Even the psychology that creates new beliefs today focuses on the necessity to change.

In the very beginning, philosophy and psychology were not seen as separate and formed part of religious and ancient teachings. The philosophical side covered themes such as ethics, universal laws and energetic principles. The psychological side covered subjects like self-study, work on consciousness, the study of a universal language and the science of meditation. Unfortunately most of that knowledge has been lost in time and is no longer that easily available to us today.

Our current, very young, modern psychology tries to offer similar solutions to work with people on change or facilitate people through times of change. What differentiates the ancient psychology from the modern psychology is its objective. While our modern psychology looks at a human being from the point of view of how individuals are supposed to function and supposed to be, the ancient psychology looks at human beings from their possibility to evolve and develop their true potential.

Elements of this ancient psychology can still be found in Christianity, Buddhism, the Tao, Hinduism, the Yoga Sutras of Patanjali, the Veda's and Bhagavad Gita, Rumi's teachings, Sufi scriptures as well as the 'Fourth Way Teaching' - just to name a few of them.

This ancient psychology's simple message is based on two fundamental statements:

- Life only evolves us to a certain point.
- Man cannot do.[61]

All other aspects within its teaching message builds upon those two expressions as well as that external life does not need us to further evolve within.

The evolution of the earth and life is subject to its own laws and time frame. No further inner evolution, on our behalf, is required in order to serve life and its events. It does not expect us to change and develop a different potential or being and become more conscious.

The world and life are perfectly equipped to feed us with plenty of food, in the form of events and external impressions, to keep us busy and engaged until we die, without anything needing to change or evolve. So through life and our external world, we only evolve up to a certain point and from then onwards it is down to our own effort, if we want to change and become more conscious.

The possibility to evolve further within and develop a different being depends on very special circumstances. We have to be at the right place at the right time in our life and need to be sufficiently prepared to even recognise the signs pointing us towards that possibility. We can't take this possibility for granted.

And the only reason that most people can't evolve and develop a different being even when it is offered to them on a silver plate is because they *simply don't want to change.*

Before we start putting effort and energy into actively changing our being, the first thing we need to know is what developing a different being and becoming more conscious means.

To be able to do that depends on certain influences, which contain specific knowledge that can reach us, through different mediums. The second thing we need to know is that meditation and work on our inner evolution can't be separated. Both have to go hand-in-hand and be applied simultaneously. The third thing we need to know is that self-study and the **study of life and its universal laws**, acquiring a **universal language**, **work on oneself** and **meditation** are the four different directions to be studied simultaneously. They are facilitating our own inner evolution.

Different Paths But No One Way

This contemporary school of thought does not believe in only one path or approach. In the same way that a surgeon can't operate on someone with a mental illness, or an osteopath can't make a client physically stronger, self-study and meditation depends on a variety of different influences and methods from different sources of expertise to facilitate and establish lasting change within. The person with a mental illness has a chance to heal with the help of a psychologist, while the client who needs to become physically stronger after his osteopathic treatment has to be referred to a fitness instructor to achieve his objective. The same is true in the science of meditation.

Due to our different individualities and mentalities a single method or technique would not do the job. One person responds to a particular approach instantly and starts progressing, whilst another person does not show any response or progress at all and requires a different approach. All of this depends on each individual's circumstances and what they have acquired and assimilated during their life.

Nature is the best example. It produces a myriad of different kinds of food, which supplies all the different species on earth. In the same way that a plant would die without the food of water, or a cat would die only feeding on plants, we would die from malnutrition if we only ate white bread.

Similarly different methods and techniques are different food for our inner evolution and growth. Otherwise our progress would stagnate and we would starve and die while still being alive, which is the case with many people today.

There are different, very traditional, paths and disciplines people usually embark on, which offer liberation of mind and thought. One is the path of the Sadhu and the path of the celibate monk, as well as the well-known path of Karma and the path of the Yogi.

The Sadhus aim is to discipline the body to such an extent, that one rises above any physical pain through hazardous methods. But the Sadhus path gives no guarantees or promises that this can be achieved in a lifetime.

The celibate monk's path is mainly based on longing, belief and faith, which are evoked by regular prayer in solitude and silence without any promises in return.

The path of karma is through surrender and acceptance and mindfulness not to commit any harmful deed, which transforms into compassion for everything that is. If one's actions and one's reactions can't be balanced in a lifetime, then another cycle of birth and death is humbly accepted and sustained by the hope of finding better circumstances to pay one's karmic debt in the next lifetime.

The path of a yogi requires constant study and practice as a disciple, in the presence of a teacher to ultimately achieve the objective and goal of the teaching.

All those traditional paths have one thing in common: *That one has to sacrifice or give up most or everything in life.*

Those traditional paths are not practical or of use to most people in our modern world.

That's why there is a fifth path available to us, which manifests itself in different forms of schools of thought. This kind of path is probably the most difficult and challenging one to follow, because it takes place right in the middle of our life, deep within the chaos and distractions of the surroundings we are individually born into. It does not require us to give up anything, yet expects us to work on all levels at the same time.

This kind of path could be called the path of the balanced person, or the path of the 'objective man'.

The notion of this path is not about others or me and them. And the only thing, which is required, is oneself and the will to work on oneself internally through self-study and self-observation, and externally through learning a universal language and practicing the science of meditation.

Cycles Of Life

Life and the universe are under the law of repetitive cycles. Examples of these include the cycle of night and day (due to the cycle of the sun) or the moon cycle, (which activates the cycle of the tide via its gravitational pull). Then there are the four different seasons evoked by the cycle of the earth around the sun, and the different cycles of nature and organic life on earth.

Our galaxy is under the influence of other galaxies, while other universes influence our whole universe and vice versa. A great display of interconnected cycles that forms an interactive matrix, which keeps everything in perfect balance through silent communication with the one source, which gave rise to creation and brought all that 'Is' into manifestation.

The tiniest interference at any given point in these cycles will influence and impact on everything else that is sustained by the matrix. These subtle changes determine the path of evolution on earth and every living being on this planet.

Our own physical body is also under the law of cycles: the cycle of the breath, the cycle of hormonal change, the cycle of digestion and the cycle of the cranio sacral rhythm. The whole creation is under cyclical cosmological laws. If we look at the life span of human beings, we discover that our own life in particular is under the law of roughly seven-year cycles.

From the moment of our first inhalation upon being born up to the age of seven, we are busy with learning to walk and move with speed: We learn how to use our hands skilfully and how to speak and interact with others. Most of what we acquire and learn during this time, we grasp and understand through the physical body and our emotions rather than through formative thinking.

As a child, between the age of seven and fourteen our sense of self or 'I', and the distinction between 'them' and 'me', is fully developed. During this time we learn about boundaries and our conditioning, and certain habitual behaviours are deepened and our intellect starts forming.

During the time as a teenager, and up to the age of twenty-one, the development of our sexuality takes place. It's a time of confusion evoked by an influx of hormones in which the sense of compassion for anybody else, is replaced by withdrawal and disinterest from the world around us and periods of self-absorption. During this time the young person is faced with many frictions, which are relating to identity and the question of 'who am I'?

In the years as a junior up to the age of twenty-eight, the world becomes an oyster and we are full of dreams. Everything is still possible and we are exploring life to its fullest extent, starting to identify with our dreams, our ideas and the ideals of others. We are in search of a role model, which helps us to form our identity and strengthen our personality.

We reach the stage of a grown up woman and man, between the age of twenty-eight and thirty-five. During that time, we start assuming the responsibilities of creating and sustaining our own family. Our habits in life become even more deeply engrained, and it is our turn now to condition and teach our children everything we have learned and acquired, both consciously and subconsciously in our life. We are firmly established in our profession and disperse our focus and time between family and climbing up the career ladder.

During the years as a senior leading up to the age of forty-two, we are increasingly faced with periods of disillusionment, realising that the dreams and objectives we had in our twenties are worlds apart, including what we believed to be, and where we wanted to be, at this stage in our life.

The years between the age of forty-two and forty-nine are years of great significance. A profound period of transition is about to take place, initially induced through hormonal changes in both man and woman and the realisation that our youth has become part of the past. The energy available to us has decreased and certain wear and tear in the body can no longer be ignored.

This phase is described as the midlife crisis. The state or level of consciousness we have evolved into by that time, determines the way we will spend the rest of our remaining years. On the one hand our whole identity and the way we have lived our life is in question during this time of crisis. On the other hand we are offered the possibility to formulate a completely different question, in regards to meaning and purpose of our life, and to use this possibility to put it out there into the open and unknown. Recharged by the energy of a renewed spirit of curiosity, and without fear of the unknown we embark on a new adventure, which might lead us to the true meaning of our very own purpose in life.

At the age of forty-nine we have reached the stage of an elder and the years leading up to the age of fifty-six are called the Golden Years in which we can express and live our full potential while joining the remaining dots. We are no longer interested in the dramas of life's events and are much more relaxed in the way we respond to external impressions of life.

During the next seven years we are partly occupied with the completion of our worldly duties and responsibilities in life and start preparing and planning our retirement.

Between the ages of sixty-three and seventy we settle into our retirement and have time to deepen and assimilate our life experience. We give more time to contemplating the internal world and meditate over the question of life and death. Our personality moves increasingly into the background and our true state of being is shining through the very obvious physical manifestations of our aging body. The work on oneself and one's inner evolution has fully internalized, and can find its expressions via different ways of transmitting this knowledge, making it available for the greater good.

The remaining years are called 'the Age of the Wise' in which our attention is drawn increasingly inwards. It is the time when our work on our own inner evolution and transformation is allowed to crystallize, waiting to be taken with us through the passage from life to death after our last exhalation.

Life And its Different Influences Acting on us

Long ago mankind stopped living in perfect harmony and synchronicity with nature, and created its own world and laws. We are no longer driven primarily by animal instinct, are not forming a natural part of organic life on earth and don't belong, like everything else, to the food chain of creation.

Our lives today are not based on primitive survival - having to hide from dangerous predators or the forces of nature. Within the world of nature, mind has created its own artificial world and way of life, which has produced countless new influences acting on us from the day we are born.

This first category of influences profoundly differs from the influences of nature and organic life and can be called *Beta-Influences*. They are comprised of material attractions and must contain objects such as fashion, cars, gadgets and properties. Other 'must-have' attractions in this category are security, health, success, fame, physical beauty, influence and power. Beta-Influences invite us to serve this mind created life explicitly and keep us constantly engaged with it. The more attracted we are to these influences, the more we participate in sustaining them.

The second kind of influence is called *Theta-Influence*, which is pure untouched nature. This influence has a profoundly balancing and healing impact upon us, it takes us out of our limited state of mind and teaches us about the beauty of creation, which awakens our finer emotions and possibly gives us a glimpse of our insignificance in relation to the whole. Nothing can teach us more about pure states of being than nature itself, and nothing can put us faster into a state of awe, than the overwhelming scale of a mountain range or the infinite horizon of the sea and the depth of the sky at night.

The third category of influences can be called *Alpha-Influences*, which are much more subtle and refined. They are comprised of organic life and everything we find in this world, which result from an influx of inspiration, acts of creativity and schools of thought, filled with meaning such as art, literature, science, geometry and architecture as well as philosophy, poetry and religion.

The fourth category of influence acting on is mainly hidden and is the most difficult to find. In actual fact it usually finds us if the conditions and circumstances are right.

This influence can be called *Gamma-Influence* and reaches us in form of a school of thought, which is entirely dedicated to facilitating people through the process of their own inner development. In the past, these schools were known as mystic schools and the life and heart of them were their teachers, who held the knowledge of how to further evolve within one's own being. Their own teachers who guided them through their extensive apprenticeship gave this precious knowledge, which they themselves had to earn through hard work, discipline and effort. And our world has never been and will never be without these sources of knowledge.

It is very important to know that as far as the bigger picture is concerned there is nothing wrong with whichever line of influence we are mainly attracted to. The reason is that for life and the evolution of the earth, it is not necessary that we personally further evolve within. Things are just fine as they are.

You only need to observe for a while, until you realize that most people are mainly attracted and exposed to *Beta-Influences,* the reason being that these influences surround and act on us most of the time. We almost can't avoid being influenced by fashion and gadgets, or striving towards name and fame.

Depending on the way we grew up and what we have learned during that time determines if we will ever be attracted to *Alpha-Influences.* The chances for a person who is only drawn to *Beta-Influences* to further evolve within and become a more conscious being, are very limited. By the time they have reached the last third of their life, deeply engrained habits and ways of thinking will have occupied most of the available space in their minds and as a consequence will govern their way of everyday life. This can reach a level in which everything within these people has become utterly and unchangeably mechanical and inflexible; hence all those mechanical patterns and habits have irreversibly crystallized.

That interface from flexibility to mechanicalness is called 'dying while still being physically alive', which happens to a lot of people in this world, yet does not mean that this kind of state of being is a state of suffering, pain or absence of pleasure. In actual fact, and everyone who has done any self-study or work on oneself for a reasonable length of time, will agree with me on this. It is probably the most comfortable and effortless state of blissful ignorance within to live.

This situation arises because of these people's total immunity to *Alpha-*

Influences, hence the impressions of *Alpha-Influences* simply can't enter and act on people, who have become immune to them. They are filtered out, get stuck or bounce off via '*Padding*[62].

True knowledge is formed of a substance called **The Substance of Gravitas**, which gives it its weight. This means that knowledge turned into experience, via conscious effort, has gone through an alchemistical process that creates the substance of Gravitas. The weight of this substance is so substantial that its gravitational pull annihilates everything that is not true or based on illusion and imagination.

There is only a defined quantity of the substance of knowledge available to us. It is not an infinite resource and its value considerably outweighs the weight of gold. It is so precious, that it is next to impossible to put a price on it. Due to its weight we only can absorb and assimilate small quantities of it. If we get too much of it in one go, we won't be able to digest it. If we received the full knowledge of the whole truth about ourselves in one flash of a moment we would die instantly because of its weight.

Due to the value, weight and impact of this substance, it is usually *well hidden and disguised*.

One example of carriers of Alpha-Influences are many ancient, and some modern, structures and monuments. The original purpose of these monuments was to preserve the knowledge of ancient teachings, their methods and ideas encrypted and humbly hidden within their architecture. Every shape, form and space, whether forming a window, or an exact number of pillars erected in a circle, opening pathways to the direction of the northern, southern, western or eastern hemispheres - everything contains a special meaning and forms a part of the knowledge. Geometry and symbols, colours, light and sound, inscriptions and paintings are the transmitters of this precious Alpha-Influence. Other carriers of Alpha-Influences include literature and poetry. They preserve the knowledge and teachings of religions, philosophies and psychology in form of parables and verses, sutras, aphorisms and similes, stories and poems. Another powerful transmitter of Alpha-Influence and knowledge is art and science, which can touch us on many different levels.

The impressions that Alpha-Influence leave in us grow and accumulate over time, creating a counter weight to the impressions that Beta-Influences have created.

The more Alpha-Influences we absorb, the more inspired we become to explore other areas in life and the less we are impressed by and attracted to Beta-Influences. Our way of thinking becomes much more spacious, and we become open to new ideas and can maintain our interest towards a particular subject due to its weight of meaning to us.

Once Alpha-Influences have overwhelmed Beta-Influences they start penetrating deeper into our personality and form a place called **Inner Longing**[63] within our hearts (around the solar plexus area). Inner Longing possesses a magnetic pull like qualities and the more it grows and expands it can't help but pull us deeper within and towards *Gamma-Influence*.

Inner Longing should not be mistaken with External Longing. Every kind of longing contains magnetic pull-like qualities. External Longing pulls us further into life and the world of external attractions, whilst Inner Longing pulls us deeper into our being and is attracted by the mystery of what lies beyond.

This takes us to *Gamma-Influence*, which, due to the way our world functions, only reaches a very limited amount of people. Gamma-Influence only reaches those people who want to further evolve within - to become more conscious and develop a different state of being by way of their own personal effort. Because this can't be done alone, help is required. This kind of help comes in the form of people, facilitators or teachers who have gone through the process of inner evolution themselves, and are able to transmit this kind of knowledge from the depth of their own being and actual experience via applicable methods, exercises and via communicating through a universal language.

To prevent this knowledge from being mis-interpreted a specific language is required to truly understand it. This language is traditionally taught through word of mouth, which reaches us through Gamma-Influences in the form of a school or a teacher. Like the medical student needs dedication and longing to go to university, to be taught by an experienced professor to become an accomplished doctor or surgeon, a man who desires to work on his inner growth, requires an accomplished and truly experienced teacher to succeed and accomplish his objective.

It is important to know that Gamma-Influence turns into Alpha-Influence the moment it is put on paper or into a form or shape.

Once a medical student has graduated, he puts all of his studies into practice and assists senior surgeons to be taught and introduced to more refined techniques, until he is ready to take on the responsibility to lead his own team in theatre. He has mastered the techniques, the theory and practice of surgery, and is free to develop his own research and new techniques, without the guidance of a professor or senior. After years of practice, lecturing, research and publications he progresses further to become a professor. Now it is his turn to hand down his precious knowledge, based on years of experience, to his own students. By the time he has reached the peak of his academic career, he has become an expert and living example of his profession to his students.

Similarly a teacher of the science and philosophy of meditation had to master the theory, the methods and the practice in the same way as did a surgeon. The moment his work has internalised after decades of disciplined effort and extensive studies, his apprenticeship is over and an external teacher is no longer required. He will then have spent many more years assimilating and progressing within, until a connection to another influence he was familiarised and connected with during his times of study, is firmly established.

This kind of influence, which can be called *Sentrum*, can't be found or be discovered anywhere in the external world. It teaches and transmits knowledge from within and forms part of that which is not subject to change, called the unchanging nature within.

Nothing can be told about Sentrum without feeding peoples imagination or an empty belief. After being well connected with Sentrum, and having turned 'Mind and Thought' into a friend, the teacher might form a school to teach, or will start working with small groups of people. Whatever form it takes, now it is his turn to hand down his precious knowledge, and facilitate people through the process of their own work on themselves and their work on consciousness.

Exercise 5: Validating different influences

- *Which of the five influences described above are acting on you in your everyday life.*

- *Spend half an hour a day under Theta-Influence and two hours a week under Alpha-Influence.*

- *Observe what impact that has on your life and your being.*

Our Main Issue With Life

We can't control or change life since life literally just happens. There are no guarantees to what life has in store for us on any given day or as a whole. We have no influence on our destiny, and whatever happens, happens.

This unpredictability causes great difficulties and frictions in our private lives, as well as in our professional lives, since it constantly interferes with our plans and objectives. We usually don't know that the company we work for is about to close, or that we are about to be sacked.

We can't predict that our much deserved holiday somewhere hot and sunny, is spoiled due to a cabin crew strike, followed by food poisoning, which, once recovered, is replaced by a hurricane, followed by losing our passports and consequently missing our return flight.

Similarly, we are surprised by winning the lottery, or receiving an award, which might be followed by a massive inheritance from a distant relative, we didn't even know existed. Anything can happen at any time, whether it has a positive or negative impact on our plans and consequently on us.

Then there is the constant possibility of our death, which is usually blanked out, denied or non-existent in our ordinary state of mind. Yet death is the only thing which is guaranteed in our lives and might meet us a few steps away, which puts an end to our plans and to the plans of a variety of people we were professionally and privately involved with. So, what goes around just comes around and we find ourselves being nothing more than a Ping-Pong ball life is playing with.

Now, we said before that we can't control or change life, but what we can change and slowly learn to control is the way we respond to the ups and downs of life and our attitude towards the ever-changing nature of life.

To be able to do that, we have to grow something within us which functions as a counter balance to the impacts the rapidly changing events of external life impose on us. That something, needs to contain enough gravitas and consciousness to prevent us from being totally absorbed and overwhelmed by the external happenings.

It is Inner Longing that in time starts penetrating through all those habitual patterns, which form part of our personality and mind and slowly transforms into **Unchanging Gravitas**[64]. The expression, "I am completely out of myself," or, 'I am all over the place,' is the best example of absence of Unchanging Gravitas in people. Hence in time, this powerful counterbalance prevents us from losing our connectedness with our true sense of self, so that we can react or respond to whatever happens in a more conscious way.

We have already talked about life being nothing more than a succession of events. From the day we are born to the day we will die, we experience nothing more than one event after another. To be more precise, we as individuals can look at our immediate personal experience of life as a succession of events. Having our breakfast in the morning is an event, which might be followed by the driving to work event, which is replaced by the five hour meeting event, followed by the receiving an award event etc. Life's uninterrupted succession of events, creates and makes us experience the illusion of time.

Now ask yourself – "How often are you actually aware, that your present situation is nothing more than an event, that you are simply part of an event"?

The answer is, if you are really honest to yourself, "Never."

Why is that?

The answer is very simple. We usually become the event due to its gravitational pull and its powerful external stimulus acting on our physical body, emotions and thoughts. Within seconds we become immersed in the event and are literally out of ourselves, which usually turns a simple event into one of the many dramas in our life. Being the event is where we spend most of our time in our life. This means that we are out of ourselves, which means we are out of balance. This, in turn, absorbs most of our precious energy and leaves us in a state of stress and depletion.

To summarise:

- We can say that by being regularly nourished by events of Alpha-Influence or Theta-Influence, the weight and magnetic faculty of Inner Longing grows stronger and stronger and in time will attract Gamma-Influence, which in return facilitates the manifestation of Unchanging Gravitas, which is connected to a far greater power in the background: the Sentrum.

Unchanging Gravitas keeps us slightly further removed from the events of life, allowing us to keep a more spacious view of things so that we can keep our connection with our true sense of self and not become constantly overwhelmed by external life.

Exercise 6: Detachment Exercise

- *While you are sitting in a coffee shop enjoying a cup of tea, observe the happenings around you from an attitude of mind of 'this is me in the having a cup of tea event'.*

- *Apply the same to 'this is me with spending time with my family event' or this is me in being in a difficult meeting event'.*

- *Observe how that impacts on the way you respond to the event or situation.*

The Necessity Of A Universal Language

Ancient philosophy and psychology is based on a new and universal language. This language is constantly changing and upgraded to the requirements of our times. The reason why it is so difficult to understand the teaching of the Upanishads or the Sutras of Patanjali, is that its symbolic language belonged to an ancient time. Without studying and practically applying and integrating this new language into our way of thinking, we won't gain access to true knowledge.

We are living in a world in which everybody speaks a different tongue. People know a lot but don't understand each other. This is due to the fact that to a large extent, **Knowledge has outgrown Action**, which prevents us from *transforming knowledge into actual experience.*

Each individual person has accumulated a massive amount of intellectual knowledge, which is mainly based on theoretical concepts, and interpreted by our own limited personal understanding. If we want to change knowledge into **True Knowledge** three different forces are required, which form a triad.

- The first force being passive by nature is **Knowledge** and connects to our intellectual brain.
- The second force being active by nature is **Action** and connects to our movement/instinctual brain.
- The third force being neutral by nature is **Experience** and connects to our emotional brain.

The third force Experience only manifests itself when Knowledge and Action are in balance. Acquired knowledge must be put into action so that experience can manifest. If one of the first two forces is absent or weak and without substance, true experience won't manifest. And without actual experience true understanding is impossible - hence we will end up speaking different languages and won't understand each other.

So, the new language we are talking about is the language of *true experience*, which requires conscious effort to be taken into action. Any vocabulary or terms used in this new universal language are neutral and free of any connotation or judgement. True Experience plays a part in producing Substance of Gravitas, through which knowledge can be transmitted by means of the universal language.

Exercise 7: Revisiting the vocabulary of the universal language

- *You have come across quite a lot of new terms in this book like Inner Longing, Unchanging Gravitas or Beta-Influence, which are based on new ideas and create different meanings. Write them down and make sure that you are very clear and conscious about their meaning and avoid explaining or interpreting them with your own personal understanding.*

9. The Process – Stage II: Understanding The Internal World

Know Thyself

According to history, 'Know Thyself' was inscribed in the forecourt of the Greek temple of Apollo in Delphi. The maxim forms part of most ancient teachings and world philosophies and its profound meaning contains probably one of the most encompassing and densest forms of knowledge. It encompasses the sum total of all mystic teachings and philosophies.

In Plato's work six different dialogues discuss the saying of Delphi referring to it as 'a long established wisdom', or 'a piece of advice that the god gave'.

The Latin term for know thyself is 'nosce te ipsum', and Thomas Hobbes used it in his famous work *The Leviathan* as 'read thyself'[65], while Alexander Pope referred to it as 'the proper study of mankind is Man'[66], and Benjamin Franklin relates it to an observation which states: 'There are three things that are extremely hard, steel, a diamond, and to know one's self.'[67]

The maxim 'know thyself' is deeply rooted in Jñāna Yoga the yoga of knowledge as well as in Buddhism it is embedded in one of the ten stages of Jñāna.

Christian theologians likened knowing thy true self along with knowledge of God. For example, Clement of Alexandria interpreted it as "if one knows himself, he will know God'. Similarly Augustine expressed it through the words 'let me know myself, let me know thee', and Calvin stated, 'nearly all wisdom we possess consists of two parts – the knowledge of God and of ourselves'.

The Yoga-Sutra of Patanjali clearly reveres to 'know thyself' in Chapter Two The Path to Realization as 'yogic action has three components – discipline, self-study and orientation toward the ideal of pure awareness'.

Modern terms like introspection, self-reflection and contemplation could be seen as the active expression of 'know thyself'.

In the science of meditation 'know thyself' is a fundamental principle, which can't be ignored, avoided or left out.

'Know thyself' in meditation is applied to self-study or self-enquiry, by means of specific work on oneself and self-observation. Work on one's self and self-study is the first direction of our practice, and if applied regularly it will soon lead to actual and obvious results.

Ralph Waldo Emerson wrote a poem referring to 'God in thee', which was based on his belief that to 'know thyself' means to know the god which exists in every person.[68]

To avoid any misunderstanding, self-study the first direction of the process does not mean to study other people at the same time. Our attitude towards others and whatever we see or observe in others, should be utterly neutral, yet we never should become indifferent to other people. If we don't like what we see in someone else, and if what we see triggers lower emotions in us, we should immediately ask ourselves: 'What is it in Me that does not like what it sees, and what do I have to do, to change that kind of response in me?' Remember, *we only can work to change ourselves, we can't change others.*

To summarise:

- We can say that the teaching how to 'know thyself' can be found in almost any ancient teaching, philosophy and religion and forms an inseparable part of meditation. Self-observation and self-study executed and applied correctly will lead to more depth and quality in our meditation practice; hence it is the ideal method to work consciously with obstacles, which stand between us, our piece of mind and meditation.

Exercise 8: Self-study

- *Define your own understanding of the aphorism 'know thyself'.*

- *Discuss the subject with other people.*

- *Enquire into the depth of the expression 'know thyself' by using the worldwide web, libraries or any other resources.*

- *Compare what you have discovered with your very own definition.*

The Different Abilities in People And Different Types of People

The evolution of human beings has created different body frames based on geographic conditions and requirements. Those body frames range from 'Jungle to Viking'[69] from a scale point of view. The Jungle frame is required in tropic conditions and the Viking frame is required in cold or arctic conditions.

Physiology has defined this even more and has created three different body types, which are called ectomorph, mesomorph and endomorph. The ectomorph type is thin and lean with a fast metabolism. The mesomorph type is athletic with defined muscles and strong. The mesomorph type has a round physique and a slow metabolism. However all those different body types have the following abilities in common, which play a vital role in our inner development.

The moment we start with the first direction of the practical work, which is self-study, we soon come across several abilities in our system, which are different to the functions of our physical body, such as the functions of our organs, nervous system, heart etc.

The abilities we want to study and carefully observe are active on a more subtle level, but have a direct impact on the functions of our physical body and its wellbeing. They can be called the ability to feel or our emotions, the ability to think or our intellect and the instinctual and external movement ability, which are closely working together. Then there are two higher abilities, which lie dormant and only can be explored and studied through higher levels of consciousness.

The first four abilities are usually working to a different capacity in different human beings and we can categorise them into four different types of people.

1. The emotional type.
2. The intellectual type.

74

3. The movement type.
4. The instinctual type.

These four different abilities manifest in a person as four different brains or four different kinds of intelligence, which act on and manifest in the physical body through the main centres of the nervous system.

The emotional brain is connected to the Entric Nervous System located in the solar plexus area. The intellectual brain is connected to the physical brain forming our central nervous system, which is embedded in our cranium and the instinctual and movement brain is connected to the spinal cord within the dura towards the lumbar/thoracic region, forming our autonomic nervous system.

We are all a combination of these four different types of people, but are usually more at home in one of them, hence a movement type naturally gravitates more towards expressing his or herself through the movement brain instead of one of the other brains. This fact does not imply that any of those four different types of people is in any way superior to another type.

Unfortunately in our Western society the intellect is seen as far superior than the intelligence of the emotional, instinctual or movement brain. To avoid any misunderstanding, from this train of thought point of view, intellect does not equal intelligence. There is a particular intelligence that is attached to the intellect as well as an intelligence associated with the emotional, movement and instinctual brains.

Most people only have one of the four brains working to its full capacity and particular intelligence, while the other brains are under developed. It is very common that the most evolved brain tries to do the work for all the other three brains.

If we observe those four brains closely it soon becomes clear that they work at different speeds, and that they have a positive and a negative component.

For example, it is impossible to dance a tango via the intellectual brain only. Every movement of the body would have to be thought out and the tango would look like a robot moving in slow motion. The intellectual brain is far too slow for that. In actual fact it is the slowest of all four, while the emotional brain is the fastest.

All scientific or artistic inspiration enters through the emotional brain and is grasped and understood within no time frame. It is a knowing beyond time. A composer knows his entire symphony from beginning to end through his emotional brain. The intellectual brain would need to read each note of the whole arrangement first before it could understand the whole symphony.

A scientist is able to grasp a complex discovery in quantum physics, that goes beyond the understanding of formative thinking through his emotional brain, yet it takes him weeks to put it on paper to make it accessible to other people.

The movement and instinctual brain has an intelligence that is so reliable that while we are walking along a mountain path we can engage in a conversation, or contemplate on different ideas, without having to be aware of what our body is doing whilst walking.

Each brain, except the emotional brain, has a positive and a negative component with which it can respond to external and internal influences. Without that division survival in life would not be possible.

The positive and negative component of the emotional brain is comprised of pleasant and unpleasant emotional feelings or experiences. There is no true negative charge in the emotional brain. What we usually consider as emotions, are in reality lower emotions, which have to be learned and acquired via imitation. So we clearly have to distinguish emotions from lower emotions.

Real emotions are void of drama and usually awaken through experiences like love and friendship or caring for others. Other experiences of real emotions are, for example, being informed of a serious illness of a friend or the death of a close person, as well as physical and mental pain or hardship.

Many people spend most of their lives living from and through lower emotions, which eat up most of our energy. They are totally artificial and not of any use or benefit for inner growth. Eckhart Tolle calls them 'The Pain Body'[70], other yogic disciplines relate to them as inferior emotions and the fourth way teaching calls them negative emotions.

Lower emotions within us have to be carefully investigated especially when they have become habitual. Once we have developed enough Substance of Gravitas, we can start transforming lower emotions and reclaim the precious energy they hold by refusing them attention.

The last kind of emotions are higher emotions, which are the most conducive to our development and meditation. Higher emotions can't be explained intellectually or be grasped by the mind. They have to be experienced and are sometimes awakened by Alpha-Influences or the 'influence of eternity' and most importantly the 'influence of grace'.

The positive and negative aspect in the movement brain is very simple. It is either movement in space, or no movement. It is important to know that all movement a physical body is able to perform, has to be learned via repetition. This starts with learning to walk as a toddler and advances to such complex moves as of classical dance.

When you first learn a new movement there is a process that involves a number of the brains. The intellectual brain has to think through every step to figure out how the next move works, whilst the emotional brain goes through all the motions of the excitement and pitfalls while learning the routine. While all that takes place, the instinctual brain is busy regulating the body temperature, the heart rate and facilitating the distribution of enough endorphins and adrenaline to keep the body going. The only brain, that actually knows how to do the job, which is the movement brain, is not allowed to take over until the movement is mastered.

The instinctual brain or our autonomic nervous system, which is divided into sympathetic and parasympathetic nervous systems, uses our five senses to activate the positive or negative compartment. This allows it to decide and choose which compartment is required to respond to incoming sensory impressions. This brain is responsible for all the inner functions of our organism, and regulates our heartbeat and circulatory system, the respiratory system and our digestive system, as well as the lymphatic system, the myo-fascial matrix and cranio-sacral system. It distinguishes what is bitter or sweet and poisonous or healthy. It knows about hot or cold and pressure or danger.

Under no circumstances should we interfere with, or try to change the workings of the instinctual brain. It knows best what to do and any interference on our behalf can lead to severe consequences. It already has to cope with all our likes and dislikes regarding diet, adrenaline kicks, drugs or taking un-necessary risks. We truly have forgotten to listen to this brain by constantly overriding its messages.

The intellectual brain depends on its positive or negative compartment to decide when to say 'yes' or 'no', or distinguish when it is the right situation for affirmation or negation. Otherwise this brain is responsible for formative thinking, conceptual thoughts, strategic planning, analysing ideas and producing an academic thesis.

As long as all the different brains are not equally developed and working to their full potential, the most evolved brain will try to compensate for what the others are lacking. This is creating a massive confusion within the different systems of each brain and will soon lead to restrictions and imbalance of the functions of the brains.

Without evolving each brain, a healthy balance and alignment between our physical, emotional and mental systems can't be achieved and established. Without balancing and keeping this complex homeostasis intact, we can't even start thinking about changing our being.

This brings us to the definition of true intelligence.

True intelligence is, when all different brains are fully developed and are working to their full capacity and in harmony.

Ancient and contemporary teachings offer a tremendous variety of methods and techniques, which concentrate on developing the different brains. For example, in the field of yoga the Asanas are practiced to develop the movement brain, pranayama is implemented to balance the instinctual brain, the teachings of being compassionate and of service to others through so called 'Seva' helps to develop the emotional brain, studying the scriptures will help to develop the intellectual brain.

The Yoga Sutras of Patanjali teach the eight limbs, which include specific instructions regarding the development of the four different brains.

Sufi teaching has designed 'whirling' to develop the movement brain and uses music and poems to evolve the emotional brain, while Sufi stories which transmit knowledge helps the student to develop the intellectual brain.

The teachings of the Tao practice Tai Chi to evolve the movement brain, and refined ceremonies were designed to stimulate the emotional brain, while a Kotao is meant to challenge and develop the intellectual brain.

To summarise:

- We can say that we all have four different brains or intelligences and can categorise human beings into four different types of people or any combination of such (emotional/intellectual/instinctual/movement). Also we can say that most of the time those brains are not working in harmony or are fully developed, which results in an imbalance in functions of the four brains.[71]
- Then we can say that we have to work actively on each of them to bring harmony and balance to the system as a whole, which will enable us to activate our whole potential to ultimately become a more conscious being.

Exercise 9: Exploring The Different Brains

- *Observe which of the four brains you mainly fall back to by default or gravitate towards.*

- *Recognise by which four types of people you surround yourself most of the time.*

- *To which type of person are you most attracted?*

- *Observe the different speeds of your four different brains.*

The Mystery of Consciousness

To most people the idea of different levels, grades or states of consciousness is very mysterious, and a lot of spiritual teachers and gurus have created a great secret around them, and are hardly ever prepared or willing to reveal the complete picture regarding the workings of consciousness.

Scriptures like the Upanishads or the teachings of Advaita had to be translated from Sanskrit to make them available to us and because they were written in an ancient and very specific philosophical terminology, they have become very difficult to grasp and require excessive explanation from a teacher who speaks from true experience.

Every ancient teaching, philosophy or even more modern approaches to meditative practice like Assagioli's Psychosynthesis, inherently carries the idea of consciousness, and aims to increase consciousness through specific work on it. This is achieved by applying definite techniques and disciplined practise.

The three examples below are explaining ideas of Advaita, the Sutras of Patanjali and psychosynthesis to demonstrate the complexity of those different teachings.

Advaita explores the workings of consciousness by allowing one's entire being to become completely absorbed by the source out of which the first 'I' thought originates. Advaita's practical approach to self-study is actively to observe the world of appearances and by asking one's self questions like, "To whom does this event arise?" Or "Who is experiencing this thought?" Staying put with the sensation and feeling the question evokes, one surrenders and merges with that moment of self-remembering and the quality of consciousness the state of self-remembering contains.

Subject and object dynamics increasingly dissolve and shift into a much more refined way of perception, in which the perceiver, the process of perception and that which is perceived fuse and become one. The pure state of 'I am' is revealed and permeates one's whole existence in which only 'pure being' will prevail. In time, and by accumulating more and more imprints of

80

experiences of that particular state of consciousness, that formless quality and pure state of perception or being, which is not subject to change within will appear and manifest as something permanent, hence the illusion of duality has transcended.

The Yoga Sutras of Patanjali base their teachings and work on consciousness on the triad of Prakriti (nature), Citta (consciousness) and Purusha (pure awareness) and their interplay with each other within us human beings. Nature or Prakriti is all that is created and subject to cause and effect, while pure awareness or Purusha is formless and motionless and free of cause and effect. Purusha's ability to perceive objectively requires a reflective medium, which is not part of nature or Prakriti.

This reflective medium is Citta or consciousness, which manifests as a symbolic screen upon which the on-goings of creation or Prakriti are projected. Both Purusha and Cita don't possess a faculty that would enable them to be aware of their very own existence and are interdependent of each other.

Consciousness requires the witnessing awareness, yet at the same time is constantly distracted by the on-goings of nature. Fortunately consciousness has the potential to evolve and expand to ultimately become as motionless as awareness itself. The Yoga Sutras utilise this reflective and motionless state between awareness and consciousness through a process called yoking or coalescence, in which consciousness reflects pure awareness back to itself, so that awareness can realize that it is not part of nature.

Assagioli's Psychosynthesis divides the different states of consciousness into seven levels, starting from the lower, through the middle and the higher unconscious, which is surrounded by the collective consciousness. Its aim is to study and to work on all these different levels.

In Psychosomatic Medicine and Bio-Psychosynthesis, Roberto Assagioli states that the principal aims and tasks of Psychosynthesis are:

1. The elimination of the conflicts and obstacles, conscious and unconscious, that block (the complete and harmonious development of the human personality).
2. The use of active techniques to stimulate the psychic functions still weak and immature.

In his major book, *Psychosynthesis: A Collection of Basic Writings* (1965), Assagioli writes of three aims of Psychosynthesis:

> 'Let us examine whether and how it is possible to solve this central problem of human life, to heal this fundamental infirmity of man. Let us see how he may free himself from this enslavement and achieve a harmonious inner integration, true self-realization, and right relationships with others.'[72]

To our Western mind those ancient teachings and the language of modern psychology are very difficult concepts to grasp, and most practical techniques and how to utilise the results of self-study and self-observation are somewhere hidden between the lines.

Now - it is much easier to understand the meaning of the different levels of consciousness if we relate them to brain wave activity.

To most of us the most common levels of consciousness are when we are awake during the day and our brain is in beta wave mode or when we are asleep at night and our brain switches over to delta wave activity. This means that the lowest level of consciousness manifests in sleep when the brain frequency range is at its lowest level and that we are on a different level of consciousness in the daytime state, when our brain frequency range is much higher.

During sleep we have very little knowledge about reality or anything relating to life, or ideas regarding the truth of our being or a higher level of consciousness. In sleep there is nothing we can do or control. Even our dreams are arbitrary and we have no influence or control over them.

In our so-called daytime state, our knowledge about the true state of things and the truth about the world and ourselves is strongly blurred by daydreaming and things we imagine as well as our 'I believes' and 'personal philosophies'.

So the level of consciousness in our daytime state is only relative from a scale point of view if we put it in relation to a higher level of consciousness. In our everyday life we only can guess or imagine how the truth of oneself and things are perceived and experienced on this next higher level of consciousness.

This next higher level of consciousness is called Self-Realization or Self-

Consciousness[73], which means the realization and experience of our true nature being free of any layers and traces such as imaginations, identifications, 'I believes' and personal philosophies our mind and personality holds.

This state only manifests during gamma wave activity, in which our brain frequency range is highest and thought and mind activity is at its lowest or completely absent. States of self-realization are very rare and the sense of time in that state is experienced as being very spacious.

The German word for consciousness is Bewusstsein, which is the fusion of two different words i.e. Bewusst meaning conscious and Sein meaning being, hence Conscious Being or Conscious of Being.

So work on consciousness automatically leads to growth of being and that is the purpose of meditation.

The German term Bewusstsein (conscious being or conscious of being) describes this well since it's literal, and clearly points to a far deeper knowledge of this state.

Conscious of being means that we have full access to the truth about ourselves in the state of Self-Realization and we will know the full truth about what we are, because we 'realize' through actual experience what our true self is.

When we are in a state of awe we automatically are in the state of self-consciousness or self-realization. When we go on an adventure and everything around us is completely new to us and foreign, we are usually in the now or present moment, which describes the state of self-consciousness.

Everybody is familiar with stories from people who have had an accident and go on to describe their experience as seeing everything in slow motion, while feeling at peace. That describes the state of self-realization.

There is one more grade or state of consciousness which can only be grasped once the third state of consciousness is fully established. The masters in India call it enlightenment or Ahimsa, while the Buddhists call it Nirvana and Christians call it Christ consciousness. Other terms for this highest level of consciousness are Moksha or God –Realization.

The most accessible term can be found in the fourth way teaching, in which the fourth level of consciousness is called **Objective Consciousness.** Hence in this pure state of utter objectivity one will have full knowledge of the truth of everything that is. This includes the earth and its organic life, man and all his internal functions and abilities, plus the sum total of the universal laws and all that lies beyond.

As a matter of principle all of us are born as conscious beings and being or self-consciousness is in actual fact the only state of consciousness we know at that time. At this early stage in life, we simply don't know how not to 'be' and everything we perceive and can be aware of is perceived as exactly as it is, in its pure state of being or 'Isness'. Soon we are taught how not to 'be' and learn a lot about how we have to be and are supposed to be, until how we have to be and are supposed to be becomes what we believe to be. All this happens in the school of 'un-be-coming', and its teachers are our life around us as well as everybody in it.

So we can say the more biased and habitual we become, the further we will move away from the actual truth of what we are including in the world around us, and as a consequence the less conscious we will become. And we can say that the more we can sustain a neutral state of mind, the less is in the way to narrow consciousness down, and the closer we will be to the actual truth of what we truly are in relation to the world surrounding us.

So work on consciousness is clearing the 'lenses of perception' from all the accumulated dust that is profoundly blurring and clouding our vision. This process slowly takes us out of our everyday consciousness into self-consciousness or self-realization by means of self-study, by actively training our different brains and by regular meditation practice.

To summarise:

- We can say that a shift in consciousness always is accompanied by a change in brain wave frequency and activity.
- So we ascend from deep sleep (delta), to a state of relaxation (alpha), to a state of day dreaming or imagining (theta). This progresses to our everyday consciousness (beta), to a higher state of consciousness (gamma), which might appear in objectless meditation practice, in a state of awe or a situation of totally unexpected circumstances, as well as hearing about the death of a dear one, or facing an own life threatening situation.
- Regular and extended times of gamma wave activity will slowly alter our brain function and lead to permanent changes in white and grey matter, hence the physical changes in the brain go hand-in-hand

with self-consciousness manifesting as a permanent state within. Consciousness requires all the different brains to work to their full potential to be able to express itself through the physical.

Before we can start working on our different brains, we need to know more about the structure, function and design of our mind.

Exercise 10: Am I conscious

- *Observe how frequently you ascend and descend during the day through all the different levels of consciousness and try actively to experience and feel the quality of consciousness you are in at those given moments during the day, and how fast you are shifted onto another level.*

- *Try to detect how much time you spend in each of them and write it down.*

10. The Process – Stage III: Understanding The Mind

We can't deny that from the moment we were born as a truly conscious being to the moment we graduated from the school of 'un-be-coming', we have acquired and formed something almost completely artificial. And once that artificial part in us had gained more weight, it pulled our sense of self away from our true nature and sense of being. We literally became what we have learned and acquired from others via imitation and repetition. Hence that acquired part turned into and mistakenly became our sense of self.

Wherever we feel or place our sense of 'I' is what we will become or will subsequently identify with, i.e. if our sense of 'I' is placed in Great Ideas that is what we will ultimately become.

Unfortunately this world we imitate and learn from does not hold any knowledge that teaches us how we can keep our true state of being, whilst simultaneously growing. So we can objectively say that we are in reality not one being or person, because we have split into two parts. An acquired part and a part we were born with.

Every school of thought refers to the acquired part as our personality and to the part we were born with as our true nature or essence.

True nature or essence consists of everything we are born with and what we were given. This includes all our natural talents, as well as higher abilities like intuition, inspiration, and the creative centre form part of its intrinsic makeup. Essence resides in 'Sentrum' and the unchanging nature or formless truth within us, is humbly expressed through essence.

Personality, which is an absolute necessity and is required to succeed in life and interact, is formed of everything else, but it is mainly animated and driven by habits and conditioning.

Personality, which occupies a lot of space in our mind, is exposed to many experiences and events in life and can adapt accordingly and change when required. Those changes in our personality are primarily caused via association and identification with others.

For example, if we meet a new group of people and are fascinated and inspired by the way they look at life, we want to become one of them and soon take on the way they speak, move, dress and even live by association and imitation.

Our true nature or true self, which in essence does not change during the course of our life, does not form any part of the architecture of the mind and is hardly ever exposed or seen, because it is hidden below the waves, noise and actions of our personality. Hence, personality is vulnerable and can easily be influenced and even hurt and sometimes damaged, while our true nature is well protected and can't be touched that easily.

Once we pierce through the illusion of oneness, we soon realize that a large part of our mind is formed of countless so called 'sub-personalities', which live according to the concept of Assagioli's psychosynthesis below the field of our awareness, within the 'middle unconscious'. Ancient schools of thought call them 'little ME's', or in certain Buddhist schools small 'I' and big 'I', while the fourth way teaching calls them different 'I's'.

We constantly alternate from one sub-personality to the other. One might wake up in the morning, as the personality of the husband talking to his wife, turning into the father while having breakfast with the children, instantly becoming the son during a phone call with one's mother, shifting into the manager at work and into best buddy with friends.

Other sub-personalities can switch the loving husband into the angry husband, the tolerant and understanding father into the disciplinarian father and the tough manager into a carefully listening colleague. Yet the most astonishing fact is, that none of those sub-personalities are aware of each other's existence. The moment one of them has taken centre stage it truly believes that it represents the whole of us, yet at the same time it might hold a completely different belief regarding the present issue or situation than the previous sub-personality, which was present half an hour ago. All of that takes place mechanically within in a glimpse of a moment without us being aware of it even happening.

On top of that, each of those sub-personalities, which form part of our mind, are attracted to a different kind of external influence. One is pulled towards Beta-Influence, while the other is drawn towards Alpha-Influence.

So we might fall asleep at night as a sub-personality, which decided to get up early in the morning to do some yoga self-practice or meditation. However, we may then wake up in the morning as a sub-personality, which believes that a long lay in leads to a much better start of the day than doing yoga first thing in the morning.

So we can clearly say that in reality we are not one person but consist of many sub-personalities, which mechanically alternate with each other, and that each of our main sub-personalities are probably aiming for a completely different objective, depending on which external influences they are attracted to.

This is the reason why many people are so full of contradictions, as well as the many frictions they experience and have to struggle with, or have to face within themselves and with others. Then we can say that it is much easier to observe the alternation of different personalities in other people, and distinguish them from each other, than it is to observe and detect them within ourselves.

This is due to the fact that they usually take over at a speed, which is so fast, that they can't be recognised in the state of our everyday consciousness. It requires a much more conscious state of perception, that is slightly further removed or above our familiar field of awareness, to catch them and their habitual response in time. This will then allow one to act from a more refined level of consciousness that is free of contradictions yet filled with integrity and gravitas.

Sub-personalities represent most of our 'I believes' and engrained habitual behaviours and conditionings. Their sum-total forms our personality, which forms the majority of our mind and is experienced within us as one undivided self, which resides within our physical body. This makes us believe and live under the illusion that we are one personality, with an individual name attached to it.

Depending on the sound and vibration our name is emanating when spoken and the way we relate and resonate with it, our body will shape itself accordingly. If our parents and most of the people in our close environment charged the pronunciation of our name with the energy of love, respect, trust and happiness, its reverberation and frequency will allow the body to grow into a more or less balanced and harmonised posture, while if the reverberation of the sound is continuously disrespectful, degrading and negative, our body will shape itself accordingly.

The same happens with the growth of our personality and its many features, appearing as individual sub-personalities subdividing and confusing our true sense of self. All those different little ME's hold a vast amount of useful energy. Each of them is directing this energy along its own direction of intent, irrespective of it being useful and conducive to the whole or not. This makes a true, or a single minded intention next to impossible, which gives rise to the question if there is any chance to develop true integrity after all. Without true integrity Substance of Gravitas can't be produced.

The term integrity comes from the Greek word 'integritas' & 'integra', which means 'whole'. It refers to a state of consciousness in which our thoughts, actions and words are congruent and free of contradictions.

At the same time the term clearly points towards a definite kind of action. We have to become active to integrate the divided self into one undivided self, hence true integrity (wholeness). In other words all of our main sub-personalities need to become aware of each other, agree with each other and speak the same language. That in return will enable them to form a cooperative, which is aiming in the same direction and is working towards a single objective. Without self-study this is impossible to achieve, and without a far greater force then the force of life, this becomes even more impossible. This force is called 'the force of meaning', which will be discussed at a later point.

Exercise 11: Studying Our Personality

- *Neutrally observe yourself and identify what you consider your main sub-personalities to be and what kind of external circumstances or events trigger them into manifestation.*

- *Please refrain from any judgement or categorisations like good or bad and positive or negative.*

- *Write them down and realise which ones are conducive to your inner development and which ones are not conducive to it.*

- *Keep observing them without trying to resist, eliminate or to change them. The more you observe and find out about the way the main sub-personalities behave and act on you and your surroundings, the higher the chances are that you can transcend them at a later stage.*

Blissful Ignorance

Besides all the little sub-personalities or ME's which are forming part of our mind there is a psychic substance, which can be described as 'padding'.

This psychic substance functions like an insulation, separating the little ME's from each other. The padding is mainly made of a fine matrix of interwoven mechanical responses and habitual patterns, creating thin layers of this psychic substance. On top of that, each conflicting want or contradiction while acting itself out, is releasing another substance created by the energy of denial, which is adding to the thickness of the padding between each little ME. The padding works as a shock absorber, which allows us to live in a state of blissful ignorance and prevent us from seeing the true impact of our conflicting wants, our frictions and contradictory actions on others and ourselves.

In ancient teachings this is known as the Veil of Ignorance, which needs to be removed because it stands between the truth and us. Other scriptures describe it as the Veil of Illusion, separating us from Brahman/Shiva/Buddha-nature/Sat Nam, the all-encompassing truth within everything we can perceive.

Each time a new sub-personality starts taking over, its gravitational pull, that is kick-started by an external event which is explicitly attuned to it, draws us into the Veil of Ignorance in which we lose consciousness of the sub-personality we embodied before and all of what it intended, promised and verbally stated.

The irony is that if all the padding were removed in its entirety, we would implode and die instantly. We would not be able to stand the weight of the shock that the realisation of the true state of our contradicting nature would cause.

The thicker the Veil of Ignorance, the more difficult it will become to change and evolve, and the further away one will move from ethical principles and conscience.

Non-Conscious States

To gain an even greater understanding of the way our mind is structured and functions, we have to study the different non-conscious states. These states are created by the mind itself, to ensure its superior position and role within our internal cosmos. All non-conscious states form a powerful counterforce, which prevent us from further evolving within, and becoming a more conscious being.

This incredibly powerful force controls and interferes in everything we do and is produced by the mind itself. It is always in action to prevent us from seeing the truth, to pierce through the Veil of Ignorance and to differentiate true knowledge from false knowledge. The Yoga Sutras of Patanjali describe those non-conscious states in detail and give clear instructions how to work with them through self-study. Other mystic teachings like Sahaj Yoga describe them as 'the negative powers'. In Christianity they form part of the Ten Commandments and the fourth way teaching calls them 'sleep producing states'. Each path and philosophy uses different terminologies, yet in essence they contain the same meaning and transmit the same knowledge.

Brainwave activity plays a major part in fuelling those different non-conscious states, and a un-balance between the different brains allows this force to have an even greater impact on us.

The first non-conscious state is called 'daydreaming'. Precious theta waves fuel this non-conscious state and shift us away from everything that is real. In this state we very often lose the connection to our physical body and the whole world around us. We become absorbed in a dream world while we are going about our daily business.

This very often happens whilst driving a car, sitting at our computer, watching TV or on a walk with the dog. We lose all sense of time and once we are shocked out of this state, by someone suddenly talking to us, or reacting to the ringtone of our mobile, or a sudden noise around us, we usually have no recollection of what had happened during the entire time of our day-dreaming. We have no idea what had triggered us into it and how long we had stayed there.

The second non-conscious state is called 'lying'. This non-conscious state has turned into our second nature. Human beings are lying all the time. We have acquired and developed many different forms of lying and have become masters in using specific lies to respond to external circumstances and situations we want to avoid.

One of the most common lies is when we feel really low, or just had an argument and someone asks us how we are and we respond enthusiastically that we are great and that life could not be better. Another frequent lie is complementing someone on how healthy they look and how gorgeous their figure is, or how delicious their food had been at last night's dinner party, while thinking at the same time that they have seen better days, could do with a workout at the gym, and that their food could had been a bit more inspiring and less plain.

These kinds of lies are not seen or regarded as lies at all anymore in our society. They have become part of a set of rules and unspoken agreements of how we are supposed to behave and interact in our social environment, so that no one ever knows and sees the true state of our feelings and emotions.

True integrity only can be established when we have become strong enough to bring lies up into the field of our awareness and face them. This way we are at least aware of the lies. If we allow this lies to go unchecked we have to invent more and more lies all the time to cover up the lies from yesterday, or the week before.

Most of our lies are mechanical and we have no knowledge of them, and unfortunately they only increase and never decrease by themselves. To become a more conscious being, we have to observe our own individual different ways of lying and slowly transcend them, so that we can build a powerful counterforce, which is called 'clear conscience'. Otherwise they will weigh us down and keep us on the lowest level of consciousness, in which conscience has died and the possibility of our inner evolution has ceased to exist.

The third non-conscious state can be called 'instant considering'. If only we could realise how much time we spend considering all sorts of things. One famous form of instant considering, is when someone is commenting on our behaviour. One tiny remark can trigger hours of inner dialogue and create hundreds of different internal scenarios regarding the way we should have responded and behaved. Massive amounts of instant considering are produced, when we feel less appreciated than someone else. Deeply engrained habitual emotions and thought patterns are brought up to the surface and throw us off balance. The confident and life embracing person we had been a minute ago has crumbled, and turned into a shadowy image of themselves. Our mind and the thoughts and feelings it produces are putting everything into question while we diminish more and more into insignificance.

Yet in reality, most of the time when this kind of considering is taking place, there is a high possibility that our response is based on misinterpretation and misunderstanding of the actual situation, due to lack of objectivity. It is usually an unnecessary event and a total waste of time. Once the waves have flattened and our mind is able to put things into perspective again, we often ask ourselves what that whole inner drama was about.

If it is the other way round and we have overstepped the boundaries and upset someone else's feelings, or things did not go according to our plan, we will go through a rollercoaster of inner dialogue, explaining and defending ourselves to justify our situation. Once instant considering is triggered and has gained its momentum, we won't be able to stop it and have to wait until it slows down and has faded out.

Instant considering has a major impact on our adrenals and is raising the stress-level in our physical body profoundly. It eats up massive amounts of energy and can deplete us completely. It often interferes with our sleep pattern and deprives us from deep sleep phases during the night, as well as possibly leading to compulsive and unconscious decisions, which don't help make our life easy and we usually regret them afterwards.

The fourth non-conscious state is 'mechanical talking'. People love to talk, and mechanical talking is something we all love to indulge in. Like instant considering, which is the internal form of mechanical talking, it is a state which most of times is uncontrollable. Once it is kick-started we will be on a ride. It is worth neutrally observing other people for a while, to get a better understanding of how it acts itself out and takes place.

People instantly go into mechanical talking to fill silent gaps in conversations. We have forgotten how to be in each other's company without necessarily having to chat all the time, we un-learned how to be silent and feel comfortable with it.

Another form of mechanical talking is literally verbalising every thought our mind produces. One can clearly witness how disjointed and incoherent those verbalised thoughts are. Many people use mechanical talking to hide and cover up their insecurities or shortcomings. If we observe a group of people who are indulging in mechanical talking, we will experience that no one is truly listening to each other, everybody is happily engaged in mechanical talking, but in reality no one is heard, understood and listened to.

Mechanical talking if not controlled, can penetrate into every aspect of our life, it can diminish the ability to listen to others, it makes people interrupt others while they are talking, and it rarely contains any meaning. Its main content is meaningless, it actually just happens.

The fifth non-conscious state is 'selling & shopping negative feelings'. Our world has become a massive market place in which we sell and shop tons of negative feelings. Most people sell more than they shop and have become extremely rich by doing so. Hundreds of reality shows have popped up, which show people throwing their negative feelings at each other and we find great satisfaction and pleasure by watching them.

Many people have nothing else left to do in life than spreading their negative feelings wherever they go. If someone is exposing their negative feelings about others and the world on us, soon our own negative feelings are activated and come into life. Slowly they enervate every part of our being and undermine everything we have established within. They try to poison our integrity, our sense for what is right and wrong, and everything, which is noble and divine in us.

Negative feelings have to be carefully evaluated and observed. They have a major impact on our physical body, which becomes prone to attracting illnesses and they weaken our immune system, as well as our emotions by diminishing our ability to be compassionate and aware of other people's suffering. The damage they can cause on our psychological makeup and personality spans from dogmatic thinking to inability to interact, as well as destructive and self-destructive behaviour, to acts of violence and aggressiveness. Nothing constructive and creative can grow on selling and shopping negative feelings and any inner development will come to a standstill, or stop completely, if this non-conscious state is not brought up into the field of our awareness, before it has become irreversibly mechanical.

The sixth non-conscious state is 'imagination', which is one of the most powerful non-conscious states. Our society promotes and fosters the ability to imagine and has turned it into a positive and very useful ability. The noun imagination contains the word 'image' within the context that the image is not actually present to our senses, hence it is not real, but rather a blueprint of fiction perceived by our inner eye or by visualization. In other words it is simply the image-making power of the mind itself, which is projecting the image onto the screen of consciousness to be perceived by our awareness.

Before we go into further exploration of this particular state we have to clearly point out that in this train of thought imagination should not be mistaken with intuition and creativity or creative force.

On a path of self-enquiry…

"too much imagination only leads to disappointment".

Most of what we believe we are, how we are and the way we think that others perceive us, is mainly the creation of our own imagination.

The 'image' or idea we have created in our mind and the way we see ourselves is far removed from the actual reality and the truth of what we represent to the world, ourselves and to other people.

Now that imagined image we call our 'self' imagines all sorts of other things. It imagines our future, as well as many parts of our past, which we in actual fact can't properly remember. It also imagines itself to being utterly objective and truly conscious, and it imagines that it possesses great knowledge and has reached the highest levels of consciousness. It imagines itself sitting for hours in meditation, and it even imagines that it has found inner peace and stillness of mind and thought, and that it has transcended all frictions, conflicts and contradictions and also that it is in constant communication with the 'management upstairs'.

Unfortunately what that imagined part does not realise, is that it does not walk the walk, that it does not see the need to put what it preaches into action, and that it lives in a self-created world of blissful ignorance.

Other forms of imaginations are what we imagine and project into others. If we are taught by a teacher, or committed to follow a spiritual master, our imagination has the power to turn those people into someone far superior or even into a god like manifestation. The disillusionment will hit the moment the teacher or master does not behave or act according to our imagination, and we end up being upset and disappointed.

We spend a lot of time imagining and projecting our imaginations into other people. And if we imagine an idea often enough we start believing that it is true and real.

Now, no human being has the energy to keep up all the different layers of imagination forever. One day, reality will catch up and this safe haven will be flooded by the power of the reality of life and things will crumble.

We have to observe carefully when we fall into imagination, especially during important events, while talking or working with other people and when we sit in meditation. It has to be remembered that the power of the mind can reproduce whatever it wants to, and for us, this will be perceived as real as our own physical body.

The seventh non-conscious state is the most powerful and is called 'Identification'.

Our negative feelings, which control a great part of our life, only can do that because we identify with them and in due course we become them. All the other non-conscious states derive their life and energy because we identify with them and ultimately become them.

We embody our lies, our instant considering, our mechanical talking and daydreaming via identification. We identify with external events, people, impressions and emotions through the power of our five physical senses.

Our mind, which is comprised of different sub-personalities, layers of padding and an interconnecting matrix, accommodating the non-conscious states is directly connected to our five senses.

Those five senses constantly draw our attention outwards and towards external objects, events and people and give us plenty of opportunities to identify with whatever attracts our attention. Whatever we identify with can give us a strong sense of self, whether it is the identification with our profession, family, friends, possessions etc.

We have to study identification very carefully because the more we understand about it, the more we understand about ourselves. Ultimately understanding and utilising identification will be the key to our inner transformation.

All non-conscious states have one thing in common, they have a life and a momentum of their own, they occupy and rule most parts of our life and we have little control over them. The moment any of those non-conscious states takes over, we are taken out of the present moment and lose our connection with true sense of self.

One non-conscious state can ignite and activate another, hence they work very well together. For example, we usually identify with what we imagine, and let's suppose we suddenly recall an unpleasant experience, which took place decades ago, our negative feelings awaken and take over. If we happen to be in the company of a friend while that vague memory fills our mind and emotions, we will spread this negative feeling and share it with our friend. Because we cannot properly remember what really happened in the past, and while being controlled by the state of negative feelings, we start lying to our friend by inventing and adding to what we vaguely remembered from the past. *Are you slowly getting how it works?*

So as long as our mind supports and is in cahoots with these non-conscious states, true balance and self-consciousness can't be established and manifest.

Inner Stories

One large department within the structure of our mind is occupied by our inner stories. Everywhere we go we are selling our inner stories. Everybody we meet has to buy at least one of our inner stories, and people we have known for a long time like friends and our family, know our inner stories in and out and have heard them and their many different versions hundreds of times before.

In return, we have had to listen to the inner stories of our friends and relatives again and again. We are sometimes surprised by the way they are garnished in a different way each time they are told, and we even can tell under which situation which inner story will be sold.

Very often the inner stories of others are hitting a nerve within us and we become very annoyed when listening to them. What we are not aware of, is that we are in no way different from them and are doing exactly the same.

Our inner stories give our life a certain meaning and a great sense of self. They are something we can rely on and by selling them to others we are getting a lot of attention. People respond with compassion to very specific stories and feel sorry for us and pity us for others. The very powerful stories, which always hit their target get people on our side, and it's usually the stories we have in common with others, which turn people into our companions or friends.

Every sub-personality has free and twenty-four hour access to the department of inner stories, and they pop in and out on a regular basis. It decides which category of stories is the most efficient one to choose from and will sell best. Unfortunately the sub-personality which is just about to sell a new story has no knowledge about which story was used by the last personality that was visiting the department of inner stories before, due to the thick layers of our 'padding'.

Most of the time we don't even realise that we are repeating the same story again and again to the same person. All inner stories we tell have become mechanical and are expressed as a matter of habit. Most of them have gone through many transformations and changes and have hardly anything to do with the actual truth to how the original event or experience took place.

The department of inner stories has a massive influence on the way we interact and behave. Its purpose is to sell as many stories a day as possible and to turn as many of the current events of our life, especially dramas, into an inner story. By doing so the department of inner stories has the potential and capacity to expand to such an extent, that in time it will start buying all other departments, and by the time we have reached the last third of our life we have turned into our own inner story.

We all know an elderly relative who has become trapped by the past and has turned into his or her history. It is interesting to observe that the older people become, the more accessible and vivid their memory of the past becomes. What initially had turned into an inner story is gradually being believed as the actual truth of the past event. This sees the story turning into real history and becomes authentic. Nevertheless people, who are permanently living in the past, have lost their connection to true sense of self and their current life has become irrelevant. They have become immune to any of the different external influences, which could reconnect them to the present moment again; hence their present life has become meaningless.

Inner stories require constant attention to still their hunger. If one of our close friends has changed within and is not buying them anymore because he or she has understood that it is not helping us to move on, the relationship starts crumbling. We start losing interest and soon find other people, who will happily buy into our story, which keeps us satisfied throughout our life until we have turned into and become our own history.

To summarise:

- We can say that the department of inner stories, which occupies a large part of our mind, stores every dramatized event, which is emotionally charged and loaded, as well as occasions that we personally interpret and judge as iniquities.
- Then we can say that it converts this kind of events, via a refined method called 'blissful denial', into one of our personal stories. The more often each story is told and sold, the more weight it gains and the further away it moves from the actual truth.

- Furthermore we can say, that in time the sum-total of all inner stories together become so dense, that they form their own artificial organism within our personality, with which we identify more and more until we derive our whole sense of self through this densely charged structure.
- And in addition we can say, that most people attract, relate and communicate with each other through this body of inner stories, which is comprised of highly charged dramas and blatant injustice.
- Ultimately we can say that nothing constructive and healthy can grow on the energy of drama. It is unavoidable to work consciously on the body of inner stories and vital to study its functions and its impact on our state of being.

Exercise 12: Giving Scale to Inner Stories

- *Observe how often you feel the need to tell one of your inner stories. Study the inner stories you sell most and discover how much satisfaction you gain from that.*

- *On a percentage scale from 0 to 100 how much do you derive your full sense of self from your inner stories?*

- *Try to remember not to sell any of your inner stories for at least two weeks. What did you learn from that?*

About Book Keeping

Another department, which occupies a large space in our mind, is the Department of Book Keeping. Our mind's operation can be compared to that of a computer, just millions of times more advanced. Everything, which enters through external influences, sensory perception and internal moods and emotions is monitored, stored, documented and filed within this amazing instrument.

Massive amounts of information are not consciously recognised. This is due to the existence of alternating sub-personalities, which each individually, once present, believe it represents the whole. They only see what they are inclined to want to see and absorb only what strengthens their presence and extends their shelf life. The majority of valid information enters unrecognised by the temporary presence of the little 'ME's', and is immediately absorbed by the darkness of our non-consciousness. That does not imply that this kind of passing information will be lost, or can't be accessed.

However, much information is stored if not acted upon. It is also like we have a huge spread sheet on which we keep a check and balance. In fact, human beings excel in bookkeeping.

For example:

- "**I** have given you a precious gift and **you** haven't given me anything in return."
- "He owes me an apology."
- "She only gave me something insignificant last Christmas, so I won't bother with her this year."

Other matters that will be documented on our spread sheets are hundreds of un-kept promises in written and in verbal form like: "You have promised to be more considerate in the future," or "You have committed yourself to helping out every Saturday morning," the list can be endless.

Other issues, which will be documented, are any form of lip service, every penny of what people owe us, all lies and exploitations and ultimately all of what we believe or imagine life and people should do for us will be added on to one of our spread sheets.

Very little is documented of what we owe and have promised to others, as well as hardly anything is written down of what we have promised to ourselves. This includes not being so self-absorbed and ignorant anymore, not constantly taking things to our advantage, being more understanding and compassionate with others and to stop lying all the time.

Our little 'ME's' are always right and don't owe anything to anybody. So we justify our own actions by constantly considering what other people have not done for us or owe us.

We can well imagine what kind of un-balance within our psychic nature this creates and how much energy we could reclaim if our books could be balanced.

How can we possibly find stillness in body mind and being, without balancing our books?

"Transcend and include"[74] that is what is required in meditation. We include everything, which benefits a faculty in us called experience. Actual experience is what we usually can rely on, at least most of the time. Everything else falls into the domain of theory or belief, and true experience forms an important part of our psychological makeup and our personality. The most honest expression of us is the sum-total of our experience.

So we aim to transcend the so called 'little me' which is singing our story and blames life and everybody in it through countless mechanical repetitions.

To summarise:

- We can say that all of us store a nice bundle of spread sheets in the department of book keeping in our mind, which document in minute detail what other people owe and have promised to us in the past.
- We then can say, that we are not as precise with our documentations regarding what we owe and have promised to others.
- Furthermore we can say that we forget to document most of the things we owe and have promised to ourselves.
- Ultimately we can understand that without keeping our books in

balance, or raising above all this unnecessary book keeping, lasting harmony and balance within cannot be established.

Exercise 13: Balancing our spread sheets

- *Observe how often you document what other people owe you or you believe they owe you.*

- *How much time do you spend thinking about the issue?*

- *Observe the lower emotions that book keeping evoke in you.*

- *Stick to one of your main promises to yourself for one month and be surprised how that impacts on your life.*

The Power of Opposing Forces

Cause and effect, the law of action and reaction, plus and minus charge in electricity, active and passive forces are all different forms, expressions and manifestations of 'the law of opposition' or 'the law of opposing forces'.

In Hinduism it is represented by the divine interplay between Shiva and Shakti, in Taoism it is known as the balance between Yin and Yang, as well as the symbolism of the sun and the moon, which can be found in most philosophical systems and in shamanism or paganism.

Duality can only exist on the notion of subject and object awareness. The law of opposition is two-dimensional and its scale of interaction is mainly linear. Black and white only manifest due to the absence or presence of intensity of light, neither form part of the colour spectrum in a prism or within the appearance of a rainbow.

Opposing forces govern and influence all cyclical appearances like day or night as well as our seasons of winter opposed to summer and spring opposed to autumn. Other examples in which the opposing forces are expressing themselves can be found in nature, in which water turns into ice and metals become liquid under extreme heat and solidify when cooling down.

One of the most powerful opposing forces is life itself, which starts with an inhalation and death that we enter with an exhalation. Within our life span we can experience phases of hunger or satiety and periods of illness or health. Depending on what life has in store for us, we might become rich and educated, or are destined to be poor and un-educated. Independent of our possessions we might experience times of war and sadness and decades of peace and happiness. Regardless of which country or way of life and culture we are born into, an opposing force is present to everything we do, decide or passively observe.

The law of opposing forces could be called the law of friction since friction is produced in large quantities. It constantly pushes us towards the opposite extreme along the line of two opposing manifestations, and once we arrive there we are pulled back towards the other end again, due to the friction it generates within this process.

The energy of friction plays a major role in evolution, whether it is our own inner development or the evolution of the earth or the universe. It is friction that creates a special kind of pressure, which is required to facilitate change. To transform flat land into a mountain requires a tremendous amount of friction, within the seismic dynamics of our continental plates, until enough pressure is produced, so that the increasing energy within the friction can transform to manifest itself as a mountain.

The law of opposition follows us everywhere and it seems to be impossible to become free of it and rise above its influence. This law contains and sustains the whole of creation and everything we perceive as the external world and the whole universe is under its influence.

We are inclined to believe that the law of the opposing forces governs our internal world to the same extent that it rules the external world. This is only true as long as it is based on the way we are conditioned and taught by example of others and the world around us. We simply don't know better and by imitating the external world and everybody we know, our mind is applying the same laws that are governing the external world to all the internal functions, which results in friction.

'Yes or No' questions and conflicts of 'right or wrong' as well as decisions like 'should I or shouldn't I' and upsets relating to 'them or me' all of this creates our ups or downs and highs or lows. We alternate between being negative or positive, between being happy or unhappy as well as fluctuating between conscious and non-conscious levels of perception.

The moment two sub-personalities become aware of each other they start opposing each other to create resistance and friction until one of them gains the upper hand and is in charge until an external event requires a different little 'ME' to take the centre of the stage for a while.

It is obvious that we can't control and change the opposing forces of nature and the external world. But what we can develop is, and this only can happen when we are under the influence of the right circumstances, to evolve within and become a different being.

Being, is a state, and **there is no opposing force** in being or within the 'Isness' of this state. And the more our state of being evolves through conscious effort and work on oneself, the more we are able to transcend the dynamics of the opposing forces within our mind and ourselves.

Being does not attract resisting or opposing force, because there is no real opposite to being except inexistence, which is void of any idea or concept of state. The origins of true being go beyond the borders and limitations of duality, and the way to develop a different being is by means of the scale and power of meaning, which will be discussed at a later stage in this book.

To summarise:

- We can say that the laws of opposing forces are acting on us wherever we are and wherever we go, as well as governing and containing the external world and the universe.
- Furthermore we can say that self-enquiry, self-observation and conscious work on one's self is synonymous with work on friction and the law of opposition.
- Then we can say that the law of opposition does not necessarily apply to our inner world, due to the possible evolution of our being.
- Ultimately we can say that in becoming a different being by means of the power of meaning we can include and transcend all friction within, and channel the energy it contains via the direction of ease, which manifests as lasting peace with ourselves.

Exercise 14: Studying The Law of Opposition

- *Observe the most obvious opposing forces in your external life.*

- *Observe what kind of circumstances are causing friction within and how often are you caught in a 'yes or no' and 'should I or shouldn't I' situation?*

- *Give each of your main frictions a name, which makes you smile and does not carry any connotations.*

- *Neutrally recognise them as such when they repeatedly appear again in due course, without trying to resist them.*

Impressions of Life And The Way They Act on us

To gain an even better understanding of the way our mind functions, we have to discuss how the impressions of life act on us. Everything we experience in life, whether it is the visual, auditory or sensual expression or appearance of the external world, is nothing more than a constant flow of impressions entering our system through at least one of our five senses.

A succession of impressions are perceived by our mind and grasped usually by one of the four brains as the present event, of which the most recent impression has been already filed as a past memory in the library of our history department.

The Yoga Sutras of Patanjali describes the matter of impressions as a process of Prakriti (nature) projecting its on-going impressions and events onto a screen called Cita (consciousness), which is then perceived by Purusha (awareness). And that everything manifesting as Prakriti (nature) is transient and subject to change, hence an illusion. Further it is mentioned that the moment Cita evolves, and instead of displaying Prakriti's impressions reflects Purusha back to itself, the truth of the unchanging nature behind all illusion can be realised.

Illusion in Sanskrit is Maya, meaning ma (not) ya (that). In Advaita Vedanta Maya is seen like a veil and represents all physical and mental appearances. Maya keeps consciousness embroiled in its ever changing play and conceals Brahman the true self from realising the truth.

The Hindu scripture Devi Mahatmyam says that the Great Maya (Mahamaya) is covering Vishnu's eyes in his divine sleep (Yoganidra) during the cycles of creation until all what has manifested within this dream is re-absorbed into one. Hence Maya seen as an aspect of Devi (Divine Mother) can both keep us and free us from the veil of illusion.

In Buddhism the experience of illusion depends on the level of consciousness of the practitioner. In everyday consciousness one becomes what one perceives via identification and attachment, while on higher levels of consciousness Buddha is neither attached nor non-attached, hence not effected by illusion, which represents the path of the middle way in Buddhism.

Most of the impressions that enter don't leave a strong imprint or groove in our mind. The impact each impression creates depends on our state of consciousness and which sub-personality is present at a particular moment in time, as well as which of the four brains is active and tries to assimilate the information, or pass it on to another department.

In other words, each individual impression, every event and the way our life unfolds is perceived through our own individual lenses. Those lenses change constantly, because each little 'ME' prefers to wear its individual style of lenses and has different optic requirements.

For example, in the non-conscious state of daydreaming most of life's impressions enter almost unrecognised and we aren't able to clearly remember the actual event, which took place while we indulged in daydreaming. We only remember that something has happened during our daydreaming and depending on more deeply engrained imprints of memories like scent, colours and noises, we vaguely know what happened and that at least something has happened. But the moment the impressions of life contain traces of information, which need to be documented in one of our spread sheets, we instantly shift back into our 'day-consciousness', yet have little control over which little 'ME' has taken centre stage and had interpreted and documented the impression, according to the lenses it is wearing.

For example, it is important to know that each individual person perceives the impression of a tree and absorbs the impression of a tree in an entirely different way than we perceive it and assimilate it, even if they were to stand at the same angle and same distance to the tree as we do.

The way one perceives the different impressions and events of life depends on what kind of association and experience one has made with that kind of impression before. If we had successfully climbed a tree in the past, we will perceive all future impressions of a tree in a completely different way than a person that was hit and severely injured by a falling tree in the past.

In the same way, we might perceive the impression of a person we don't know very well differently than a friend of ours who has known that person for a long time. To us the first impression of that person might be very inspiring and will leave a pleasant imprint in our mind, while it might cause a massive upset in our friend, due to a recent unpleasant experience caused and initiated by that particular person.

The majority of people respond to most of the different impressions of life with one of their habitual patterns or mechanical responses. If a present impression, which is about to enter, has got the slightest similarity with a past impression we will respond to it in the same way as the one which has left an imprint in the past.

In other words, if we are introduced to a new person at a dinner party, and the first impression of that person reminds us of another person we know very well, our response to the new person, will be extremely influenced by the association we have with the person that the new person reminds us of. We might invent a polite excuse to get away from the new person as soon as we can and tell the friend who has introduced us that we can't stand that type of person at all etc. If we have responded in a less conditioned way, soon we could have discovered that this new person was holding the key elements leading to a window of opportunity we could only have dreamed of.

If an impression of life is perceived and grasped for what it actually is while it enters, which implies that we respond to it very consciously, than it will naturally find its way to the correct brain.

For example, if an impression, which is loaded with signals of danger enters, it will automatically be received by the 'instinctual brain', which activates the fight and flight reflex and we will respond accordingly. As we said before, the 'instinctual brain' knows exactly what it needs to do and we should not interfere in the way it works. However the 'instinctual brain' regulates the intake and requirements of our food and uses likes and dislikes that are keeping things in perfect balance to sustain a healthy body. If the 'emotional brain' tries to do the work for the 'instinctual brain', because it developed a passion for sweets, it will override the alarming dislike response of the 'instinctual brain', due to its identification with sweets.

The more confused the brains become via conditioning the more they try to do the work for another brain and the less conscious we will respond and deal with the incoming impressions of life.

To summarise:

- We can say that regardless of what conscious or non-conscious state we are in at each given moment in time, the uninterrupted stream of life's expressions never stops and acts on us in one way or another.
- Then we can say that each impression or each succession of

impressions, which form an event, enter our system through at least one of our five senses.

- Furthermore we can say that depending on the level of consciousness we are in and which feature or little 'ME' is present to perceive the impression, as well as what kind of lenses we are wearing and what state of emotions we are in, the impression might not fall into the right department.

- This means the different brains might assimilate or accumulate impressions, which do not belong there.

- To conclude we can say that the majority of people haven't developed something permanent within themselves yet, hence whichever part of us perceives the impression is probably not established in a neutral state of mind and, will respond according to its level of ability. i.e. non-conscious.

- And finally we can say that as long as there is no unity within ourselves, we won't be able to respond to the impressions of life in a conscious way, and we won't perceive things as they truly are. Our view on things will be obstructed by the different lenses we habitually wear, which means that we safely and comfortably can hide behind the Veil of Maya or illusion.

This gives rise to the question of what would happen if we were to perceive and recognise everything as nothing more than a fleeting succession of life's impressions forming an event. I leave it up to you to find out.

Exercise 15: Being an actor on the stage of life

- *Observe how often you are identifying with the impressions of life's event, which are currently acting on you.*

- *Imagine yourself being an actor on stage in a play called "My Life". For example, choose one event a day whether at work or in your private life in which you can shift into a mind set in which you can feel and say; 'This is. ...... (your name) having a coffee with his best friend event" or "This is........ (your name) in a meeting with her colleagues event'.*

- *What impact does this have on you and your day?*

Illustration: Erika Shapiro

11. The Process – Stage IV: Understanding The Physical Body

The mystery of what animates the human body can't be grasped, because whatever animates the human body is invisible, at least to our physical eyes. What is obviously always visible to us is each other's physical body.

112

Our association with ourselves is mainly through the association with our own physicality we experience through our five senses and our name. It is the physical appearance of a person we identify with, attach and connect to and perceive as real, because we can see, smell, hear, feel and even touch the person. Based on what we see in this physical appearance we instinctively like or dislike the person in front of us.

Considering the idea, that there is *something* that is animating the physical body and using the body to express itself, to move about and to interact.

Many philosophies consider the body as an obstacle or something irrelevant, and usually describe it as nothing more than an illusion. Other religious teachings go to great lengths in the way they preach how to suppress and refrain from any physical experience that might be pleasant or pleasurable. A lot of different spiritual approaches work with techniques, that help to overcome the physical body.

From the idea of a higher consciousness point of view, this clearly indicates that those kinds of religions, philosophies and spiritual teachings are working on the level of consciousness of the law of opposition, which only results in friction. And as long as there is no alternative or greater perspective available to the followers of those teachings, life can easily turn into a never-ending battleground in which the deeply engrained belief fights the body.

Regardless of what we believe in and whatever teaching or religion we follow, the very fact remains that as long as we are alive and relatively conscious, this body is not going to disappear. So wherever we go and whatever we do we never will be without this physical body.

From the moment we are born into this world, the physical body and all its internal functions are regulated and taken care of by the highly developed 'instinctual brain'. This brain is responsible for our whole nervous system, our body temperature and circulatory system, as well as all the organs, the reproductive system, our heart function and the five senses. If the whole homeostasis of the body is kept in balance the 'instinctual brain' will fulfil its task to its full potential until the day we die.

Everything we learn and acquire happens through this body, even our inner evolution and meditation practice happens through and within this body. The truth is that we completely depend on our body and its functions.

The body encases that invisible being, which is conscious, aware and perceives the impressions of life through the five senses of the physical body, as long as it continues to exist.

The question arises: *Why do we have to evolve and acquire a different being within this physical form?*

The answer is simple:

The physical body is our reference point to the now!

Wherever we are taken during our fluctuating non-conscious states our body always stays in the now, and because we have no doubt about the 'Isness' of its existence, unlike the possible doubts we might have regarding the existence of a soul or something within, which is not subject to change, the body might be the gateway to understanding and experiencing higher levels of consciousness and a different state of being.

So all the work on oneself, self-study and meditation practice is done within the domains of our physical body. And to be able to utilise our physical body as a gateway to higher levels of consciousness, meditation and stillness of mind and thought as well as change of being, we need to look at the power within the functions of our five senses.

Inner Growth And The Power of The Five Senses

After the communist dictator Nicolae Ceausescu was executed in 1989 in Romania, human deprivation experiments were discovered in Romanian orphanages. The children under observation had been fed and cleaned, but were deprived of any other stimulus and the results were shocking. The children were grossly delayed in their physical growth and motor and mental development. They rocked and grasped themselves, grew up with strange social behaviour and were unable to form permanent attachments.

These terrifying discoveries proved that we cannot evolve in a healthy way, if we don't receive the proper external stimulus through touch, attention and social interaction.

As mentioned before, the functions of our five senses are perfectly regulated by our 'instinctual brain'. But ever since we stopped living in harmony with nature and the artificial mind created life started influencing and affecting everything on our whole planet, the natural functions of our senses have changed.

Mind created life is imposing a different demand on our senses as well as it has created habits that are superimposing new impressions on our senses. These impressions are in no way related to nature and are alien to our senses.

We can call these new impressions Electro/Virtual Impressions. They differ in speed and frequency from the impressions of nature. This has led to an increase of sensual overload that has gone way out of balance; hence our senses are stimulated by external impressions of mind created life, that were not produced by nature and are not very compatible with the way our five senses work.

If we look at some very rural communities, which are still living in harmony with nature and still cultivate and work with Great Ideas, yet don't depend entirely on gadgets, fashion, mobile phones, TVs, game consoles, gym regimes and PCs, their sense of time is still spacious and their five senses are allowed to work as they were designed to work in the first place.

A balanced life led in harmony with nature allows time for contemplation and assimilation as well as time for stimulation. Those vital components had to be sacrificed by mind created life and the outcome of that does not require any explanation.

This incompatibility of mind created life with the natural functions of our five senses and the way they have to deal with the Electro/Virtual Impressions it produces, has a massive impact on us and the way we function, as well as affecting us on all levels, physically, emotionally and intellectually.

The result is that our five senses have turned from being fluid and responsive to being highly-strung and hardwired.

Scientific research in medicine and psychology is just beginning to understand how much and to what extent, constant sense overload and 'hardwired-ness' caused by Electro/Virtual Impressions impacts on our health and wellbeing. They seem to play a much greater role in increasing the risk of cancer, heart attacks and developing mental illnesses and addictions, as well as preventing us from evolving emotionally and physically.

Our brain hasn't had the time to evolve and change its brain function to be able to absorb and assimilate the massive quantity of Electro/Virtual Impressions.

To summarise:

- We can say that the increasing pressure Electro/Virtual Impressions are creating can be utilised to the advantage of our inner growth and be directed towards meditation. Then we can say that due to permanent overload caused by Electro/Virtual Impressions, our five senses are constantly desperate for a break and are longing for a chance to shut down and recover by practising meditation.

- Furthermore we can say that we can't change life and the impressions it produces, but we can make a conscious effort to be under more Alpha-Influences or the influences of nature, which allow our senses to spring back to their fluid responsive nature.

- And finally we can say that once our five senses find stillness in meditation and stop sending any stimulus to our brain, gamma wave activity will increase, which slowly will lead to permanent changes in brain function, hence change the way we will respond to the stimulus of the impressions of life.

Exercise 16: Escaping from our mobile phone

- *Observe how much time you spend under Electro/Virtual Influences and how much you rely on them.*

- *Be in the presence of Alpha-Influence for a couple of hours at least once a week, as well as making an appointment with nature for an hour two to three times a week.*

- *Experience what impact that has on your state of mind and your everyday life.*

Our History is Stored in Our Connective Tissue

There is scientific evidence that suggests each of our cells has its own intelligence.

One example of this is the research from Albrecht Buehler Ph.D. who says:

> "My research for the past 30 years or so was devoted to examining whether cells have such signal integration and control centre(s). The results suggest that mammalian[75]cells, indeed possess intelligence."[76]

His research documents that cells have the ability to see and respond to light as well as possessing special awareness, and can change their direction towards a different object if required. Other research indicates that each cell in our body contains traces of cerebrospinal fluid and can function like a mini brain containing a definite level of intelligence.

Bruce H. Lipton PhD discusses the matter of intelligence in each of our cells in detail in his book *Biology of Belief*. In one of his interviews about his book he says:

> "We think of ourselves as a singular entity, but the reality is that we are an interactive community of 50 trillion individual cells. It is their technology and their intelligence that created us. The reflection of their intelligence is in their technology—they can manage their environment and manage their world with technologies that we haven't even comprehended yet".[77]

As a therapist myself, having specialized in post-traumatic stress disorders for ten years, I am constantly witnessing how much unconscious memory is stored and can be held by our connective tissue, and how intelligent this tissue memory is.

The body's inner self-healing ability seems to play an integral part within this process, as well as it seems to be an intelligence in action, which aims for a resolution and completion of the bio-emotional process.

Every force that is impacting on our body has to be dealt with in one way or another by our physical system.

If it is a light force, like someone accidentally bumping into us in a crowded department store, we might be pushed slightly off balance, but otherwise our body can easily deal with this impacting force. The energy of such a nominal impact will go straight through our body and won't leave any traces behind. But if we happen to walk down a flight of stairs and accidentally miss one of the steps, the impact of the force of that fall might not only lead to a lower back injury and some bruising, but the physical and emotional trauma that fall has caused, will be stored within the connective tissue. The energy of the impact of the fall will enter our body and instead of travelling all the way through it to dissipate on the opposite side again, it will enter and be directed along a certain vector and will get stuck somewhere in the connective tissue.

The place where it gets stuck is usually quite a bit further away from the actual injury. The same is the case regarding the impact of forces like surgery, food poisoning, any verbal abuse or physical abuse as well as sexual abuse or severe illnesses.

Most of these extreme impacts force us into a state of shock and, depending on its severity, we may not remember a thing afterwards. People describe this experience as if a large part of themselves froze in time and was paralysed during the traumatic experience. What they might be left with after the physical injuries have healed and their life has gone back to normal, are feelings of anxiety, minor to major changes in behaviour that can be triggered by certain situations or unexpected circumstances.

Severe trauma causes our mind to blank and can lead to complete loss of memory of what actually happened. This can result in experiences of paranoia, feelings of being polluted within, aversions to touch and affection as well as mood swings and phases of deep depression.

To therapists those areas of trauma are called *active lesions* manifesting as hardened tissue within the body's connective tissue structure. And once those lesions are detected and palpated, they usually display a specific movement pattern.

By applying specific tissue release techniques to these active lesions, as well as simultaneously implementing very specific non-invasive therapeutic dialoguing and imagery techniques, the client's tissue gently will reveal and shift the dormant memory up into the field of the client's awareness, to enable the person to release the stored energy the traumatic experience had caused in the past. In time, and with regular treatment sessions, the symptoms that had been causing a lot of problems to the client's wellbeing completely cease to exist.

The capacity of tissue memory is vast and very precise. Nothing is forgotten, yet not everything is required to be remembered. But rest assured, only what we no longer need, and only what is of no further constructive use to us will be brought up to the surface by our self-healing faculty, that forms part of this amazingly intelligent organism called our physical body.

Organ transplantations and obvious changes in behaviour of the organ receivers, has attracted the attention of the medical world. Candace Pert[78]says:

"Memories are stored not only in the brain, but in a psychosomatic network extending into the body, all the way out along pathways to internal organs and the very surface of our skin."

She discovered neuropeptides[79] in all different kinds of tissue and fascia, which gave rise to her conclusion that:

"...through cellular receptors, thoughts or memories may remain unconscious or can become conscious-raising the possibility of physiological connections between memories, organs and the mind."

Paul Pearsall, MD, a psycho-neuro-immunologist and author of *The Heart's Code*, has researched the transference of memories through organ transplantation. After interviewing nearly 150 heart and other organ transplant recipients, Pearsall proposes the idea that cells of living tissue have the capacity to remember.

University of Arizona scientists and co-authors of *The Living Energy Universe*, Gary Schwartz PhD, and Linda Russek PhD, propose the universal living memory hypothesis in which they believe that:

"...all systems stored energy dynamically and this information continued as a living, evolving system after the physical structure had deconstructed."

Schwartz and Russek believe this may explain how the information and energy from the donor's tissue can be present, consciously or unconsciously, in the recipient.[80]

To summarise:

- We can say that the ability to store memory might not only be exclusive to the brain and its neurons, but also to different tissue types throughout the body.
- Then we can say that this newly researched cell memory ability does not only store trauma caused by an external physical or psycho-emotional force, it stores all the memory and the blueprint of different states of consciousness.
- Furthermore we can say that the impact gamma wave activity has on our cells and different types of tissue requires further research, yet the impact of gamma wave activity on permanent changes in brain function does not require further proof.
- And finally we can say, that increased memory of higher states of consciousness in our cells, might play a major part in the formation of something, which is not subject to change within induced by objectless meditation.
- And we can say that regular meditation can have a powerful impact on the way we assimilate and integrate the stored memory, which was brought up to the surface by the connective tissue while it processed towards release.

Suggestion:

If you have the feeling that you are inhibited by certain Somato-Emotional, or Psycho-Somatic patterns to develop into your full potential, it might be worth considering talking to someone who is specialized in post-traumatic stress disorders. The relief and freedom you might gain out of a few sessions with an experienced therapist can be phenomenal. Throughout this process you only rid yourself of something you no longer need that is not conducive to you and your life anymore.

The Importance of Asana And Movement Practice

We have already established that all four brains have to be trained and developed to their full potential to establish balance. However each of the four brains requires a specific training approach and teaching environment in order to become balanced.

Our body is designed to move, and if we look at movement from a scale point of view, than there are multiple levels and dimensions to movement. On a two-dimensional level we can perform movement in slow motion even down to micro movements. On a more three-dimensional level we can train the body to such an extent that our body almost defies gravity, such as in gymnastics and classical dance. The fourth dimension of movement is the ability to master speech and train the vocal cords to sing like an opera star, as well as executing skills like painting and drawing, or performing surgery as a surgeon, and repairing cars or computers as a mechanic.

The potential of movement possibilities is almost infinite. Most of those kinds of movement skills require focus and concentration and the ability of the movement brain to communicate with the intellectual brain, hence both have to be trained to be able to work with each other. In this mind created world, we have added another dimension to movement, which is the movement of thought, however this does not require the participation of the movement brain.

Most of us are mainly using this newer kind of movement and the only physical movement required are micro movements of the physical body and the movements of our eyes. We became masters over this kind of movement and our mind activity has overpowered any other activity and is dominating almost every given moment.

This is part of the reason why we became unable to sit still in meditation, or experience periods of absence of thought. We can literally physically feel the movement of our thoughts in our head, and the more it speeds up and the more compulsive it becomes, the more pressure builds up within our skull.

Simultaneously each little 'ME' and all the different departments within the mind are going into overdrive until, we risk a mental burnout. The movement ability and speed of our thoughts has outgrown and is dominating the movement ability of the physical body in the majority of people today, hence we have lost the connection with the only true reference point to the now, which is available to us.

Essentially the present moment could have a tremendous power over the mind, if the mind allows it to enter its domain and welcomes it into its court. Unfortunately the mind knows that the only thing you will discover in the present moment is - that you simply are, hence that realisation of the state of being of 'I am', could drive the mind out of its kingdom by which it will realize that in its essence it always was a wonderful and humble servant in the first place. Within this momentary simple state of being, we realize that our body is the physical expression of that 'I am' state of being, void of any connotations.

Regardless of the true position of the mind along a scale of hierarchy, the mind has found empowerment and contentment in the complexity of its own movement. It finds less and less satisfaction in physical activities, which could leave some imprints of present moment experiences behind, especially in the younger generations as well as in contemplation and meditative assimilation, which ultimately could lead to a different state of being.

To summarise:

- We can say that in our ordinary state of mind our body is the closest connection to the truth or the 'Isness" of all there is to know.
- Then we can say that the five senses, which form part of our physical body, perceive external impressions as precise and accurate as they are.
- Furthermore we can say that essentially there is no fundamental difference between the 'I am' state of the self felt as the subject, and the state of being of the 'Isness' of things, perceived as the object or an external expression.
- Ultimately we can say that it is not the five senses which alter, change and modify what they perceive to our liking. It is the faculty within our being that perceives the external impressions, which are correctly delivered by our five senses, that is clouded by the veil of illusion. By default our five senses only can transmit objective information.

- Finally we can say that the veil of illusion that is clouding our ability to perceive things as they are, is created by those new and recently acquired uninterrupted movements caused by the highly charged activities within our mind – our non-conscious states.
- To conclude we can say that there is a profound message to be found in Patanjali's teaching that yoga Asana or any other form of conscious physical practice was only developed to channel and focus the scattered energies of our emotions and our mind towards meditation out of necessity.

This can only be achieved by utilising the most obvious and closest access to the now – our physical body and its five senses – consciously, hence by implementing conscious effort. This is the reason why it is so important to develop our movement brain to its full potential as well as recognising that this physical body was given to us as a window of opportunities, or as a gateway that might lead us to what might not be subject to change within.

Exercise 17: Developing The Movement Brain

- *Engage your body in physical activities four times a week, by practising yoga, pilates, running in nature or swimming etc. Always implement flexion, extension, side bending and spirals.*

- *While you train keep your attention within the spaciousness of your physical body and challenge it now and then with coordination practice.*

- *Avoid repeating the same routine and order of exercises or the same protocol. The movement brain requires variety to evolve and by implementing new challenges it is much easier to stay in the present moment.*

- *Include ten minutes of assimilation and integration after your practice.*

The Mystery of The Breath

Our life starts with an inhalation and ends with an exhalation, and there is great significance in this fact. Our breath is invisible like the wind yet it makes us part of something mysterious and undiscovered, which we call the 'Unknown' that forms an intrinsic part of infinity, which is the never ending spaciousness surrounding all there is to be seen in the macro-cosmos and beyond, as well as the spaciousness surrounding all there is within the micro-cosmos.

The air has free access to enter our body and whatever is contained in, or is part of, the air seems to keep us alive and enters into every part of our physical body. Science calls this exchange of gasses respiration, or to put it into very simple terms our respiratory tract takes oxygen in via the inhalation and expels carbon dioxide via the exhalation.

Yet there are other Great Ideas regarding the meaning of the breath to be found in yogic disciplines, world religions, ancient philosophy and the science of meditation.

In yogic disciplines the breath is the key to all different forms of yoga practice. Through yoga Asana, we open the body and master the postures via the help of the breath as well as we synchronise the movement with the flow of the breath. By utilising different Asanas that flex, extend, side bend and rotate the body, all the different energy channels (Nadis) are cleared and the different nerve centres (Chakras) are activated and illuminated, hence the physical body is strengthened and hydrated, which allows the energy to flow freely through the different channels and nerves.

Asana practice prepares the practitioner for a more refined practice called pranayama (breathing practice). The term Pranayama comes from Sanskrit and consists of two words. Prana, which means life force or vitality, which is literally everywhere surrounding us, and Yama, which is Prana's intrinsic active component or its engine. Prana is contained in our food and carried by the air, as well as the rays of the sun, and water distribute it. According to the yogis it is not a part of matter but can be found within the spaciousness of matter, even down to the infinitesimal space of an atom. This vitality, or life force, infuses life into our body and all the refined pranayama techniques utilise Prana in a very specific way, and should be taught by an experienced teacher, hence this kind of in depth knowledge can't be properly explained in a book.

The profound depth of the symbolic meaning of the word breath can be discovered in all world religions and their respective languages.

In Christianity God created the five elements first and thereafter all living beings including man, and 'he breathed into his nostrils the breath of life and the man became a living being'[81].

The word breath in Latin means spiritus and has a variety of different meanings. It always relates to a non-corporeal or immaterial substance, which explains the level of consciousness of a living being as well as it reveres to its state of being. This includes the whole scale of living manifestations, including bacteria and cells as well as plants and all animals.

The Judaeo-Christian Bible uses the word 'ruach' (wind) as the spirit whose essence is divine. As well as Scandinavian languages, Baltic language, Slavic languages and Chinese language use their word for 'breath' to explain ideas relating to 'the spirit'. Similar concepts can be found in languages like Greek using the word pneuma and Sanskrit akasha or atman.

In philosophical and metaphysical terms the word spiritus or breath relating to spirit has acquired a number of meanings. It sometimes is used as a term for 'the Creator' or equates to 'Essence', as well as the term 'The Spirit' is conceptually identical to Plotinus' 'The One' or Friedrich Schelling's 'The Absolute'. In some Native American traditions the spirit stands for 'The Creator'.

In the science of meditation the access to the present moment takes place first and foremost through the physical body via the internal movement of the breath. By being attentive to our breathing cycle, we will discover a natural pause after the inhalation, which is called the full pause or Abhyantara Kumbhaka, and another natural pause after the exhalation, which is called the empty pause or Bahya Kumbhaka in yogic terms. There is no activity taking place in both of those pauses and if we observe a bit deeper we will discover that it is very difficult to think within the duration of the pause, hence each pause is a moment in which nothing happens – a moment of absence of thought or meditation.

To summarise:

- We can say that whatever we do and wherever we are we are breathing.
- Then we can say that we cannot stop breathing for longer than approximately three minutes even if we try to do so.
- Furthermore we can say that there is a possibility that we might be 'breathed' by something, which is unknown to us and can't be grasped in the state of our everyday consciousness.
- Finally we can say that we are permanently connected with, and are consequently an inseparable part of the universe, and the spaciousness surrounding all there is externally and internally via the rising and falling away of our breath.
- Ultimately we can say that there is no such thing as a physical boundary between the external and the internal, except the concept of subject object awareness in our mind.
- And last but not least we can say that that infinite spaciousness that is surrounding all matter and all there is might not be subject to change.

Exercise 18: Breath

- *Regularly visit your favourite place with a beautiful view and simply be aware of the spaciousness surrounding things.*

- *Try to be aware of the spaciousness surrounding things in your everyday life.*

- *Observe what impact it has on you and your breathing.*

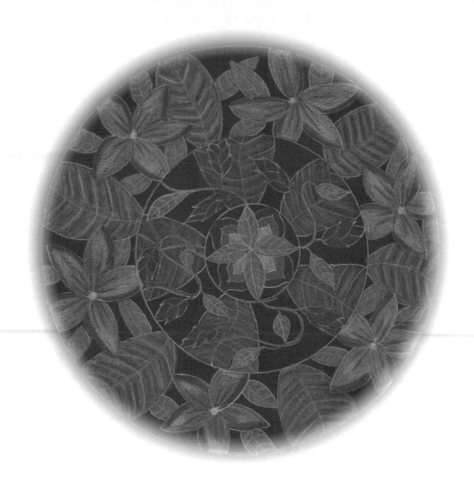

12. The Process Stage V: Stilling The Mind

Human Beings Cannot Do

'Human Beings Cannot Do', is a powerful statement and will challenge every person when they come across this aphorism. People's immediate response will be of opposition. They will feel very strongly about how much they do every day and how much they have done already in their lives, as well as how much they have more or less achieved, which is visible proof of their ability to do.

In reality it is a miracle that anything is accomplished and completed by anybody in this world considering the many universal laws we are under.

We have already discussed the law of opposing forces we meet with every step we take, and there are many more less obvious laws we are not aware of, in the state of our everyday consciousness. For example, the law that we definitely die, regardless of how much effort is invested by the scientists to prolong our life span. The awareness of the law of the death of our physical body has been eradicated in our Western culture, and no matter how much we 'will' not to die, we definitely will die due to opposing forces and this law.

Other famous laws are the law of cause and effect and the law of action and reaction, which form a fundamental part in every philosophy and world religion as well as in social ethics and mystic teachings. Ancient cultures were very aware of those laws and based all their decisions on the idea of how much this action would affect people who are born five generations later.

There is another law, and this is the law that 'life simply just happens and unfolds', and regardless of what our plans are we won't change that unfolding, which only is revealed to us in every occurring present moment.

The outcome of what each given moment of unfolding will reveal is constantly subject to change depending on which state of consciousness we are in at any given moment in time, hence what will meet us at some point in the future automatically changes according to the state of consciousness we are in each given moment.

Being in a non-conscious state will affect the way life is going to unfold, in the same way than being in a conscious state of being. The former might produce a more mechanical or incidental outcome, while the latter might lead to a more objective outcome. So whatever is going to be revealed to us at each given moment in time is, in the hands of the unknown to which we have no access to after all. Ultimately the outcome of our future is determined by our fluctuating states of consciousness. Less fluctuations might result in less arbitrary outcomes. In the end everything depends on our own effort and the help we are receiving from others.

The last law I want to mention, one we should not forget, is that not one moment passes without us having killed a living being. Whether it is a germ or bacteria, a plant or an insect or a mammal. We keep ourselves alive by the expense of another life. That is a law. We can't live on Praná only; the minimum we need to keep this body alive is water and air, as well as greens and vegetables, which are living beings. These are only a few examples of laws acting on us and I leave it up to you to discover and define all the other laws that act on us.

Exercise 19: Blanking The Mind

- *Now – close your eyes and blank your mind for exactly two minutes. Simply be aware that you are a living being, and do not allow any thought to enter during the duration of this exercise.*

The majority of people are not able to complete this exercise successfully, which simply proves the truth of the initial statement that human beings cannot do, and have absolutely no control over their thoughts and their own mind.

This is what we are dealing with, and as long as we are not developing a different kind of strength, to be able to extend the times in which we have more control over our thoughts by means of conscious effort, the mind won't give in and be still. Consequently we will stay under the control of our non-conscious states until the law of death acts on us while life unfolds.

In other words, how often do we witness, less in ourselves than in others, for the fifth time in three years an announcement of an important life changing intention of a dear friend, which he never has put into action or could see it through to the end. Regardless of his strong intentions, each time half way through the process something seemingly more important interfered and brought the whole plan to a hold until it was forgotten, to be announced again six months later with a little bit of a different take on it.

In our everyday state of consciousness shifting from one non-conscious state to the other, while simultaneously one little 'Me' replaces the other, it is next to impossible to formulate a strong sounding true intent and see it through to the end. We need a much stronger force and strength, as well as more 'substance of gravitas' and something within, which is not that much subject to change, to be able to state that we truly can do.

To summarise:

- We can say that there is only very little we can do.
- Then we can say that we haven't developed enough strength yet to be able to still the mind.
- Furthermore we can say that as long as we don't work on our non-conscious states, by applying conscious effort to catch them in time before they try to take over, lasting change won't happen.
- Finally we can say that regardless of the fact that we cannot do and are able to still the mind – we can at least try to do to still the mind.

Exercise 20: Pause Exercise

- *Make yourself stop for twenty seconds two to three times a day and instantly be aware of the fact that life unfolds in front of you.*

- *Observe what happens within this moment.*

The Mind Has to Become Our Best Friend

Even the leading scientists admit that we are far away from using the full capacity and potential of our human brain. Each neuron of the brain is stimulated, not only by the impressions of life, but also by the mind itself, and each neuron of the brain has become an employee of the mind and feeds it with whatever it thinks fit.

Let's go back to where we started right at the beginning of our life.

We said that we were born in a pure state of being and by imitation we soon acquire a strong personality, which we need to interact with life, hence personality represents an active part, while pure being is passive.

In time we are more pulled towards the active part and completely forget the pure being part of our essence. Throughout the first seven months of our life our mind lies dormant and motionless, but the more we acquire by imitation the more will be imprinted in our mind, which could be more or less seen as a flexible disc with the capacity to grow. In time every new external impression will leave a groove in this disc.

By the time we have reached the age of two, the disc starts spinning more and more regularly and we spend less time in our pure state of perception. Once we are seven-years-old, most of our patterns and conditioning as well as our personality and little 'ME's' have formed. From that moment onwards this disc like mind does not stop spinning for the majority of people. The non-conscious states imprint deeper and deeper grooves into our rather fluid mind, and in time more areas on the surface of the disc become increasingly ridged, hence by the end of our lifetime those grooves are irreversibly crystallized. A large part of those imprints are shaping our personality, which is affected by the lack of flexibility and will become as ridged as the grooves themselves.

Initially we are born with enough substance of gravitas, which is safely stored within our essence, but the more sub-personalities are born, which are increasing the size of our personality, the more substance of gravitas is assimilated by them.

Ultimately most substance of gravitas is wildly dispersed between all the different sub-personalities, which means that each of them is in the possession of a very small amount, hence there is no real weight to personality to do the job it is supposed to do, i.e. to respond to life's impressions as a whole, or as one unit, which is in agreement.

Furthermore we have the problem, which makes it even more difficult for us to act with integrity, that each sub-personality is attracted to a different kind of impression of life and most of them are originating from Beta-Influences that are not conducive for our inner growth and development.

So what do we have to do to be able to still the mind?

The answer is simple:

The mind has to become our best Friend.

The best way to go about it is to gather as many sub-personalities, which had been under the regular transforming impact of Alpha-Influences as we can. In time these will form a strong unit and are willing to put all their scattered substance of gravitas into one place, which manifests a significant amount of this substance. This enables them to keep their interest focused towards one direction or line of interest for a prolonged and reasonable length of time.

At one point enough weight has accumulated to attract Gamma-Influence, which is connected with a much greater force than any of the other influences, which could be called the force of Great Ideas, which were not developed by mind created life.

This force will encourage us to work on all the four different brains and bring them into balance, and with the help of those Great Ideas, our mind will find pleasure in meditation and a lot of satisfaction while absorbing and assimilating those Great Ideas. Thus, by regular practice of meditation and by applying and implementing the Great Ideas into our everyday life, our mind will slowly regain its flexibility.

The power of meditation and the impact of Gamma-Influences will slowly iron and flatten out all the deeply engrained grooves, which had been imprinted in our mind until it has turned back to its original form, hence the mind will ultimately slow down its activity and stop spinning.

To summarise:

- We can say that as long as there is no unity within us, we won't be able to keep our interest on one subject for very long, due to the law of attraction.
- Then we can say that the more we study and explore the functions of our own mind, the more we will be able to understand what is required to turn it into our best friend.
- Furthermore we can say that regardless of how interested we are in a specific subject, our mind and personality will become bored and dissatisfied with it and wants to move on to the next best thing, which can give it enough of a kick.
- Finally we can say that by keeping company with people who share the same interests and are able to inspire us, it becomes more realistic to bridge the dry times when things have lost their spark until, we have regained our enthusiasm.
- And last but not least we can say that the more often we have come out of the dry times or the desert, the deeper and more profound our understanding of our subject of interest will have become, hence it will have penetrated through all the different layers of our mind and personality deep into our essence and will have transformed the initial superficial knowledge and understanding into true experience.

Exercise 21: Avoiding Falling Asleep

- *Develop new ways to keep infusing life into your main field of interest, which originated out of Alpha-Influences.*

- *Form or join a study group, which is meeting up on a monthly basis to nourish yourself with new inspiration.*

- *Don't forget to give regular time to each of your different brains.*

The Matter With Discipline And Effort

'The idea of laziness does not exist within the concept of the work on oneself' – this is a law!

There is a simple reason why this law is of outmost importance:

We simply don't have any time to waste in this lifetime.

Considering that you have applied some of the exercises described in this book already, you will have come to the realisation, that all this applied self-study and self-observation, as well as regular meditation and work on all the four different brains, plus dealing with the demands of life and enjoying some time out from all our good intentions and obligations, requires lots of time.

The other realisation you might have come to is that this inner evolution process is a very slow process and that twenty-four hours a day are in actual fact not enough to pack all of this in. In addition, we are dealing with the fact that 'we cannot do', because we have such little control over our mind, our thoughts and our little 'ME's', which is the reason why we have to study the different kinds of effort in the first place.

There are four different kinds of effort we have to look at, which will help us to understand the importance of the kind of discipline that is required for the work on oneself, as well as helping us to counter-balance the pull to be caught and trapped by extremes via the law of opposition.

The first kind of effort is called **non-conscious effort** and we are all mainly under the control of non-conscious effort. This kind of effort relates to everything we do mechanically. Most of the time we are not even aware that we are doing something, such as watching TV or going shopping with our inner stories.

Initially it looks as though non-conscious effort does not require loads of energy. In reality it is ultimately depleting us and drying us out until we are completely dehydrated. This process of dehydration will lead to the crystallisation of all our conditioning, as well as our deeply engrained habits and patterns. Without the right nourishment and food, such as impressions from nature, and without plenty of Alpha-Influences, we will lose all our mental and emotional flexibility, and as a consequence we simply become unnoticeably frozen at a random point in our precious life.

Non-conscious effort is what brings laziness into our life and has to be carefully studied in minute detail, because there are many layers to it, which are not necessarily obvious.

The second kind of effort is called **conscious effort**. It is this kind of effort that we usually apply when we have worked on something for a while, have given it a lot of thought and have put a lot of effort into it, such as learning a new language.

Initially we are excited to study and learn all the new vocabulary because our imagination of seeing ourselves speaking fluent French with a waiter, who is serving us dinner at a restaurant overlooking a beach in Cannes, is still fresh. Once that initial imagination has lost its attraction, we are faced with the reality of learning a new language, and it only is a question of time until our mind gets bored and laziness is about to take over.

Well – in this instance we apply conscious effort and common sense, because being fluent in French does not only mean being able to have small-talk with a waiter, it actually will enable us to explore different ideas which were produced by a different cultural background, as well as it might open the doors to different career possibilities or possibly become a life saver at some point in the future.

By applying common sense and implementing conscious effort we gradually move towards our objective and might even master the language after all.

This process won't happen in a straight line and it will teach us great skills in flexibility and that we will have to pay for everything we intend to do. In this particular example we might pay with little sacrifices or face a lot of friction, which can be seen as a form of payment, as well as we might have literally to pay a teacher who can help us to understand the different rules of grammar regarding the foreign language

It is conscious effort, which requires a certain amount of flexible discipline that might ultimately lead to results. Conscious effort is what we have to apply once we are on our path of self-study and work on our inner evolution. This second kind of effort requires loads of energy, due to the fact that it has to work above the level of our non-conscious states, hence without a certain amount of substance of gravitas and the help of several neutrally centred supporting 'MEs', as well as support from others who speak the same language and work with Great Ideas, non-conscious effort will soon take over, regardless of how much we would like to succeed.

The third kind of effort is called **inspirational effort**. Actively implementing and applying regular conscious effort will gradually take us to inspirational effort. This kind of effort is unique in its kind because it does not deplete us of energy at all.

The dynamic of inspirational effort is effortless, regardless of how difficult and demanding the actual tasks are. This is due to the fact that the respective subject itself has become so full of meaning to us, that we can't help not contemplating it, and we can't help exploring and enquiring as well as allocating as much available time as possible to it, just to be able to be in its company and under its inspiring influence.

Inspirational effort will be given to us once we have paid for it, that is once we have put enough conscious effort into our respective subject as well as great or new ideas have become more important to us and full of meaning and have taken the place of our own individual small ideas.

My teachers always said that conscious effort or disciplined effort invites Grace. With Grace help can enter, which leads to more effort that invites more Grace, which leads to…

The fourth kind of effort is called **selfless effort**. This kind of effort is available to us once all the Great Ideas of the teaching have internalised and become active within us, that is years of inspirational effort will ultimately result in selfless effort.

There is not much, which can be said about selfless effort except that all the little 'MEs' have become passive and our essence and state of being have evolved to such an extent, that they are humbly present and active in everything we do.

Great things can manifest through selfless effort, such as we see in the work of Mother Theresa or the manifestation of a piece of art or literature, which transmits Alpha-Influences. In addition, people who have reached a level of consciousness by means of inspirational effort, which has turned into selfless effort through which Gamma-Influence can transmit itself to facilitate sincere people, who long to evolve within, through the ups and downs of their own inner evolution and change of being.

Self-less effort always has the greater good in mind, whether this takes place on a small scale or on a large scale. The 'ME-thought' has become irrelevant in comparison to the meaning the respective subject holds, which does not mean that that person is completely free of the 'ME-thought', the 'ME-thought' still might be present in other areas of the person's life. From a Great Idea point of view, there is nothing wrong with a healthy 'ME' or 'I', as long as it does not claim to represent the whole and knows its place.

To summarise:

- We can say that the different kinds of effort are powerful tools once we have studied and worked with them for a certain length of time.
- Than we can say that sheer discipline, which is based on a superimposed protocol won't lead to any results and will only invite opposing force and resistance to enter, which will lead to a build-up of suppressed energy that will find a way to free itself.
- It is an utter flexible and spacious discipline, which is conducive to the work we intend to do that we have to develop in time.
- Furthermore we can say that once we have neutrally explored and studied Great Ideas for a significant amount of time, we will realise that work on consciousness can't be carried out without some help and support.
- Finally we can say that a lazy attitude of mind and laziness itself is non-existent in Great Ideas and belongs to the level of non-conscious effort.
- Last but not least, we can say that by regularly applying the technique of conscious effort we will receive help through which we will ultimately develop inspirational effort, as well as once the right time and the right circumstances have arrived, selfless effort will be given.

Exercise 22: Effort

- *Observe how much time you spend in the state of non-conscious effort.*

- *Set yourself an achievable small task like learning one or two words of*

French everyday for a month and document your observations about non-conscious effort.

- *Set yourself a real task like studying new or Great Ideas for an hour every day and applying some of them into your life. If you feel that you start losing interest, switch and work with a different brain so that the brain that is required to complete the task can recharge itself.*

- *Observe how that impacts on your life and what is gradually changing within you.*

Definition of Thought

At the beginning of this section, and this concept has to be grasped symbolically, we compared the mind with a flexible rotating disc, which can grow and expand. Every external impression of life that enters our system via our five senses is triggering a specific activity in our mind and will be instantly compared with charged imprints of impacts of similar impressions that have been left on that disc previously.

As a result the incoming impression will activate a specific sub-personality, which is attuned to the charge of the present incoming impression, as well as to the similar charge of accumulated imprints that have created a significant groove in our mind.

The sub-personality or little 'Me' then functions like a lens or filter and adds its own subjective charge to the present incoming impression and will respond to it accordingly using one of our non-conscious states.

Our non-conscious states are made of a low frequency, which our inner sense of perception perceives as thought or thought impulses.

It is believed that:

Man is the only creature that thinks,

and thinking can be seen as a mental activity or intellectual process involving one's own personal subjective consciousness.

The word comes from Old English *þoht*, or *geþoht*, from stem of *þencan* "to conceive of in the mind, consider".[82] The idea of thought includes concepts like cognition and imagination, as well as consciousness and sentience. The process of thinking allows us to make sense of what we perceive and enables us to explain ideas and concepts subjectively.

'What is most thought-provoking in these thought-provoking times, is that we are still not thinking'[83]

This statement refers to the idea that we are still not thinking properly due to the fact that we are still half asleep and are spending most of our precious time in the state of our everyday consciousness. This is that our thoughts are nothing more than an uninterrupted stream of mainly mechanical and conditioned thought patterns, triggered by internal and external impulses, which act on us randomly and are usually linked to sub-conscious and vague memories of experiences and events in the past.

In addition, Heidegger's statement seen from a Great Idea point of view, points to the notion that Great Ideas, which are not produced by mind created life, teach us that we have to learn to think properly to be able to think differently, hence to think objectively. That is we have to start thinking through our four different brains simultaneously, which is a totally different way to think and in actual fact the only real way to think.

But 'four brain thinking' depends on our present state of consciousness, the development of our being, as well as on substance of gravitas and the balance and proper function of all four brains, which will be explained at a later stage.

Nevertheless ever since we left the pure state of being as a toddler, and mind activity started predominating our ways of perception, and rapid streams of thoughts increasingly captivated our attention, thoughts or random thought patterns became our constant companion.

This companionship became so symbiotic that we gradually turned into our thought patterns hence we became them.

I am what I think and believe, that is - I am my 'I-believe' that gives me a strong sense of self.

A lot of what we think is imagined, as well as a lot of thoughts our mind produces are not conducive to our inner evolution and are useless in facilitating the change of our being.

For example, all the negative thoughts that are produced by Lower Emotions, which are undermining our integrity and are upsetting our associations with others, and are only nourishing our non-conscious states.

All thoughts that are a product of non-conscious states are not real. That is we are not real, as well as our sense of self is not real because it is constantly changing as long as we believe to be what we think. One of the purposes of Great Ideas is to re-establish our connection with our sense of being, and to root our sense of self in the true state being, instead of our sense of self 'being' our thoughts or thought patterns, which are constantly subject to change.

141

To summarise:

- We can say that in our everyday state of consciousness we are not really thinking if we apply the idea of scale to the underlying concept of thought.
- Then we can say that by observing and studying the way we think as an individual person by means of conscious effort, we will get proof and re-confirmation regarding the fact that we are mainly randomly thinking, as well as that we have very little control over our thoughts and thought patterns.
- Furthermore we can say that the moment when we observe our thoughts by means of inspirational effort, we are able to be aware of our thoughts, that is we have further removed ourselves from our thoughts and have created a distance between that which perceives the thoughts or ourselves as the subject, and that what is perceived hence the thought itself as the object.
- Finally we can say that by having created that distance between ourselves and our thoughts, which could be defined as a state of divided attention, the observing part that is simply aware of the thought must be in a state of absence of thought or non-thought.

Exercise 23: Taming ones thoughts

- *Observe what kind of stimulus triggers very intense thinking and thought patterns in your mind.*

- *Make yourself stop twice a day and be aware of your thoughts and recognise how that impacts on your state of mind.*

- *In a quiet moment, or even better once you are out in nature, consciously catch your thoughts and ask yourself the question, 'To whom, does this thought appear?' Absorb the quality of 'Being' the question evokes within yourself for the following twenty seconds. Then keep enjoying your time in nature.*

- *Implement the 'question exercise' described above into your everyday life if you can remember to do so.*

The Vibration of Thought

Every individual thought is charged with energy and a rapid flow of thought patterns can be literally felt in our head as a form of tension combined with an increase in charge. The more friction and both internal and external pressure we have to deal with, the more random thoughts are produced by our mind. This is due to the fact that our mind desperately tries to find a solution and a direction, through which the accumulated thought energy can dissipate and be released.

The more emotionally charged our thoughts are, the more our whole nervous system will be affected, which increases the stress levels in our physical body. Expressions like 'my head is about to explode' or 'my brain is driving me nuts' as well as 'my thoughts are giving me head ache', are more than common to us.

This state of mind is created by what we call 'subjective thinking', by which things can't be put into relation to anything else anymore, as well as they can't be seen from a greater perspective.

The limiting and depleting effect of rapid subjective thinking can be felt everywhere in the body, as well as in our emotions and psychic structure and is taking the last bit of energy out of us. It makes us highly strung and wired and keeps us in a constant state of survival, as well as robbing us of our ability to sleep and relax or unwind. During subjective thinking we are usually completely absorbed and entirely under the control of our increasingly narrowing thought formations, and it does not come as a surprise to us that subjective thinking is mainly triggered by our non-conscious states.

Objective thinking or 'clear thinking' is less charged and dramatic. It enables us to understand concepts and theories and is much less judgmental towards the different information and impressions. It can put a train of thought aside for a while if a different thought formation is required, and can come back to it to put the two together, once it makes sense and is thoroughly understood. There is a much more neutral attitude of mind in clear or objective thinking and it is this kind of thinking which will initially help us to work with Great Ideas. Please note the word 'initially', because to truly grasp and understand Great Ideas and the depth of their inner meaning, four-brain thinking is required.

It is the practise of meditation that will help us to transform subjective thinking to still the mind, so that we can establish ourselves in applying objective thinking, which is far more conducive to dealing with the uninterrupted stream of impressions of life.

Meditation practice[84] is <u>one</u> of the best ways to study our thoughts and thought formations, and with regular practice and a bit of conscious effort we soon discover that each chain of thoughts carries an emotional charge, which will be reflected as a physical sensation in our solar plexus area and sometimes in our throat.

In time we will realize that each thought formation has a major impact on the way we breathe. The more our thoughts are emotionally charged the more it will impact on the way we breathe and the more we will be identified with what we think, hence the event in life or any internal event that is triggering those thoughts has a strong hold over us.

The less emotionally charged our thoughts are the more spacious and relaxed our breath will be and the less identified we will be with our thought patterns, hence the appending event in life will have less or no hold over us at all.

Once our mind activity has gradually slowed, via the impact of alpha-brainwave activity, the tension and agitation in our head has calmed, our physical body has found contentment in sitting motionless as long as required, and our five senses have learned to be much more indifferent to external stimulus, as well as that our thought formations will have become much more spacious.

In this state of consciousness, which takes place slightly above the state of our everyday consciousness, we have stopped being one with our thoughts or thought formations and we are more or less resting in the state of divided attention in which we are able to observe our thoughts in more detail. With a bit of patience we might discover that to be able to understand and make sense of our thoughts, our mind projects our own voice into each thought, which is one of the reasons why we believe that we are our thoughts.

Usually when people start practising meditation they say that they can't stop their own voice in their head. We perceive this inner voice in the form of words. If we study this voice neutrally we soon realize that each of our sub-personalities can be discovered in this voice in our head, we only need to listen to the change in intonation and the different words it produces the moment we face a different situation in life.

If a strong sounding thought appears and we give it our whole attention, it will produce an image that contains traces of the energy of all the historical imprints of emotions, which are attached and related to this image. Instantly that flash of an image the sound of the thought has produced, is projected or spreads itself out on the screen out of which the thought has appeared, to be perceived by our inner eye and to be heard by our inner ear, hence by our awareness.

This voice will disappear or better dissolve once our thought process has become even more spacious via the impact of theta-brainwave activity, which is a particular state of consciousness in which the awareness of anything physical starts diminishing and our thoughts have moved further away into the background.

A sequence or succession of thoughts, are usually perceived as a movie like scenario displaying itself in front of our eyes. This can take place simultaneously, while we execute a task, which does not require too much of our attention, as well as during daydreaming.

Being further removed and distanced from our thought activity, our way of perception will have ceased to be linear and will become three-dimensional. In this state of perception we recognise and can see thought for what it truly is and realise that our thoughts are nothing more than vibrations made of the energy of light and sound, that are created by the spinning movement of the mind, which is relentlessly harvesting and consuming different influences and impressions produced by mind created life.

To summarise:

- We can say that to understand the difference between subjective thinking and clear thinking puts a different perspective on the way we can grasp and understand things.
- Then we can say that objective thinking might transform the way we express ourselves and talk to others, as well as it might help us to respond to the events of life less predictable and mechanical.
- Furthermore, we can say that exploring and studying the matter of

thought via meditation practice and in life itself, will allow us to experience the different layers of thought formations and the way we think and the way our thoughts act on us, as well as it will validate the theory of Great Ideas and transform them into actual experience.

• Finally we can say that the more we study and experience the vibrational nature of each thought, the more we will be able to work with thought formations that randomly appear in our everyday life, as well as in our meditation.

Exercise 24: Creating Distance to Thought

• *Consciously listen to the sound of the voice in your head and experience that you are not your thoughts.*

• *In times when you feel that your head is about to explode switch into your movement brain and go for a run or practise your yoga allowing the breath to take over. Observe how that has impacted on your state of mind and the way you think.*

The Gaps Between Our Thoughts

When we sit motionless, with our eyes closed in a state of deep meditation, we will witness that our thoughts appear out of nowhere in form of a vibration that consists of light and sound as long as our attention is not triggered into action by them.

A single thought impulse can't sustain its appearance for very long and will dissolve or be reabsorbed by that nothingness out of which it appeared, to be followed by the appearance of another thought impulse.

The moment we are attracted to it and start resonating with its vibration, rest assured that within a glimpse of a moment we will be flooded with a stream of thought formations we soon take as entirely real and identify with their content. Whether their content is the product of imagination or any of the other non-conscious states is totally irrelevant.

In a meditative state in which our body is at ease with sitting still, our breathing cycles have become very subtle, and the thought process has relaxed and slowed down, we might become increasingly aware of the gaps between our thought impulses and a certain gravitational pull, which emanates through them. The more we are willing to undo and the more we gradually detach and are freed from our inclination towards selfhood, as well as that we have become profoundly tired by the conviction that we can do and that we know via the power of meditation, the more we will become receptive to this gravitational pull that is emanating from and reaching us through the gaps between our thoughts.

To summarise:

- We can say that the more we meditate, the higher the chances are that we become more and more indifferent to our thought impulses during meditation.
- Then we can say that as a result of that, we are less prone to be swallowed by a stream of thought formations.
- Furthermore we can say that the gaps between our thoughts are of

great significance at a certain stage within the process of meditation and must be revisited and experienced again and again throughout a long period of time.

- Finally we can say that a deep meditative state can't be produced by sheer will or disciplined effort, as long as we haven't developed something permanent within us, which is not subject to change.

- Ultimately we can say that without self-study, self-observation and work on being, by means of inspirational effort we won't progress in our meditation and we won't progress and succeed with our self-study and work on our inner evolution, without regular meditation practice by means of not doing and undoing. Both lines of practice, the external and the internal, have to be applied simultaneously, hence they have to go hand-in-hand.

Exercise 25: The Two Second Gaze

- *It takes between one and a half and two seconds until we start identifying with any object we perceive through our eyes and will start labelling it. After a maximum of two seconds our mind will give a name and ignite a flood of thought formations, which relate to the object or event we perceive.*

  If it is a person we don't know but observe during a bus ride, the first thought relating to the person we observe will trigger an inner dialogue and might lead to an opinion about the person or judgement, but most times it will lead to imagination.

  If we see a tree or an object we want to buy, we certainly will be captivated by an inner dialogue our inner voice is having within a couple of seconds. The same is the case when we listen to a person during a conversation. One specific word mentioned by that person would in no time trigger a flood of inner comments while we are listening. This exercise will prepare us to be able to detach from our thought formations, during times when our thought process is not necessarily required, as well as it will benefit our meditation practice.

  While you are walking on top of a hill or in an open space, allow your gaze to wonder and avoid looking at any object you perceive for more than two seconds.

Once you feel comfortable applying this technique in open space apply the same technique on a bus ride or when you are talking to your friends.

Advance to apply the same technique when you are seeing signposts or displays of advertisements, or anything written which catches your attention while you are on your way to work. Don't let your gaze rest for more than two seconds and instead focus more on perceiving the space surrounding the words you see, without being tempted to read them.

This exercise will take some practice before you start getting it, due to the habit of labelling or thinking about everything we see. The moment you master the technique it will become a powerful tool for clear thinking.

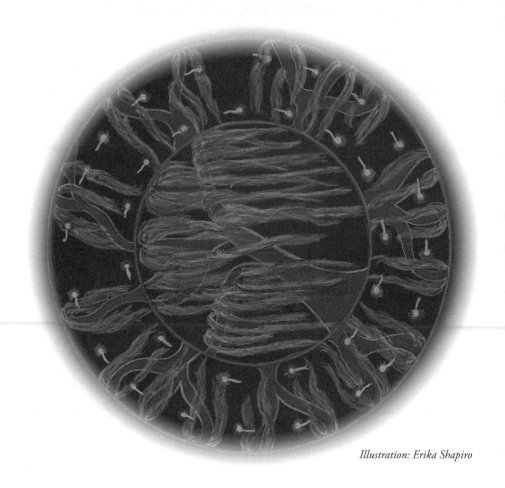

13. The Process – Stage VI: Consciousness

To be able to understand the process of meditation, as well as all that is happening and is experienced during the process of meditation, we have to understand and study the workings and functions of consciousness.

We have explored the different levels of consciousness before and came to the conclusion that our state of consciousness is constantly fluctuating, depending on external stimulis and our own state of mind, as well as our state of being. But what we haven't explored is consciousness itself and all the different qualities and attributes attached to it.

Different dictionaries define consciousness as:

- Aware of one's own existence, sensations, thoughts, surroundings.[85]
- A term that refers to the relationship between the mind and with the world it interacts.[86]
- The state or condition of being conscious.[87]
- "What is meant by consciousness we need not discuss - it is beyond all doubt."[88]

As we can see, the term consciousness hasn't been clearly defined and probably never will, which is based on the current fact that it lies beyond the understanding of our mind and intellect, hence it can't be grasped by it.

'Consciousness is like the Trinity; if it is explained so that you understand it, it hasn't been explained correctly.'[89]

What our researchers, scientists, physicists, linguists and academics forget is that at one particular point in history, they chose to inquire and research the external world or the world of matter, in order to get to the bottom of the truth of things and the way they function and interrelate with each other.

In contrast to that, and in much earlier days, philosophers, mystics and yogis started researching the workings and the nature of consciousness and all that is attributed to it, as well as the scale of consciousness that includes the different levels of consciousness, by means of the science of meditation.

This was done by simply meditating for extremely long periods of time and monitoring, as well as discussing and comparing their findings and experiences with each other. They gained their access to different levels of consciousness by taming the body, mind and thoughts in the first place. By having fully mastered the skill and ability to shift into the state of self-consciousness with ease, they then used their higher faculties or different sense of perception, which lie dormant in every human being, to explore consciousness from within consciousness itself.

By having fully transcended all non-conscious states they gained an objective view of exactly what happens and has to be done at each stage of the process of meditation, to get such and such definite results. To them the prerequisites and rules applied to the science of meditation, are exactly the same as the prerequisites of the science of biology to a biologist. The only difference is that to the mystic and yogi the laboratory is the internal world, while it is the external world to the biologist.

Each experiment requires the right order and the right ingredients and exact amounts or quantities of substances to be successful and lead to the same result, regardless of how often it is repeated. The only difference between the external and the internal science is, that the former can be monitored by instruments, while the latter can't be currently monitored by any instrument, because the sensors are not refined enough yet, and may be never will.

The external science is governed by mind, intellect and thought, which is subjective and much more subject to change, while the internal science is governed by the state of absence of mind and thought that is objective and much less subject to change the more refined its level of consciousness becomes.

To summarise:

- We can say that the workings of, and all that is attributed to consciousness, only can be studied and known from within the dynamics of consciousness itself, hence we have to raise to each respective level of consciousness ourselves in the first place, which is a presupposition before we can come to any conclusion.
- Then we can say that we are all conscious beings in one way or the other, which can be easily proved by asking someone the question, "Are you a conscious person?" The person will probably place one or even both palms of the hands on her or his chest and will clearly respond with the answer, "Of course I am a conscious person." Before we asked the question the person probably was absorbed in daydreaming or in one of the other non-conscious states and not really conscious, but the moment they heard the question they instantly woke up to the reality of their own existence and remembered their own state of being or pure state of 'I am', confirmed and strengthened by placing the palms of their hands on their chest or solar plexus, hence they experienced a moment of 'self-realisation'.
- Finally we can say as long as there is no electronic device that can measure the workings and dynamics of consciousness we have to use

our own device, and by applying step by step what the mystics and yogis have known for millennia find proof of their teachings within ourselves and turn it into our own experience.

The Nature of Consciousness

Consciousness is not a concept or merely an idea that can be analysed by our mind and thoughts and interpreted accordingly by them. On the contrary – consciousness seems to represent much more of the truth of what we are, than our mind and thoughts ever possibly can be.

Consciousness can exist without our mind and thoughts as well as without our different brains and vice versa. Consciousness is such an intrinsic part of the truth of what we truly are and what the unchanging nature within us is comprised of, that it can only be experienced, hence consciousness can't be objectified.

Consciousness even can be seen as a faculty or function within the 'Isness' of our being.

**"Consciousness is the name of a nonentity… a mere echo,
the faint rumour left behind by the disappearing 'soul' upon the air of
philosophy".[90]**

This formless quality can be experienced in the state of absence of thought as a frequency and motionless pulsation and the very nature of it is to expand by means of the so called 'Stream of Consciousness' that interconnects all there is.

The scale of consciousness is literally limitless, ranging from 'Deep sleep' to 'self-consciousness', which both are still within the domain of our intellectual understanding, to more refined levels of consciousness that go beyond the understanding of our mind and thought, as well as it ranges from a subjective state of perception to an objective state of perception.

We can become conscious of the world around us and all of that exists in it, as well as we can become conscious of our own physical body and our internal world. But whatever we are conscious of, or are conscious about always seems to appear to us randomly and out of nowhere, yet we seem to have little understanding or say how this takes place. All we know is, that most of it takes place through the subject object dynamic, which is a very linear dynamic that is mainly influenced by the law of the opposing forces. To gain a greater understanding about the workings and the nature of consciousness we have to study the functions of Awareness and Attention, as well as their inter-relationship with each other.

To summarise:

- We can say that consciousness is always at work literally twenty-four hours a day, whether through us or within us and around us is irrelevant.
- Then we can say that the whole scale of consciousness is at our disposal at each given moment in time.
- Furthermore we can say that when the expanding nature of consciousness is inhibited, it takes us towards the lower end of the scale and when it is uninhibited it takes us beyond our habitual way of perception.
- Finally we can say that the way out of our habitual perception is by means of regular meditation and self-study.

Awareness And Attention

The attributes attached to each of those qualities within us could not differ more. Each individually belongs to one end of the extreme the moment we apply scale to them. We can be aware of something or someone and we can give someone or something our attention, as well as we can be attentive to something or someone around us. Both qualities are worlds apart from their function point of view, but never exist without each other and have to be studied in great detail.

Awareness is the state or ability to perceive external and internal impressions. These impressions can be validated by an observing faculty, without the necessity to grasp or understand what is perceived. It is the quality of the state of being aware that counts without, having to translate it into a concept or idea.

Awareness is a relative concept from an intellectual point of view and provides the building material for qualia, which are recognisable characters of the given and are mainly universal. *Qualia* is a term used in philosophy that refers to a subjective conscious experience, like a 'raw feel' that is unique to the individual, like the taste of water or the colour of a sunset.

Throughout our life we have accumulated countless imprints of external qualia, which are fundamental to be able to live a congruent life. Very often it is the qualia that we have in common with other people that interconnects us with each other. The faculty of awareness is required to build internal qualia by means of meditation and self-observation.

The mystics know about all the different qualia we meet during the process of meditation within us as well as the qualia we meet during self-observation. These are signposts of our inner world that function like reference points, guiding us through the jungle of our non-conscious states towards more refined levels of consciousness. These inner qualia are available to everybody and can be individually experienced by means of the science of meditation.

Awareness is receptive and intuitive in its nature, yet passive in its force, as well as motionless in essence and does not possess the ability to be aware of itself or act. Its energy is feminine being symbolised by the tranquil light and quality of the rays of the moon. From an energetic point of view it manifests as an energy channel or Nadi along the left side of the spine known as Ida, and plays a vital part in different pranayama techniques.

If we fall too much into awareness, we will become more and more passive and inactive, as if we are drifting through life without any direction or sense of belonging. Our whole demeanour will come across as indecisive and unreliable, finding it difficult to commit and complete what we have intended to do or to achieve. We will increasingly rely on the good will of others, who will have to do most of the work for us.

Attention is the taking possession by the mind, in clear and vivid form, of one out of what seem several simultaneously possible objects or trains of thought. It implies withdrawal from some things in order to deal effectively with others, and is a condition, which has a real opposite in the confused and dazed scatterbrained state, which in French is called 'distraction', and 'Zerstreutheit' in German.'[91]

The workings of attention, is one of the most explored and researched subjects within the field of neuro-science and psychology. It plays a vital part during the cognitive process. Scientists are exploring areas within education, neuroscience and psychology in order to determine the source of the signals that ignite attention into action, as well as the effect these signals have on the tuning properties of the sensory neurons in the brain.

Other areas of research are the impact of disruption of attention in early development and how that affects our learning and might lead to all sorts of attention related disorders. Other research proved that nothing around us is ever really filtered out and will be stored to start within our short term memory, yet it is attention that becomes selective and prioritises to which impression it will respond and which one has to wait and might be addressed by means of reflection at a later point in time.

Attention is always ready to respond to any stimulus by nature hence it is active in its force and dynamic in its essence. The energy of attention is masculine, being symbolised by the reflective light and quality of the rays of the sun. From an energetic point of view it manifests as an energy channel or Nadi along the right side of the spine known as Pingala.

If we fall too much into attention, we will start biting our teeth into the small print and the minute details of little things. Our behaviour might become extremely compulsive and we won't allow any room for other possibilities to enter. We will lose the ability to work with others, because no one else could fulfil our unrealistically high expectations and will ultimately end up imprisoned in our self-created dogmatism as very lonely people.

Awareness and attention together create a state – awareness in the background and attention in the foreground.

This state is called the state of *divided attention* in which our sense of perception is split between two things at once. Walter Benjamin, a German Philosopher and Intellectual, describes this state as 'reception in a state of distraction', which is an obviously limiting, linear, very static and two-dimensional state of perception that can't be sustained for very long, as well as requiring a lot of energy and creating a vacuum in which there is no room for movement.

The quality of awareness and the quality of attention, as well as the state of divided attention, on their own seem not to be able to lead to a meditative state or a more refined level of consciousness, yet they play a major role within the process of meditation. To be able to utilise these two forces in meditation as well as to satisfy our mind and our intellect, we have to study the triad of awareness, attention and concentration.

To summarise:

- We can say that the proper function of the two qualities of awareness and attention are vital for our orientation in life and the world as well as for our cognitive behaviour and the fact that without both of those qualities working to their full capacity, a conscious perspective on life and on ourselves would be impossible.
- Then we can say that once we look at the two qualities as active and passive forces, we will be able to see their interplay in everything around us.
- Furthermore we can say that energetically representing the masculine and feminine energy, they seem to oppose each other within their co-dependency, each individually taking their position at one end of the

scale of possible activity and passivity.
- Finally we can say that without understanding those two forces, work on consciousness becomes next to impossible.

Exercise 26: Exploring Awareness And Attention

- *Observe in which of both qualities you spend most of your time.*
- *Observe in which of both qualities you find yourself, while interacting with others.*
- *Discover the workings of the two forces in different things and events around you.*
- *Sit still and divide your attention between you as subject and a tree as an object in front of you. Don't allow yourself to lose your perception of one of them. Stay in that state of divided attention for a few minutes.*
- *Write down your experiences of the divided attention exercise above.*

The Triad of Awareness –
Attention And Concentration

Within the dynamics of awareness and attention - awareness is the passive part while attention is the active part and in our 'everyday consciousness' they hardly ever come even close to reaching a level of balance.

Most of the time in our life we are governed by the energy of attention. Our mind is uninterruptedly captivated by external impressions delivered by our five senses, while attention constantly responds to whichever impression it prioritises.

One of the primary abilities of attention is to zoom in, and the more it zooms in, the more it loses its connection with awareness as well as its ability to put things into a greater perspective.

In actual fact attention requires the receptive and motionless quality of awareness as a reference point, to be able to see things in relationship. Unfortunately nothing stimulating is ever happening in awareness, and due to its lack of motion and passiveness, attention hardly ever sees the necessity to be attentive to it and has become the slave of our five senses, as well as of our mind and thoughts, hence both of them are caught in a constant struggle as active and passive forces, male and female energies symbolised by sun and moon, bounce back and forth within their very linear and two dimensional way of interaction.

Nothing in this universe can happen and manifest without having formed into a triad. To truly establish a healthy balance between awareness in the background and attention in the foreground or between passive and active forces, a third force is required.

In the case of awareness and attention this third force is called *concentration* or 'neutralizing force', which is symbolised by the quality and the rays of the light of the fire.

Concentration in this school of thought, in order to avoid any misunderstanding, has nothing to do with the ability to focus, or with zooming in. The development of concentration is literally the result of the fusion of awareness and attention, caused by the increasing pressure of

160

friction between the male and female energy, creating more and more heat, which consequently produces fire manifesting as the state of concentration or a concentrate during the process of meditation.

The moment awareness and attention meet in perfect balance by means of meditation, neutralizing force can enter, hence concentration appears.

This alchemistic process, in which the male and female energy are fused, distilled and transformed by the power of the fire ultimately manifesting as a concentrate, or the essence of both male and female qualities cum scent. The Nadis (energy channel) Ida (awareness, passive, moon, feminine) and Pingala (attention, active, sun, masculine) fuse by the power of the fire (concentration, neutral), resulting in the manifestation of Shushumna (an energy channel along the centre of the spine).

In less symbolic words, and coming back to the workings of the three forces, we said that we have awareness as the passive force (subject in the background) and attention as the active force (object in the foreground) along a two dimensional way of perception, as well as we have concentration as neutralizing force (the space surrounding both subject and object), which takes it onto a three-dimensional way of perception. Subject, object and the space surrounding things in which all there is to be perceived within the scale of that spatial awareness - is allowed to simply be.

If we apply the workings of the three forces to the preliminary stages of meditation we have the awareness or the perceiver as subject in the background and the thought activity or the perceived as object in the foreground, as well as the spaciousness surrounding thoughts perceived as the omnipresent infinite as the neutralizing force, which manifests by willing to undo and soften further back into the formless motionless quality of awareness.

Please take a few minutes to reflect and contemplate on the meaning of the last paragraph.

To summarise:

- We can say that awareness, attention and concentration form a triad that consists of the dynamics of the active, passive and neutralizing force, which manifests a three-dimensional way of perception that is

161

shifting us out of the linear or two-dimensional subject and object way of perception onto a more refined level of consciousness.

- Then we can say that this three-dimensional way of perception is free of any friction, transcending the law of opposition and creating a state of tension free balance, manifesting by the fusion of both active and passive forces.

- Furthermore we can say that the alchemistic process of that fusion of both opposing forces transformed into concentration cum essence that is gently filling the spaciousness with its subtle scent of oneness (unity).

- Finally we can say that only the mind is able to narrow consciousness down by means of attracting attention and make it zoom in, hence a much stronger force is required to resolve this pattern, which can be found within the functions of consciousness itself.

Exercise 27: Inviting Neutralizing Force

- *Sit still and divide your attention between your sense of self as subject and an object of your choice.*

- *Feel the static and two-dimensional tension arising within this state of divided attention.*

- *After a couple of minutes release the state of divided attention by becoming aware of the spaciousness surrounding the object.*

- *Be aware and recognise what has changed.*

Triads

Philosophical teachings and ancient scriptures are using a lot of symbolism and similes to transmit their knowledge as well as different concepts of cosmological laws that can be observed externally and internally.

One of these symbolic ideas is that of the **triad**, which weaves its appearance like an interconnected matrix, through different teachings and philosophies that evolved separately, and without having any connection, on different continents at different times in history. A few of them turned into universal laws and one of these laws is the triad.

To our knowledge the term triad is defined as:

- A group or set of three.[92]
- A trivalent element, atom or radical.[93]
- A three-note chord in music.

In Christianity the triad can be found in the concept of the Trinity or three as one, which expresses the belief that God is one being comprised of three distinct expressions that exist in co-eternal communion as the Father, Son and Holy Spirit.

The whole yoga Sutra of Patanjali is based on the idea of a triad that describes the friction and interplay between pure awareness (Purusha), consciousness (Cita) and Nature (Prakriti) that culminates in a process called yoking or coalescence, in which pure awareness is freed of the illusion of duality and time as well as subject object perception, and realises that it is not part of creation and nature.

In many yoga teachings the triad is symbolised by the sun, the moon and the fire as well as the Nadis Ida, Pingala and Shushumna, while in the science of meditation the idea of the triad is applied to the attributes of consciousness defined as the qualities of awareness, attention and concentration.

Georg Wilhelm Friedrich Hegel, a German philosopher, described and defined the triad in philosophical terms in form of the idea of the thesis. His concept on the triad is based on the thesis considered as an intellectual proposition, the antithesis seen as the negation of the thesis, hence a reaction to the proposition, which manifests as the synthesis that solves the friction between the thesis and antithesis, by reconciling their common truths, and forming a new proposition.

A triad always seems to appear when three different equally powerful forces or components meet and generate via their perfect balance of power a manifestation.

Friedrich Hegel's thesis is the active force of the triad, the antithesis is the passive or resisting force of the triad and the synthesis is the neutralising force of the triad, which results in the reconciliation of their common truth and manifests as a transformed new proposition.

Another analogy that illuminates this Great Idea beautifully is the seed seen as active force, the soil in the ground seen as the passive force and the water that penetrates through the ground and reaches the seed seen as neutralizing force, which transforms into a plant that is seen as the new proposition, carrying new seeds.

To summarise:

- We can say that the moment we look at things from a different perspective, let's say the perspective from a Great Idea like the triad, we can see the workings of the triad everywhere around us.
- Then we can say that only one aspect of the triad, whether it being active, passive or neutralizing force can't do anything out of its own. If active and passive force is forming a dyad, that is something consisting of two, they immediately manifest the law of the opposing forces evoking a linear interaction between the two qualities opposing each other.
- Furthermore we can say that the moment we find ourselves caught in a state of friction bouncing back and forth between 'is it the right thing to do' or 'isn't it the right thing to do', without neutralizing force entering in one way or the other the friction won't be resolved and nothing ever will happen in regards to that particular matter, unless a reconciliation takes place.
- Finally we can say that understanding the different dynamics in a

triad, help us to understand different events and situations in our life, as well as when it comes to formulating a 'strong sounding intent' or undertaking, hence the intent can be seen as the active force, our little 'ME's' might represent the passive force and inspirational effort might be the neutralizing force, that will lead to a new proposition of the physical manifestation of what was initially the vision of the intent. In regards to 'strong sounding intents', there are many possibilities that could appear as the passive or neutralizing force.

Exercise 28: Triad

- *Observe the dynamics of the three forces in your everyday life.*

- *Observe what impact neutralizing force has the moment it enters.*

- *Set yourself a small task like cooking a meal or travelling from A to B and observe the appearance of passive or resisting force.*

Consciousness and Conscience

Every philosophical system, every religion and every psychology is based on a concept of morality mainly known as the *golden rule* or ethical code, a maxim that essentially states that one should treat others as one would like others to treat one's self.

The golden rule can be found as different concepts of morality that are supposed to prevent us from falling back into, and transcending our intrinsic animal nature (we are still hunters and gatherers).

One of the first concepts of morality was explained in the 'Yoga Sutras of Patanjali" in form of the Yamas that are covering the external disciplines and the Niyamas that cover the internal disciplines.

The moral code for Buddhists, from both Theravada and Mahayana traditions that are not monks or nuns, is called the five precepts or Pali. People who practise Buddhism strictly follow eight precepts, and monks as well as nuns follow ten precepts.

In Islam the moral code called 'Sharia law' is explained in the Quaran and covers every aspect of life, including law, human behaviour, marriage etc., both Sunni and Shi'a follow those laws.

The moral code in Christianity is described as the well-known Ten Commandments in the Bible. In the Middle Kingdom of Ancient Egyptian (2040-1650 BCE) the golden rule is expressed in the concept of Maat as 'do to the doer to cause that he do thus to you'.[94]

The existence of the golden rule can be found in all major philosophical schools in Ancient China, for example, Confucius worded the golden rule as follows; 'Never impose on others what you would not choose for yourself.[95]

In Judaism the ethical code is expressed in the following terms; 'you shall not take vengeance or bear a grudge against your kinsfolk. Love your neighbours as yourself: I am the Lord.'[96]

And in Plato's philosophy the golden rule is a central concept based on the words 'one should never do wrong in return, nor mistreat any man, no matter how one has been mistreated by him'.[97]

In Hinduism we find the code of ethics expressed by the words 'one should

166

never do that to another, which one regards as injurious to one's own self'.

In reality conscience is not a concept of morality – it is something present deep within us, something very alive within our essence that can produce a 'bitter flavour' the moment it is compromised or undermined by our attitude of mind.

We all know about that bitter flavour that can penetrate through every cell in our body, and can make us feel truly miserable. We don't feel miserable because something happened or was done to us. We feel terrible because we have done something, which undermines everything we stand for including our integrity and our truth. As long as that bitter flavour is poisoning our system our conscience is not clear, and we wish from the depth of our heart of hearts that this self-inflicted bitter flavour is taken away.

The only way to free ourselves from this poisonous manifestation is to face up to and take responsibility for what we have caused. The fact is, we can only be conscious when we have developed a clear conscience, hence when something is not weighing us down.

'A clear conscience is a powerful reference point for every action in life'

Every action will produce a sweet flavour or a bitter flavour within us. Conscious actions produce a sweet flavour and keep our conscience clear, while non-conscious actions are producing bitter flavours and weigh our conscience down until it is buried, hence consciousness and conscience are in essence the same yet differ in their expression.

If every future action is fuelled by the power of our clear conscience, our meditation practice will deepen profoundly.

All past actions happened and can't be changed anymore. If some of them caused us sleepless nights and profound feelings of guilt, then we should not waste any time anymore and move on.

Great Ideas are not working with the power of guilt or intend to implant guilt within us. We are all in a position to judge perfectly when we have overstepped the boundaries and undermined our conscience. The right thing to do is to take responsibility for it, regardless of how uncomfortable the outcome of that will be for us.

It is 'mind created life' that has disconnected many people from clear conscience. As a consequence, the manifestations and outcome of that can be seen in the way we have exploited and treated the earth and how many animals we have exterminated, as well as in the ever increasing gap between the poor and rich, the increase of crime, and in the state of our economy.

It is our contradictions and the thick padding all those contradictions have created that have buried our clear conscience and as long as we contradict ourselves we won't be able to keep our conscience clear, hence be considered a conscious person.

To summarise:

- We can say that with the increasing disappearance of conscience, consciousness is diminishing more and more.
- On the one hand we can say that with the decline of consciousness on our planet the possibility of more people wanting to evolve within diminishes as well.
- On the other hand we can say that external pressure and friction might cause people to remember their real values and meaning in life again as well as it might trigger their 'inner longing', which in return will attract the right influences that excavates conscience and ultimately leads to work on consciousness.
- Furthermore we can say that a clear conscience is required to be able to sit in meditation and find stillness in body mind and thought.
- Finally we can say that without clear conscience consciousness is not able to expand and take us towards the unchanging nature within.

Exercise 29: Bitter Flavour

- *Observe the impact 'bitter flavour' has on your state of mind and the way it makes you feel.*

- *Are there non-conscious actions in your life that don't leave 'bitter flavour' within you anymore?*

- *How do you respond to actions of others that are not connected to clear conscience?*

- *Define your own personal golden rule for life.*

The Screen of Consciousness

The reality regarding the subject of consciousness is that it is very difficult to understand and be grasped by our mind and intellect.

Consciousness is a formless state that, once not limited by the mind, can transcend our three-dimensional way of perception. Consciousness only can be experienced by means of our state of being that is 'being' in its evolved state of expression.

In other words from one particular point in our life onwards, usually when we have learned and acquired all there is to acquire to be of use to mind created life, we have to use our own effort to further evolve within, become more conscious and develop our being.

The more we work on becoming more conscious the more our being can grow and consequently the more we will be able to grasp and experience the initial intellectual concept or Great Idea of consciousness. Both have to go hand-in-hand and always need to take place simultaneously.

Still without an intellectual or philosophical concept that can be validated by practising the science of meditation we would not know how to distinguish either of them.

'Being is the passive part and Consciousness is the active part of what represents the truth of what we are in 'Essence' or in 'Quint-Essence', which is the neutralizing force that manifests as the unchanging nature within as a new proposition.'

As an analogy we could consider consciousness as a neutral screen or field that has reflective properties and the ability to infinitely expand. We can become aware of that screen the moment we close our eyes as well as when we open our eyes in the morning and it usually stays with us all day, without us being ever aware of it.

In each condition the field appears or will be in front of us displaying a different kind of scenery. With our eyes open, it is the scenery of creation or the external universe and with our eyes closed, it is the scenery of our

169

internal world displayed right in front of our sense of perception.

With our eyes open we experience and see the external world as a three-dimensional space, filled with solid objects including our own physical body, while the moment we close our eyes the experience changes and the internal world is experienced and seen as more fluid and spacious, as well as energetic, vital and etheric, including the way we experience the inside of our body. The concept of muscle, bones and organs has disappeared once our eyes are closed, and re-appears the moment we open our eyes again.

The idea of the screen or field of consciousness can be utilised while sitting in meditation and has been known to the yogis and mystics since ancient times.

What we initially see reflected or appearing on that field, are our thoughts, imaginations and different reflections of our mind, as well as little glimpses of the state of absence of thought. The moment our body has settled and relaxed, whilst sitting still and absolutely motionless, it might take a while until our senses start relaxing as well. By default our attention follows what our senses primarily pick up and our physical eyes will follow it as well, hence whatever appears on this screen or field in front of us once we sit with our eyes closed, will trigger an impulse that will make our eyes move.

The same happens when our meditation technique is initially based on following the breath cycles. The moment we direct our attention towards breath observation our eyes will move along the pathway of the rising and falling way of our breathing during the inhalation and the exhalation.

It is vital to train the eyes to switch off and relax to such an extent that no sensory impression triggers them to move. Every movement of the eyes during meditation will otherwise initiate the *identification with what the physical eyes perceive*, hence identification with all our thoughts, emotions and images appearing on that screen or field of consciousness.

So, by initially remembering to soften further and further back into the skull and instead of engaging our physical eyes to look onto that screen in front of us, we want to look through these physical eyes, like looking through an open window from far behind perceiving that vast and laterally expanding field of consciousness in front of us.

As long as the depth of the screen of consciousness can be perceived without the engagement of our physical, eyes we will be present to the present moment and the seemingly nothingness on that field, and the part of ourselves that observes and perceives the field, already is in an altered state, in a state of absence of thought.

The very moment the screen disappears we are in the process of identifying with what our mind projects onto that screen and our physical eyes will have gone back to their default response, to follow what they see, as well as our breathing pattern will have changed and thought activity will dominate again.

Once that has happened, we have to wait until the part in us that loves and enjoys to sit in meditation, and supports Great Ideas, is activated and remembers that we are in actual fact supposed to be sitting in meditation right now, and not indulging our thoughts and emotions. This will help us to detach our attention from the thought impressions bringing it back to the screen of consciousness. The more imprints of experiences we get from that receptive state the easier it will become to relax into that field of consciousness in front of us, out of which all there is to see appears, whether we have our eyes open or closed.

With regular practice and patience our mind will find pleasure in sitting still and will produce less thought activity. In time our attention is increasingly drawn towards the spaciousness between the thoughts, which is a gateway from the physical into the non-physical, as well as from the world of matter, shape and form into the formless and transcendental.

To summarise:

- We can say that the screen or field of consciousness is constantly within the field of our awareness whilst we are in our everyday state of consciousness.
- Then we can say that the moment something within that field of awareness catches our attention, we will become identified with what we see and will attach a concept and emotion to it.
- Furthermore we can say that we have the possibility to remember to keep our awareness more continuously on that field of consciousness, which in return will help to establish a more neutral state of perception of things. In addition, it helps to bring attention back into its natural equilibrium - that is becoming receptive to awareness as well.

- Finally we can say that once we sit in meditation, we initially have to continuously train our senses and sense organs to disengage into a stand by position by means of further removing oneself deeper into oneself, as if we want to observe the 'Isness' of things or the spaciousness surrounding our thoughts from the depth of our solar plexus by means of undoing.

- Ultimately we can say that the concept of consciousness is very difficult to understand, due to the fact that it leaves a lot of room for imagination and interpretation, hence only Great Ideas that are not produced by mind created life, can help validate the actual existence of its expression by means of action and conscious effort.

- And last but not least, we can say that our level of consciousness as well as our level of being, determines the possibility to realise the depth of knowledge that is transmitted through those Great Ideas, so that they slowly and continuously transform into true experience and ultimately become permanent in us.

Exercise 30: Field of Consciousness

- *While you are driving your car or while you are on a bus ride, make use of this time and take your attention towards the way the world around you is passing by. Observe how that changes the way you perceive things.*

- *Apply the same technique during your walks in nature. See the world passing by and be aware how the appearance of life each single moment of it is moving through you, how the objects and scenery around you are simply moving through you. Observe how that impacts on your state of mind and being.*

- *Keep your eyes utterly relaxed in both of the above exercises, as if you perceive the appearance of the world from a place deep within you.*

- *Sit still with your eyes closed and be aware of the field of consciousness in front of you. Disengage your physical eyes and become aware of both outer corners of your eyes simultaneously, do this while you are looking through your physical eyes from far behind.*

14. The Process – Stage VII:
The Stream of Consciousness

Ramana Maharshi, one of the greatest teachers the world has seen, who was a living representation of the teachings of Advaita, refers to the home of the mind as being in the solar plexus.

Babaji a mystic in the north of India explained to us that when we start falling asleep at night, the mind first drops down into the throat while shifting into the dream state and then down into the solar plexus in deep sleep, while the Surat (the soul or that that is permanently conscious) separates itself from the mind and moves up.

The true origins of the thought 'I' can be physically sensed and felt as a weight just above the vicinity of the naval, that is when people talk about themselves they very often refer via their body language to the solar plexus the moment they use the term 'I', hence 'I' with all that it has acquired and is attached to it is synonymous with mind.

We can find many different examples of similar analogies in ancient scriptures. Another analogy describes the mind tantamount to will and that that will is scattered, being divided into many little wills and has to be gathered and transformed into one single will or 'I-thought", which can be seen expressed in martial arts in which the scattered will (mind) is gathered and tamed within the Hara (solar plexus).

There are two different streams or currents at work within us, the one is the uninterrupted stream of thought and mind activity, the other is the more subtle stream of consciousness. Both streams appear simultaneously on that field of consciousness within our eye-centre and while the former hardly ever gets our attention the latter is very familiar and well known to us.

The current of the stream of thought usually takes us further down into the non-conscious states, while the current of the stream of consciousness takes us towards more refined levels of consciousness, that is towards a more neutral and objective state of perception. The field of consciousness is the place where the stream of consciousness can be experienced. Remember that the very nature of consciousness is to expand and the moment it flows deeper into the world of shape and form the more it will be narrowed down by the mind and its many different 'ME's'. There, in our limited state of being, is nothing the stream of consciousness can meet within us that recognises its infinite nature and could be carried away by it.

We are simply not attracted to the gravitational pull this omnipresent current is emanating twenty-four hours a day. The beat of the heart of awareness pulsates from within the formless manifestation of our being in synchronicity with the universal pulse of consciousness and merges in coalescence once it has evolved to its full potential.

Exercise 31: 'I-thought'

- *Observe the body language of your friends, family and people around you and be aware of the gestures arising the moment the word 'I' is verbally expressed.*

- *Observe where you feel your own 'I-thought'.*

The Universal Pulse of Consciousness

'Spanda', which means vitality, oscillation or vibration, is the universal pulse of consciousness, emanating from the stream of consciousness can be perceived by the heart of our awareness. This universal pulse of consciousness carries all possibilities of manifestation symbolically expressed in the timeless mantra and silent inner sound 'AHAM' (I am), as well as all different levels of consciousness.

M.S.G. Dyczkowski[98] describes this mantra as the giver of life to every living being and that the resonance of its sound is there at the very beginning of every manifestation. The letter A, which is the first letter of the Sanskrit alphabet symbolises the absolute, while the Sanskrit letter HA is the final letter that symbolises completion. The sound of A-HA contains all fifty letters of the Sanskrit alphabet, which symbolises every aspect, level and phase along the vertical scale of consciousness. The letter M represents the individual sole within each living being, while the little dot or Bindu below the letter M stands for the subtle vibration of 'I'.

The 'Bindu' is the infinite nature of the 'I am', a motionless pivot point, around which the circles of all subtle levels of consciousness from A (absolute) to HA (manifestation) rotate. The depth of the Bindu can be seen as the void or infinite nothingness, in the centre of the vibrations of consciousness from which all the powers emanate and collapse back into. Further it is explained that the three aspects (triad) of AHAM constitute a movement from A the transcendental consciousness to HA the expansion or emission of its power, to M the subject that contains and makes manifest the entire universe of experience.

M-AH-A, which is the reverse of this movement, describes the notion of withdrawal (like the withdrawal of our life). Thus all cycles of creation and withdrawal are contained in the mantra AHAM. The Bindu and the AHAM together are a perfect example of the three forces that form a triad (A-HA-M) to manifest as a new proposition (bindu, dot) as well as a great description of the subtle pulsating nature of Spanda, as the universal pulse of consciousness emanating and retracting out of one infinitesimal point behind our eye centre.

176

Spanda induces consciousness to expand and is as such expressed by the quivering of the ultimate Reality, which is inherently creative and carries all the potentialities of being within 'Non-being'. The motionless beat of the heart of awareness within the depth of our being, pulsates in synchronicity with the universal pulse of consciousness.

In our linear way of understanding this might sound like a paradox, yet the moment we rise above the domain of mind and thought our more spacious, and altered way of perception will prove it otherwise. The 'one', who recognises the recurrent pulse of spanda as the movement of his own consciousness, as well as the consciousness of everything and everybody else, merges ones dualistic and linear way of perception into the universal or transcendental way of perception. That is it merges with the ever-expanding nature of that stream of consciousness. The initial access to that experience is through a specific manifestation within our breath cycle, which will be explained in the following section.

To summarise:

- We can say that the dynamics and expressions of consciousness can only be explained symbolically and by means of analogies, of which we can find thousands beautifully expressed in different philosophies and ancient scriptures.
- Then we can say that as long as we try to grasp these Great Ideas via intellect only, understanding is not going to manifest.
- Furthermore we can say that the powerful symbolic nature of these analogies can result in a sudden experience of the inherent truth of the subject they express, by inducing the mind to blank, due to its inability to grasp the meaning of the symbolic nature of the analogy, manifesting as a transient experience of the actual expansion of consciousness.
- Finally, we can say that we have reached the point at which theoretical and intellectual knowledge have reached their limits and actual experience is required to validate the truth by means of conscious effort.
- And ultimately we can say that without doubt every person has experienced the quality and feel of this expression or expansion, by

having simply been in a state of awe, such as being lifted into a state of higher emotions, while listening to a beautiful piece of music or witnessing an outstanding sunset.

Exercise 32: Movement of Consciousness

- *After your yoga or movement practice sit comfortably on an armchair with your spine upright arms resting on the armrest or hands in your lap.*

- *Rest your attention behind your eyes while keeping the eyes totally relaxed. Soften further back into awareness and become aware of the field or screen of consciousness in front of you.*

- *At the same time be aware that your awareness can emanate beyond the limitations of your physical body.*

- *With a gentle inhalation feel the screen of consciousness and your awareness expanding laterally and around you, with an exhalation relax. Inhale through your subtle body. Exhale undo.*

- *Keep gently inhaling and exhaling, feeling yourself expand during the inhalation.*

- *Then let go of all breathing and rest behind your eyes, keeping your eyes relaxed.*

Asana Practice For The Subtle Body

Within this body, that we perceive as our physical body, another body can be found that could be called the invisible body. It is invisible to our physical eyes, yet can be measured by electronic devices and photographed by specific cameras, as well as it can be felt by the palms of our hands as a subtle energy or electro-magnetic field, that extends beyond the surface of the physical body.

It is that second body, which forms the matrix, which is connecting the energetic with the physical by utilising the different brain wave activities, the neurological and respiratory system, as well as the fascial network, through which the pranic life force can be distributed and dispersed to animate the body. Within this invisible body exists another body, that is called the formless body or third body, which lies dormant and is hardly ever activated or recognised.

The third body usually stops growing once personality starts outgrowing it around the age of three. From then onwards, it remains underdeveloped in its dormant state like a seed, until we start working on our own inner evolution. It is activated by Gamma-Influences and strengthened by different Asanas for the finer body, that ultimately leads to a deep state of meditation and the expansion of consciousness.

Our third body is activated and nourished the moment awareness and attention is brought into balance by concentration. This balanced state that consists of the triad of active, passive and neutralizing force allows a fourth force to enter, that manifests as the new proposition. This fourth force is the universal pulse of consciousness or Spanda that manifests within the pause after the inhalation.

In the space between the two breaths another breath is taking place. According to the yogis without that third dormant breath life would end. While sitting motionless in meditation, and the five senses being at ease, as well as with regular practice, we come to experience that in the inhalation is a rising, an almost motionless very subtle whiff of increasing breathing taking place.

The exhalation and inhalation become one in the centre through focused attention that manifests as concentration by which consciousness starts arising. Initially we have to find the centre between the two breaths. Just like the yogis are seeking the centre that can be found in the 'Bindu' between Ida (awareness) and Pingala (attention) and just above Shushumna (concentration). It can be found there in form of a seed (spanda) just behind the eyes, where the pineal gland can be located. The reason why the yogis want to find this seed, is because the fire (concentration) is there.

To the yogis the moon is knowledge and the sun is practice or action, while the fire is will. Not our personal will but the transpersonal will. The willingness to undo the doer as well as every latent and non-conscious intent, even the intent or feeling that one is the one who is meditating during meditation. Within this third breath, within that Bindu or seed, transformation takes place in the form of the energy of bliss, induced by our higher emotions or 'inner longing' in which shape and form turn into the formless, and mind and thought transcend via the expansion of consciousness.

To summarise:

- We can say that regular meditation practice will take us to the profound experience that we can't meditate regardless of how much we try to meditate, but are being meditated by surrendering into the willingness to undo, not do.
- Then we can say that we only are meditated once we surrender to the gravitational pull of the stream or field of consciousness, which can be accessed through that third breath after the inhalation, within the spaciousness of the gaps of our thoughts.
- Furthermore we can say that the moment we experience the quality of the energy of bliss or 'inner longing' within the expansion of consciousness, our sense of time becomes spacious and our mind as well as our whole sense of 'I' softens further down and finds stillness and contentment within the depth of our solar plexus.
- Finally we can say that once our mind is at peace within it's true home the higher faculties of 'Intuition' and 'Pre-ception' become active and awaken.

Exercise 33: Third Breath

- *Once you have practiced your yoga or movement discipline, sit in a comfortable chair with your spine kept upright and while keeping your eyes closed take your awareness and attention towards the tip of your nose without engaging your eyes and take a slow and very subtle inhalation through your nose. Feel the rising of the third breath after the inhalation and exhale gently until the next natural inhalation meets you. Repeat for five minutes then rest behind your eyes.*

Intuition And Pre-ception

Intuition can't take place when we are biased. It only appears when we are in an unbiased or neutral state of mind. The moment we are biased or judgemental, opposing force has entered and nothing can happen or manifest hence intuition won't appear. A neutral state of mind and objective perspective, which is the neutralizing force in that triad, is the prerequisite for the possible appearance of intuition.

We are very often told that we have to become more intuitive, or have to use our intuition more often. What we don't understand is that intuition is part of a higher faculty and only appears on a higher level of consciousness. That is, a neutral state of mind automatically contains the reverberation of a more refined state of consciousness. We once said that everything has to be earned via conscious effort, and when we are told or want to be more intuitive or use our intuition more often, we won't be able to do so out of our ordinary will.

If I am telling you right now to be intuitive, that is to use your intuition, you won't be able to do so, due to the fact that we don't really know what intuition truly means to us. In our ordinary state of consciousness, in a state of 'yes or no' or 'shall I' or 'should I' and 'either this' or 'better that', we have to struggle with the law of opposition, which most of the time leads to a massive culmination of thought formations creating a vacuum, the more urgent and desperate we try to come to a resolution.

The friction and our struggle within that vacuum forces our battling little 'ME's' to surrender (neutralizing force), which leads to a release of the thought formation in form of a 'Aha-moment', in which we grasp all we have struggled with for so long in a moment of spacious perception, manifesting in form of the gift of a resolution. The rising energy of the 'Aha' is the vibration of intuition, which is a finer or higher faculty within the third body. So we usually struggle and work hard to receive the gift of true understanding via the faculty of intuition.

Everybody knows how an Aha-moment feels. It usually is a profoundly liberating and spacious energy spreading throughout our whole system filling us with vitality and aliveness. And within the vibration of intuition we, not only understand what we have struggled with intellectually, but also understand it on all levels at the same time, instinctually, emotionally and physically. This is usually combined with an unshakable depth of knowing, that includes not only the resolution, but the required energy to see it through to the end as well.

From a Great Idea point of view, the meaning of intuition is that we are 'in-tuition' hence we are receiving tuition from within and are taught from within by something that is able to 'pre-ceive'.

This kind of inner tuition takes place in an altered or enhanced state of perception, in which the idea or concept of time has been transformed from perceiving to 'pre-ceiving', hence we receive information of something in advance that has not actually manifested along a so called symbolic linear timeline that forms a triad.

This linear timeline consists of a more or less continuous chain of dots, that each individually once had been an actual very alive present moment in time, which simply has turned into nothing more than a corpse of a memory we can access and perceive or experience as the past.

Furthermore the timeline contains the timeless present moment as well as the possible manifestation of an event in the future that has not materialised or manifested yet. On that timeline, each given moment in time, the present moment or 'the now' that is represented as a space or gap, meets a vertical ray called the 'ray of eternity'. The 'ray of eternity' contains the scale of consciousness, in addition Grace, help and intuition can enter and meet us through this infinite ray.

In our ordinary state of consciousness we are hardly ever aware of this vertical ray. Through meeting alpha and Gamma-Influences and by putting conscious effort into work on oneself, the 'ray of eternity' increasingly illuminates the higher levels of consciousness. The moment we rise up a step on the 'ray of eternity', we shift onto another level of consciousness taking the linear timeline with us, which will change the outcome of our future, as well as the way we perceive our past, according to the frequency or pulsation (Spanda) of each particular level of consciousness.

The further we internally move up the scale of consciousness during the process of meditation, the more the linear scale of the timeline, which manifests as a point representing the past that is connecting to a point representing the future, is reabsorbed by the present moment.

To summarise:

- We can say that through the process and the science of meditation we gradually shift from external tuition to internal tuition or 'in-tuition'.
- Then we can say that 'in-tuition' has to be earned through work on consciousness and meditation. Also intuition only can enter through the 'ray of eternity', once all the different brains are working to their full potential and in balance.
- Furthermore we can say that Great Ideas only can be understood and grasped by means of 'in-tuition', hence true understanding of a particular subject or event, only manifests the moment we can see it from a higher point of view or perspective. We can't truly understand self-consciousness from the level of our ordinary state of consciousness, which takes place on a much lower frequency. That is, we have to rise up to the level of what we intend to understand or grasp in the first place, before we will possess true knowledge of it.
- Finally we can say that once we have established a more permanent neutral state of mind, which in itself is a much higher state of consciousness, 'in-tuition' can reach us with less interference from the law of opposition. In other words, our life becomes less prone to the law of accident and more congruent via the gift of 'pre-ception'.

Exercise 34: Intuition

- *Observe the impact and quality of energy spreading through your whole system the moment intuition enters as often as you can and as precise as possible.*

Consciousness And Emotions

The whole purpose of the science of meditation, and its applied psychology, is to teach us to think differently and awaken our emotional brain. To think differently means not only to think via our intellectual brain, in actual fact it means to learn to think through our emotional brain as well.

As we mentioned before, the different brains work at different speeds. We still live under the illusion that only our intellectual brain can know and understand. Our instinctual brain knows instantly if the food we ordered in a restaurant is cooked well and spiced to our taste, as well as it knows when the temperature in our house has dropped in the evening and we need to switch the heating on. Our movement brain knows immediately when to put the foot down on the brake while we are driving down a steep hill, as well as it knows how to calculate distance and height to step out of the way when it is required.

In our ordinary state of consciousness our emotional brain is literally asleep narcotized by our non-conscious states and habitual ways of thinking. Most of the emotions we have acquired by imitation are negative emotions as well as we have experienced some real emotions, which usually come up in exceptional situations that interrupt our daily routine by surprise.

Nothing can grow from negative or mechanical emotions. Our emotional brain has a cognitive capacity, a potential to know as well as to grasp, and what we have to understand is that knowing and understanding has nothing to do with thinking or analysing.

Thinking is usually fed by the impressions of mind created life, that most of the time ignite a conditioned thought pattern, as well as it triggers the memory of the habitual emotions attached to it. As long as we have not learned to think differently, as long as our way of thinking is not truly connected with Great Ideas that reach us from beyond mind created life through alpha and Gamma-Influences, our emotional brain will be dead and only will react from the way we think mechanically and habitually.

The moment we are inspired by knowledge and Great Ideas we haven't heard of before, developing new trains of thought and new ways of flexible and three dimensional thinking, as well as thinking from the Great Idea point of view, a time will come when all these conscious efforts of thinking and their practical application, will transform into a new meaning and sense of purpose. That is the time when our emotional brain is involved and has woken up.

New meaning and purpose only manifests when the higher emotions are active and have woken up. Great Ideas teach us to think in a new way about life and the universe, and its objective is to change our mechanical way of thinking, as well as to profoundly change our intellectual brain to awaken the emotional brain.

In our everyday state of consciousness the intellectual brain has become a slave of our senses and of mind created life, by constantly pulling attention in, as well as dragging the emotional brain with it. This narrows our consciousness down to such an extent, that the emotional brain becomes buried below the non-conscious states, and as long as that is the condition it is subject to, it can't wake up.

Once all the Great Ideas we can derive from different philosophical sources or teachings have penetrated through the non-conscious states, and have developed strong roots within our intellectual brain, then our emotional brain can start to awaken to its full potential. So what we have to know, is that it is not necessarily the intellectual brain that has the capacity to know, grasp or understand the truth or real meaning of things. Depending on the state of the emotional brain, the intellectual brain usually compensates for it and tries to do its work.

The capacity to know and understand the truth of things and people as well as the truth of Great Ideas, belongs to the higher emotional brain that arises out of our inner longing to ultimately know the truth of what we truly are, to finally know the real purpose and meaning of our existence as well as all there is to know beyond our mind and thought.

All philosophies and ancient scriptures talk about the pang of separation, that almost unbearable longing to become one with the source or the creator. Rumi's poems document the intensity of this longing.

I am so small I can barely be seen.
How can this great love be inside me?
Look at your eyes. They are small,
but they can see great things."

Masters, mystics and yogis awaken the emotional brain of their students and disciples and plant the seed of inner longing into their hearts. Irina Tweedie's book, *Daughter of Fire*, documents her suffering and journey of years of intense pangs of separation and the burning pain of her longing evoked by her Sufi teacher, to finally find union and peace of mind after years of intense struggle.

In Christianity songs of praise are part of the service to lift our spirit by the energy of emotion directed towards God, and in Hinduism, as well as in Buddhism, chanting is practised to awaken higher emotions and devotion within.

In the science of meditation Great Ideas, like the 'ray of eternity' and the 'scale of meaning', as well as everything that transmits true knowledge, which teaches us to think differently like the influences of nature, arts, science, philosophy, literature, ancient scriptures and architecture, are gradually awakening our higher emotions, that ultimately will lead us by means of inspirational effort to a more permanent sense of self and finally to what is not subject to change within.

To summarise:

- We can say that in our ordinary state of mind we are mainly experiencing emotional ups and downs and fluctuating emotions of which most of them are negative.
- Then we can say that, as long as our emotional brain is underdeveloped and dominated by our intellectual brain we are not able to experience higher emotions that are awakened by Great Ideas.
- Furthermore we can say that without the energy and frequency of higher emotions we can't transform knowledge into being due to lack of scale of meaning, that is the more meaningful Great Ideas become to us, the more conscious we become and the more we evolve into a different being.
- Finally we can say that higher emotions are to our life what concentration (fire) is to meditation and the expansion of consciousness, that is the heart has risen above the mind and generates the energy of eternal longing, which has the power to transform and burn away everything that is not true within us. What we are

ultimately left with, is a permanent emotion that is not subject to change, which forms and beats as the heart of the unchanging nature within us in form of eternal love and compassion.

Exercise 35: Higher Emotions

- *Take a walk in outstanding nature and become absorbed by the impact it has on you.*

- *Listen to a piece of music from your favourite composer or read your most favourite book that holds a lot of meaning to you and observe the impact it has on your heart.*

- *Walk up a hill or a mountain when there is a clear night sky. Sit and look into the depth of outer space and contemplate on the meaning of eternity.*

The Simplicity of Being

Being remains once we have come in peace with ourselves. First we have to come in peace with ourselves before we can come in peace with life and the world. As we have mentioned, we cannot change life, but we can change our attitude and the way we respond to life.

To be able to do that, we first have to acquire a strong personality that has to undergo a lot of ups and downs and learn a lot from and through life. To be able to further evolve and become more conscious and develop a different being we have to get rid of our personality again and all we have acquired by imitation.

This might give rise to the question why do we have to build and acquire a strong personality as well as all our 'I-believes' and 'Personal Philosophies' in the first place?

The answer is simple we never would be humble enough to appreciate the pure state of being we were initially born with, without having experienced the ups and downs in life.

So, we have to reach a point in life at which we have learned a lot and gained a lot of life experiences and have become disillusioned enough about life and our dreams as well as our inability to 'do' and what we believed or imagined to be, to finally arrive at the conclusion that we have to change.

Being able to change requires that we become more conscious. And the very first objective to become more conscious is to become more neutral and non-judgemental to life and ourselves as well as to new ideas. In becoming more conscious by means of self-study and the science of meditation as well as the assimilation of Great Ideas, we become aware of things within us we don't necessarily like to be there.

The more conscious we become the more is brought up from the depth of our non-consciousness and is illuminated within the field of our awareness. By that time we already have gone through a long process of friction and resistance, and have become tired with ourselves and the repetitive nature and cycles we seem to constantly re-visit.

The package and wrappings of the events of our repetitions might be different, yet the theme is usually always the same. By having realised our true circumstances, we are now under the perfect condition to start our journey of self-study and work on consciousness by means of meditation, receiving the knowledge of Great Ideas with some help of others who have done this work before.

By learning to think differently and by utilising the capacity of our emotional brain to know and grasp Great Ideas, we soon realise that all we see and neutrally observe within ourselves, that all those manifestations have nothing to do with what we truly are in essence.

We realize that we are not what we have learned and acquired by imitation and identification, also we are not our non-conscious states and our conditioning. In time, and the more we study and apply the science of meditation in our everyday life, all those features and conditionings as well as all the little 'ME's' and 'I believes' become less threatening to us. We start becoming less identified with them and reclaim more of the energy they hold. This energy provides the strength and endurance to be able to stay connected with the teaching of the Great Ideas more continuously, as well as to look at all the manifestations and the events of life from a Great Idea point of view.

Soon the little 'ME's' start shrinking to their actual size and start moving into the background. It's like sitting in meditation, the moment when you give the respective thought that has come up only one second of your attention, it will increase in its size and power and will make you identify with it. Similarly all the non-conscious states and manifestations within us are putting a spell on our attention to be able to spring into life, and within less than a second we lose our sense of self, identify with them and become them without even realising that we had been carried away by them.

We literally become our negative emotions and our 'I believes' or personal philosophies by means of identification. Once most of the mechanical manifestations have moved into the background, the different little 'ME's' that stand behind the Great Ideas and are inspired by Alpha or Gamma-Influences, start forming into one entity by the power of their underlying commitment, and integrity towards the teaching, and enable us to keep working along the directions of the meaning of the teachings.

Simultaneously our regular meditation practice deepens and we experience more extended times of concentration in which our thought formations become more spacious and move further away into the background. The reiterated experience of effortless concentration starts impacting on our mind and its imprints and grooves as well as forming 'Substance of Gravitas' that gives us a more permanent sense of self deep within us. This will have a profound effect on how life and its impressions are going to impact on us during the day.

The more permanent sense of self, sustained by the energy of meditation, allows us to recognise the unpredictable and fluctuating nature within the unfolding of life's events, the less impact it will have on us and our state of consciousness.

This is the moment when we have come in peace with ourselves and consequently in peace with the life and the people around us. The friction and the struggle with ourselves has profoundly diminished. We simply are not threatened by the divided and scattered nature of our personality anymore, because we are connected with something much more powerful within which is far more meaningful than the attractions the divided self is looking for or mind created life has to offer.

We have far less time for it due to the fact that there are much more important things to do in life. We have stopped defining ourselves by what we do or what we have achieved or established in life. We define ourselves by means of the teaching of the Great Ideas, which have started to become more active within us. The need to try to change others or criticise and judge others, has transformed into the knowledge that people usually just don't know better and that we only can change ourselves and can't do the work for anybody else.

In reality all this is accomplished by the power of regular meditation that in return supports us to self-study and work on ourselves, as well as on consciousness and the development of our being.

Meditation is - to stop resisting what we truly are in Essence, while the process of meditation is, to gradually undo and die to what we believed and imagined ourselves to be.

Now the question arises what does work on our being actually mean?

Before we can answer this question we have to look at what being actually is.
Being can't be seen, measured or calculated as well as it can't be grasped

by our intellect and be put into a formula or concept. No one ever can possibly judge the state of being of any other person. Only we know and can judge the state of being we are in, yet in our ordinary state of mind being is hardly ever considered as relevant.

Being can't be visualized by our mind but we can visualize our personality. It can be visualized in form of the shape and form of our physical body.

'Being is Self cum Non-Self - that is the concept of form and shape has been taken away'.

The closest expression to the state of being is the term 'I am' without any connotations attached to it. So, being only can be felt or sensed as something very real yet formless within us. From the science of meditation point of view it simply can be defined as: 'the less thought activity, the more being and the more thought activity, the less being and the more personality.'

So how do we actually work on being and change our being?

'Being is knowledge cum knowing'

Every 'Aha' moment makes being grow stronger. And work on being, which ultimately leads to change of being, is to struggle with the friction the teaching of the Great Ideas or any idea or concept are causing, and by putting the teaching into action by means of conscious effort we again and again experience the moment, when the loose ends join together by the liberating energy of a 'Aha' moment.

The different unconnected pieces of knowledge of the particular subject we struggle with increase in density. This is caused by the friction of lack of understanding and once the vacuum can't sustain itself anymore, the different pieces of knowledge fuse and are released through all the different brains simultaneously by the powerful energy of the 'Aha' moment.

Hence the different pieces of knowledge transform into 'knowing' that becomes part of our 'being'. This is the underlying cause on which, from a Great Idea point of view, consciousness is defined as 'knowing all together in an altered state of perception' and conscience is defined as 'feeling all together in an altered state of direct perception.'[100]

Without a strong sense of being that would never be possible.

It is the energy of the 'Aha' that evokes this altered state of consciousness, which consequently manifests as true understanding and knowing, which can't be taken away from us anymore. This is the true meaning of the saying that something has become our second nature. That is, it has shifted into 'being' and become part of 'being'.

Once a certain kind of knowledge has become part of our second nature, which always involves a process of struggle and friction with the particular subject before this takes place, one has earned the mastery over what has turned into knowing, hence no effort is required from then onwards, because it has become part of our being and experience.

What has been a big deal before, has turned into no big deal at all. That's why a lot of students in any field of expertise say to their teachers, "For you Mr X this is not a big deal at all and you make it always look so easy and simple, but for us it is a big deal and we struggle a lot with the subject and have to work hard for it."

This describes 'the simplicity of being' perfectly well, and we only have to stop turning ourselves into a big deal and simply become 'no big deal' at all, to be able to experience and enjoy the state of the simplicity of being, which is very unspectacular and the most natural state to be in.

To summarise:

- We can say that the science of meditation and self-study as well as the work with Great Ideas is a gradual and gentle process of disillusionment of everything we believe ourselves to be and of everything we believe to know.
- Then we can say that gaining peace with one's self does not imply or mean that all parts of our divided self and all our non-conscious states are eliminated. With the inspiration of Great Ideas, as well as being connected with a greater source that does not originate from mind created life, but from the conscious circle of humanity, we simply have become so tired about their control over ourselves that we have become relatively immune to their impact on our state of consciousness, as well as on the state of our emotions.
- Furthermore we can say that knowledge and being should not

outgrow each other, due to the fact that a massive amount of knowledge is useless to us and will forever stay in the department of theory, as long as each bit of it has not been transformed into actual experience. If we stay in the initial state of being we were born with, which implies the complete absence of knowledge or only a tiny amount of acquired knowledge, we would not be able to evolve into our full potential.

- Finally we can say when knowledge and being are in balance we are closest to the truth of the expression of what we are in essence.

- Ultimately we can say that it is a far better preposition to live in the state of being we were born with and with only a little amount of knowledge, than having become completely mechanical and only act through our non-conscious states, because the former has not acquired the ability to identify, which makes the process of dying at the end of our life much easier.

- And last but not least we can say that once we dropped the idea and the concept of making a big deal out of ourselves and have stopped being a big deal, we automatically will experience the appearance of the state of the simplicity of being. Our little 'I's' are replaced with a real 'I' or true sense of self.

Exercise 36: 'Being'

- *Sense and relax into the aliveness and vitality within the spaciousness of your body while you are aware of how life and creation unfolds in front of you.*

- *Lose yourself in walking, sports or painting while you feel the aliveness within the spaciousness of your body.*

The Unchanging Nature Within

Everything in creation is constantly changing and nothing we can perceive or know of within our universe and within the whole cosmos is permanent. Nothing is made to last forever and every living being has only a certain lifespan at its disposal. Also every mortal being strives for survival and intrinsically does not want to die.

Quantum physics talk about an energy field called the 'Higgs Field' that pervades the universe and that, the very moment a particle is interacting with the field, it is rewarded with mass. So the quantum physicists claim that they may be close to finding the so-called 'God particle' that sustains the universe. So there always was and is a lot of research and enquiry taking place, to find the answer and discover something permanent that is not subject to change.

The whole matter starts changing the moment we look within and explore the internal world of manifestations from the timeless ancient teaching and ancient philosophy point of view.

Mythology talks about 'Aether', which means pure essence that shines, also 'Aether' is seen as the fifth element of nature or as the quintessence that unlike all the other elements is not subject to change, is penetrative and non-material. The Greek and Tibetans as well as Medieval alchemy saw 'Aether' as the unchanging part within the five elements.

In Hinduism and Buddhism 'Akasha, Akash, Akasa' is the Sanskrit name for 'Aether' and has to be considered both in its elemental and metaphysical sense. The actual meaning of the word Akasha in Sanskrit is 'Space' and its main characteristic is that of the quality of light and sound, 'Shabda' or Shabad' the substratum of the quality of sound and light. In Jainism Akasha or 'Aether is what gives space to all manifestations of the existence.

Other philosophies consider Akasha or 'Aether' as eternal and all-pervading light and sound that cannot be perceived, yet has knowledge of all there is to know, so that without it there is possibly no magic nor spirit nor soul.

Akasha also is seen as the 'Centre' as well as the Bindu or the void in the centre around which all levels of consciousness emanate from and withdraw.

In the science of meditation the concept of 'Aether' refers to the formless non-perceivable and inconceivable 'Sentrum', manifesting as the realization of the permeating unlimited might of the ubiquitous transcendental consciousness, which can be experienced in a more prolonged state of absence of thought as the state of 'the unchanging nature within.

In non-philosophical terms, the unchanging nature within, is regarded as a non-conceptual unchanging formless quality or state of being that reverberates the quintessence of the truth of what we are, once mind activity, and thought formations, have ceased to exist. This can be experienced in form of a motionless indiscernible frequency of invisible light and inaudible sound, as well as the most honest and truthful expression of what we are in essence from a state of being point of view.

To summarise:

- We can say that the idea or actual existence of something that is not subject to change is foreign to our way of understanding, due to the fact that there is nothing similar in this creation it could be compared with.
- Consequently we can say that the state of the unchanging nature can't be explained in academic terms, as well as it only can give us a hint of an idea of what it really is, when it is explained in philosophical or poetic terms.
- Furthermore we can say that it has to be experienced to be able to validate the truth of its existence.
- Finally, we can say that we can experience it by means of regular meditation practice in which we are under the influence of prolonged times of Gama-wave activity in the brain, as well as by relinquishing imagination and identification by means of work on consciousness and work on oneself.
- And ultimately we can say that our mind and thoughts have become so complex and complicated and so profoundly conditioned, that they are not able to grasp the existence of the unchanging nature.
- That is the unchanging nature is too close to us and so simple, that it has become impossible for us to understand or grasp it. The moment its concept has transformed from knowledge into knowing cum 'being', it's no big deal anymore and nothing worth talking about.

15. The Process – Stage VIII: The Art of Meditation

Recent neuro-scientific research on brain function has proved that it is the regularity of meditation practice that generates results. Whether our objective is to de-stress and find more 'centeredness' in ourselves and balance our mood swings, as well as dealing with pain, high blood pressure or depression, makes no difference.

The best habit we can create for ourselves is to sit in meditation regularly. Lots of people are very enthusiastic once they come across a new interest and initially put a 150% effort into their new objective. This approach does not work in regards to meditation due, to the fact that there are no guaranties to when we will see the fruits of what our Meditation practice produces. People usually sit a lot in meditation to start with and after a few weeks they become frustrated and give up.

Most people come to me with the excuse that they have not found the right meditation technique for them yet, which is the reason why they don't meditate. To be frank, the right meditation technique might never really come and for most people it does not exist in the first place, at least initially. Our mind always likes to bend things to its own advantage and always has its own individual take on things as well and its attention span has to be questioned.

Considering you have read at least some of the previous chapters, it must be very obvious to you by now, why the mind does not like to meditate. The mind knows that it won't run the complete show anymore once it is under the influence of the non-invasive power of meditation and the impact of gamma-brainwave activity.

What people forget is that our five senses and our attention are programmed to be aware of the external world and to focus on the impressions of life. This has become such a strong and deeply engrained habit, that initially it will take our five senses a while to relax, and it will take time to remind our attention to remember its real purpose again.

Initially we want to start sitting in meditation for ten minutes three to four times a week.

We always have to remember that it is not the quantity that counts at the beginning; it is our attitude of mind towards meditation that will bring about quality and in due time results.

How to Prepare For Meditation

The best appointment in the world is meditation.

It is an appointment with your 'Self', as well as it can be seen as an appointment with what I call the 'management upstairs', as for many people it is an appointment with 'God'.

And who wants to possibly ever miss that?

So the best way to not miss such an important opportunity is to pencil it into our diaries and consider it as mandatory and non-negotiable.

The scale of meditation is limitless due to the fact that it transcends time and space once thought formation has ceased to exist, as well as it is transgressing past and future and above all rises above matter. Along that scale are higher capabilities that lie dormant in our ordinary state of consciousness waiting to be remembered by the undivided self. Yet all of that becomes utterly insignificant once one is embraced by the boundless depth of peace, simplicity and silence that is awaiting the humble self, in the form of the realization of the unchanging nature within.

Meditation is to experience life in a new way – that is life as a means and not as an end.

Exercising: The process of meditation starts with our physical body. Our body is not happy to sit in meditation as long as its vital forces are not channelled towards sitting still by means of a balanced physical workout.

This physical workout has to suit our physical abilities and can range from a remedial practice to a high impact workout, and it does not necessarily need to be yoga. Any intelligent movement and exercise practice will do the job as long as there is a beginning (in the form of a proper warm up), a middle (in the form of increase in intensity), as well as an end (in the form of a cool down, gentle stretching and a resting phase).

A well-balanced skeletal muscle structure, combined with a healthy range of motion and joint flexibility will profoundly benefit our meditation practice. We are the best judges of our physical abilities and our biggest priority is to avoid going to any extreme.

Asana practice is to channel the energies of body, mind and thought towards meditation.

When not to meditate: It is a waste of time to sit in meditation when we are in a highly emotional state and in a state of a major upset, as well as when we are under the influence of alcohol and mind altering drugs. We have no control over certain non-conscious states under the influence of these kinds of substances and a neutral state of mind or a non-judgemental view on things is next to impossible.

It is very difficult to properly meditate while lying down, because our body associates lying down with sleeping, and the very moment we shift into alpha-brainwave activity we might fall asleep. Trying to sit in meditation with a full tummy is equally difficult as lying down, because our body uses a high percentage of energy for digestion, which makes us slightly dozy and impacts on our alertness. We won't be able to utilise the benefits of our meditation when we meditate late at night and go straight to sleep afterwards. We should have at least another fifteen minutes of wakefulness to be able to assimilate our meditation before we go to sleep.

A balanced healthy lifestyle is most conducive to meditation.

Meditating while being ill: Meditation is very beneficial during times of illness, even when we have to lie in bed or on the sofa. While we are ill our attention naturally wants to withdraw and move inwards to enable the self-healing powers of the physical body to do their job. Out of necessity it is much easier for us to detach from the physical, when we are ill and our thought process is usually not that compulsive, because the body needs to safe energy to heal. So we can make use of our time and meditate for more prolonged times while we are ill, which undoubtedly will help speed up our recovery.

Illness can be utilised to exercise detachment.

The best time for Meditation: There is no best time for meditation as such, but there is an advantage to sitting and meditating in the very early hours in the morning, best between three-thirty and five o'clock. This time is called the *time of elixir* according to the mystics, in which the so-called spiritual currents are strong while the world around us is fast asleep and mind activity around us is at its lowest. But due to the way we live our modern life this would be too much to ask for and is not very practical.

We might consider sitting in the early hours of the day once we have retired or during our holidays. So anytime that is suitable for us, and fits best into our day and way of life, will be the perfect time for us to meditate.

Meditation is to tire the mind out and rid ourselves of what we no longer need.

Where best to meditate: Human beings are creatures of habit and association, and it is very conducive to our meditation practice to be sitting somewhere quiet where we feel comfortable, safe and not exposed. At home, this should become one's special place for meditation, and after a few months we will associate this place with meditation.

Initially some non-invasive music might help us to relax, or reading a paragraph in a book that talks about Great Ideas and awakens our higher emotions, helps directs our attention towards meditation. At a certain stage we should try to sit without any music in the background, which will help the sense of hearing to deactivate, so that our whole focus can be directed within.

There is a reason why people wrap a meditation shawl around them while they are sitting still, and one can strongly recommend purchasing a warm blanket or large meditation shawl that can cover most of our body as well as a pair of warm socks. Our nervous system is gradually calming down during the process of meditation and our body might start to feel a bit cold, especially when one intends to sit for more than fifteen minutes.

'Meditation is to be present to one's own presence'.

How to sit in Meditation: People still believe that one only can meditate when one is able to sit cross-legged or in the famous lotus position. This is a complete and utter myth or a clever excuse by the mind.

Meditation is not about posture or the physical and for most people it takes years to gain the flexibility to sit in lotus or half-lotus. Even when one can execute half lotus or lotus comfortably in a yoga class, the moment one sits more than ten minutes in this posture, one's joints and knees start to ache, as well as that one's attention can be drawn towards the aches instead of the screen of consciousness.

Meditation is about transcending all physical awareness and to be able to do that, sitting cross-legged or squeezing oneself into the lotus position is not required, and is only feeding our vanity and inflates the little 'Me' being able to sit in full lotus.

Having said that, for people that find it comfortable to sit cross-legged on a meditation block or bolster for more than twenty minutes, there is no reason at all to change that and one should keep meditating sitting cross-legged. Otherwise the only requirement for sitting in meditation is to keep the spine vertically upright.

That can easily be done by sitting on a comfortable chair or armchair with a cushion on the small of the back, while comfortably resting one's hands into one's lap or onto one's upper thighs, as well as keeping the soles of the feet flat on the ground.

Keeping the light in the room dimmed, and by leaving a bit more time than we have originally planned, we are now in the perfect environment, and have created the perfect condition for ourselves to start sitting in meditation.

Meditation is not about quantity; it is the quality that counts.

To summarise:

- We can say that initially we start with ten minutes of meditation three to four times a week and increase it to six days a week within four months.
- After four months we extend the length of the appointment with our 'Self' by five minutes every month until we are happy to sit for thirty minutes six days a week.
- Furthermore we can say that one gives one's mind a rest on the seventh day of the week, otherwise it tends to rebel and will stop us

meditating for good.

- Finally we can say that if we miss one of our appointments due to 'real circumstances', and not any excuses made up by the mind, we want to keep a neutral attitude of mind and consider it as a missed opportunity and simply get along with it.
- Ultimately we can say that we have to apply conscious effort to start with, due to the fact that the mind will resist sitting in meditation and gets bored after the initial enthusiasm has worn off.
- And last, but not least, we can say that once we simultaneously start applying self-study and work on one's self, as well as actively applying the teachings of the Great Ideas, our conscious effort will turn into inspirational effort and meditation will have become an inseparable vital part of our life. Independent of whether our life circumstances are easy or difficult; meditation and the teachings will have become a powerful counter weight to calmly see us through the ever-changing nature of external life.

The Complete Process of Meditation

The following pages contain a precise description of what actually happens whilst we sit in meditation, what kind of sensations we will experience, as well as the unavoidable struggle with our mind and thoughts. It includes some of the qualia of the timeless teaching of the mystics and yogis that will be met and experienced by every meditation practitioner alike, during the process of meditation.

Furthermore, it contains the quintessence of personal experiences of thousands of hours of dedicated meditation practice during the last thirty years on behalf of the author, as well as the feedback and responses he received throughout the last decade from his students and clients, regarding their own meditation practice, as their mentor or teacher.

It is an honest attempt to demystify the process of meditation including both the actual facts and reality of the possible struggle and friction one initially and generally will face, throughout the process of meditation, as well as the rewards one receives from meditation for one's conscious efforts and dedication.

The description is not based on a specific meditation technique, and only highlights the occurrences that take place during the process of meditation that a practitioner repeatedly might experience. Concurrently the description of the process of meditation from this school of thought point of view, does not claim to be the only way the process of meditation actually takes place and can be described. This is due to the fact that there are hundreds of different cultural backgrounds and all kinds of approaches to meditation that might lead to different results and qualia.

Regardless of that, and I am sure most long-term meditators agree with this, that once one has gone beyond mind and thought formation, one realizes that there are countless ways to lead to the same objective, which can be found beautifully described in most of the ancient scriptures. This particular school of thought looks at the actual meditation process more pragmatically and less philosophically.

204

This is The Teaching of Meditation:

The first objective in Meditation is to still the body, before we still the mind. One of the main obstacles we meet within the process of stilling the body, are our five senses. By applying Asana practice[101] or any other movement practise just before we sit in meditation, approximately two thirds of the scattered energies will be gathered as well as tamed.

Due to Yoga Asana, most of our fascial matrix and Nadis will have opened and cleared, to enable the life force to circulate freely. Once we attend to our personal meditation posture, allowing the physical body to be taken by gravity, whilst simultaneously assessing that the diaphragm is not restricted by any means and is able to move freely, as well as making sure that the spine is free to oscillate and our shoulders are at ease and relaxed, we close our eyes and gradually start taking our attention away from the external world, directing it inwards into the vast spaciousness within the confines of the physical body.

More than one third of our scattered energies will be still responding to what they have to respond to by default, as well as that our sympathetic and parasympathetic nervous system will still be very active due to beta brainwave activity.

Once our eyes have softened further back into the skull and are relaxed, our attention initially will be drawn to different sensations in the body such as heartbeat, the breath, the blood circulation and certain tensions and pressures. Furthermore a fine, but almost prickly feeling of energy throughout the whole body might occur. Simultaneously our attention will be attracted to external stimulus, like light, sound and different happenings again and again, as well as internal stimuli appearing as emotions, imagination, internal considering etc. That in return will ignite a response in our nervous system and will impact on the rate of our heartbeat and breath, as well as our body temperature or any other activity in the body.

After a non-specific length of time of regular meditation practice these occurrences will gradually settle and will only appear at the beginning of meditation. By that time the body has found it likes sitting still. This is the time to increase the duration of meditation by simply staying motionless.

By doing so, the withdrawal of our life energies, that is the energies of awareness and attention and our five senses, towards one point behind the eyes is ignited. This will be experienced as an initial increase in energy in our hands, as well as certain aches and little pains throughout the body, caused by the mind's need to indulge in some external stimulus and consequently by the body's increasing wish to move. This is almost like witnessing a child throwing a tantrum because it does not get what it wants.

At this stage in meditation the practitioner experiences a crucial point of struggle and friction with the physical and mental forces, that might bring up sensations of anxiety or an overwhelming sense of impatience, as well as the feeling of a tight throat in some instances.

This is absolutely no reason to panic and the meditator is presented with two options:

1. To change posture in slow motion to avoid the activation of the five senses.
2. To stay put and motionless for another five minutes, provided the practitioner is untouched and relaxed.

Initially most people will give in to the mind and body's needs and end their meditation at this stage, with a feeling of being recharged and re-energised.

By meeting this stage again and again via conscious effort and regular meditation, the meditator becomes more and more at ease regarding the struggle with the body and the mind's desire for constant external input and food. Once one has relaxed enough to stay put and withstand the physical and mental sensations, by keeping one's awareness and attention within the screen of consciousness regardless of all thought formations, all aches and pains will vanish and our body will be at peace.

This is the stage in which the nervous system has calmed down, the influx of adrenaline has stopped and is replaced by the activation of alpha-brainwave activity, as well as our five senses have relaxed and our breath feels free, calm and at ease.

Having stilled the body the mind has to be tamed. The stage is reached in which the life forces of the body have withdrawn up to the manubrium, a point just above the solar plexus where the ribs meet in the centre, hence everything below that point in the body has died to our awareness and attention.

Due to the fact that our body and the external world does not require our attention at this stage in meditation, the practitioner is faced with his or her mind and thought formations only, as well as with the accompanying emotions.

The meditator's brain waves are fluctuating between alpha and theta, which in themselves indicate a slightly altered state of consciousness. The practitioner faces the struggle with possibly drifting into sleep, or identifying with the constantly appearing thought formations and the so familiar inner voice. Here, the seemingly unsuccessful effort to keep the awareness and attention within the confinements of the screen of consciousness is a common experience.

This is the time to focus on keeping the eyes very relaxed and soften even further back into oneself, almost as if one perceives the screen of consciousness from within the depth of the solar plexus. By being aware of both outer corners of the eyes simultaneously from within the depth of our solar plexus, we allow the life force of the body to withdraw even further up towards the third eye. Here the field of consciousness starts becoming more vivid and can be perceived as less fleeting and flickering. Those flickers are mainly caused by the interruptions of the movement of the mind and emotions, as well as our thoughts.

The meditator has now reached the stage in which mind activity and thought formations have become less invasive. This is due to the deepening realization, and by having surrendered to the fact, that as long as a person tries to meditate and believes to be the meditator, actual meditation is not taking place.

The more this realization is repeatedly experienced during meditation, in time it will penetrate through all the different brains. This is an indication that the mind has become incrementally tired at this stage, and that the meditation practice of the meditator ceases to be performed exclusively by personality and the supporting 'ME's' only. Hence awareness and concentration start coming more frequently into balance, which induces concentration to develop and consequently results in the manifestation of a new proposition.

The new proposition will be experienced by the meditator as a complete withdrawal of the entire life force into one point behind the eyes, while all thought formations become very spacious. The breath cycles will have fused into one and the breathing will have become so calm that it is hardly perceptible. Within a glimpse of a moment, the field of consciousness in front of the meditators eyes starts expanding, combined with a clear sensation of being pulled by the stream of consciousness through what might appear as an increasing gap between the thoughts. Contemporaneously all thought and mind activity stops in an instant.

Here the physical body starts to feel as light as a feather and seems to drop away and dissolve below one's field of perception. This experience can be compared with the sensation one gets on a rollercoaster tipping over the peek with tremendous speed, causing a sensation of being suspended in space. That is a perfect description of the sensation that appears when the physical separates from the formless, in a state of deep meditation in which literally - only the experience of the formless remains.

Another example is the sensation that appears when we are sitting and start nodding off to sleep. This usually causes our head to tip towards the chest, which produces a strong sensation of falling into an infinite space within us. Now one is at a level in meditation, in which gamma-brainwave activity is taking place in the right lobe of the frontal cortex that seems to profoundly alter the practitioner's perception and level of consciousness.

The meditator ultimately has reached the state of complete absence of thought, while being completely absorbed in the infinite space of the formless presence of blissful silence and peace, that is emanating from the unchanging nature within the simplicity of our timeless being.

The practitioner's sense of time has dissolved and the physical body has completely died to the perception of awareness and attention. Within the depth and simplicity of this deep state of meditation, the meditator is experiencing an indescribable sense of vigilance and alertness that does not seem to be of this world. This is combined with an influx of energy that seems to consist of a continuous wavelike stream of light and sound that exceeds all powers of imagination. Concurrently the sense of 'ME' and 'I' has disappeared as well as that what thinks. The external and the internal seem to have fused and become one, as well as all concepts of subject and object have dissolved. All that remains is a paramount connection with the 'Isness' of all there is.

Initially, the state of absence of thought will alternate with phases of intense thought formations during meditation. At this point the practitioner is going through times in which the mind will mainly keep the upper hand, in which the person only rarely experiences prolonged times of the state of absence of thought. Yet, the more conscious effort transforms into inspirational effort, the more the practitioner will be 'meditated', as well as the more experiences of the state of absence of thought accumulate, the faster this state of consciousness will be appearing and ultimately can be accessed in meditation practice at will.

With dedication and patience the state of the unchanging nature will not only manifest throughout the process of sitting in meditation but as something very real and permanent within us in form of Great Ideas.

To summarise:

- We can say that meditation is a slow and gradual process of undoing and transcending all that is not permanent within us.
- Then we can say that initially, the very moment when the experience of the expansion of consciousness appears we will try to grasp it, which will make it disappear in an instant.
- Furthermore we can say that it usually requires patience and a long time to transform conditions like intents, wants, expectations and all forms of doing, or being the doer, as well as trying to grasp into becoming the understanding that one cannot 'do' meditation.
- Finally we can say that only after a few weeks of regular meditation practice its benefits can already be experienced during the day. This is regardless of how much we struggle during meditation, or think that the quality of our meditation has not been very good.
- And ultimately we can say that to a lot of people, especially in recent times, meditation comes surprisingly naturally and gives them a welcome break creating a counterweight to their stressful life.
- And last but not least we can say that we sometimes can avoid a lot of waste of time by being introduced to meditation by an experienced teacher, as well as joining a meditation group to start with.

'There is no aim in Meditation apart from just to 'Be' in meditation'

Alpha-Influence Meditation

Meditating does not necessarily mean just sitting still and motionless. We aim to access a meditative state in all different kinds of circumstances, and one of the most powerful open eye meditations, is the so called 'Walking Meditation'.

The only prerequisite that is required for walking meditation is that we are comfortably dressed and warm. Otherwise our attention will be drawn to the freezing parts of our body instead of being contained while walking. The other thing that has to be considered is that our clothes are not too tight, so that the diaphragm is not restricted and squeezed in, as well as that the air can circulate around our body.

Walking Meditation

- *Once we have arrived at the starting destination of our walk we take our attention into our feet and start walking while being aware of the way our feet touch the ground and bear the weight of our body. After a few minutes relaxing into our feet we completely let go of our feet and take our attention further up to the calves, which are known as our second heart that helps keep the blood circulating, and we want to be aware about the way they engage, as well as they contract and relax during walking. We fully let go of our calves and slowly work our way up towards the knees and let go of them after a few minutes, then thighs and hips, our waist and chest, from there towards the arms, and last but not least the head. Each time letting go of the body part below.*

- *Once we have arrived at the head we soften our eyes and take our attention and awareness into the spaciousness and vitality of our body, looking through our physical eyes from deep within ourselves, enjoying the impressions of nature. After a forty-five minute walk we want to sit somewhere quiet for ten minutes to assimilate. Just to consciously be with ourselves and the spaciousness in our head, as well as the feeling of contentment to 'be' and being part of the creation.*

Another wonderful Alpha-Influence meditation is to visit a gallery or a museum, to simply allow the art pieces or artefacts of history to act on us. We are not particularly interested in analysing the meaning or the reason behind their creation. We are more interested to sense the way they act on our state of mind while being in their presence. We want to keep our eyes relaxed and want to be aware of the spaciousness surrounding the object, as well as wanting to monitor if a silent communication between our presence and their presence takes place and the knowledge we receive from that.

We can apply the same technique while listening to music, or watching a theatre performance as well as watching a movie that does not fall into the blockbuster category. Other possibilities are being under the influence of architecture or watching the stars at night.

Deep Relaxation - Alpha-brainwave Meditation

All forms of deep relaxation techniques fall into the category of alpha-brainwave meditations. The simplest form of them, is by simply listening to a piece of music that makes one relax. Other possibilities are finding a deep relaxation CD that we like and following their instructions.

Alpha-brainwave Meditation

- *A very effective deep relaxation technique is to lie on a yoga mat in 'Savasana'[102] being covered by a blanket. We start with gently lifting one leg slightly up and letting it fall back into gravity, allowing it to become very heavy, becoming one with the ground. We do the same with the other leg. From there we move up to our pelvis and gently lift it slightly up and let it drop, allowing it to become very heavy. We go further up along the body and do the same with the chest, followed by first one arm, then the other arm and at last the head.*

- *Once our whole body has become very heavy and one with the ground we take our attention inwards. We start by visualising our muscles, then our bones and after that our cells. From there we imagine ourselves to consist of atoms and take our attention into the spaciousness of one atom. Then we want to dive into the spaciousness of neutrons to be taken by the all-pervading matrix of infinity, in which we want to rest for five minutes.*

This kind of deep relaxation technique is ideal during times of study, or when we have to complete a project. It helps us to assimilate what we have learned as well taking our attention away from a subject we have become too close to and requires some detachment, to be able to see it in a different light or from a different perspective again. Furthermore this technique helps us to recharge our batteries, by having switched into a different brain, without having to compromise too much with time that is not available. On a physical level it helps to balance our nervous system and reduces the influx of adrenalin, as

212

well as profoundly reducing our stress level.

Alpha-brainwave meditation activates alpha waves within our brain. Those brainwaves put ourselves in the ideal position to learn new information, memorise facts and save data as well as making us more able to perform difficult tasks, analyse complex concepts and ideas and learn new languages. Alpha-brainwave meditation induces an enlarged mental clarity and creates formation of remembrances as well as creating an ideal state of creativity and the proper function of the right brain hemisphere.

Theta-brainwave Meditation –
Meditation on an Object'

In former times meditation on an object was mainly used to generate devotion. Worshiping an object or a religious symbol is a form of Meditation on an object. The Christian cross and the sculpture of the Buddha as well as the black stone known as Ka'ba, became symbols of devotion. In India the 'Lingam' and 'Yoni' or in very ancient cultures the sun and the moon became objects of devotion and worship. Tibetan Buddhists are using Tanka's and Yantra's as a means to focus the attention to develop concentration that consequently takes one from the world of shape and form into the formless, represented by the Bindu, forming the centre in each Yantra and Tanka.

If one is not initiated into these specific meditation techniques by an experienced Buddhist teacher, by just simply staring at the specific object of our attention, we only create a state of divided attention, which can't be kept up very long and ultimately will create tension in the eyes and head.

The Object Meditation we are talking about that activates Theta-brainwave activity is - meditating on an object within. The specific object within us is simply our formless breath, which generates a continuous movement that in itself forms the breath cycle, and within this cycle the different pauses of the breath.

Within each pause after the exhalation as well as within each pause after the inhalation, we can meet a moment of 'Dhyan'[103] – a real moment of meditation.

In all Meditations described in this book it is absolutely vital and necessary, that we train our eyes to stay relaxed and become inactive regarding their intrinsic nature to follow everything that moves. So we have to learn to switch off our rapid eye movement by relaxing and softening the eyes back into the skull, and instead of perceiving the movement of the breath with our physical eyes, we want to solely perceive the rising and falling away of the breath via the faculty of our awareness and attention.

The same applies to all experiences or appearances in meditation that might come up in form of light, sound or subtle shapes and forms. Our physical eyes are looking at things, while the 'Self' perceives things and furthermore, on a higher level of consciousness, the 'Self' 'pre-ceives' via a higher faculty within the finer body. So looking is active or doing, while perceiving is passive and not doing or undoing.

Throughout all different meditations explained in this book, the physical eyes have to be kept at ease and relaxed. As long as our eyes still move as they would naturally move, while looking at the external world during meditation, we will remain the doer during meditation, and never will reach the stage of 'unbecoming', i.e. Meditation won't take place and consciousness won't expand.

Always remember – relax your eyes and switch off all movements of your physical eyes during the whole duration of meditation. Simply disengage them.

Theta-brainwave Meditation- Full pause Meditation:

- *We only want to breathe through the nostrils during this meditation. After we have settled into our sitting posture, we close our eyes and allow them to soften and disengage, becoming aware of the rising and falling away of our breath.*

- *We gently start increasing the length of the inhalation to a comfortable length, feeling the belly rising, without any force, and gently ease into a nice long exhalation.*

- *Once our breath has found a slow motion kind of rhythm, we want to relax and totally undo in the pause after the exhalation, as well as allowing the whole body to become heavy.*

- *There we wait and surrender into the pause after the exhalation until the inhalation meets us again.*

- *We feel the whole body slightly expanding during the inhalation without forcing it, and ease into a long exhalation, becoming completely absorbed by the silence within the pause after the exhalation.*

215

- *After ten minutes we simply want to assimilate the theta waves for a few minutes before we end our meditation.*

It is important to know that we do not want to impose too much on the breathing. The inhalation and exhalation has to be very gentle and relaxed. We don't want to spend much time in the pause after the inhalation, and the exhalation should be comparatively a third longer than the inhalation.

If our breath feels shallow we probably haven't done any exercises. Sometimes, even after having exercised, the breath is still shallow due to different circumstances in life.

In this case we want to do pretty fast inhalations and exhalations through the nostrils for approximately twenty to thirty seconds. This will usually balance our breathing and solve the problem. If it is still shallow after that, we should practice some belly breathing before we go to bed by placing the palms of our hands onto our belly to just feel how the belly is moving by the natural flow of the breath. If belly breathing does not help, then we should learn all different ways of breathing from an experienced yoga teacher.

This meditation technique is ideal in times when our immune system is weak and when we are lacking energy, as well as when we are in a phase in life in which inspiration and intuition is required.

Theta-brainwave Meditation activates theta waves within the brain. The powerful healing properties of theta waves are able to impact on all different levels, as well as connect us with our so called sixth sense and most important, can help detaching us from the external world and take us into a deeper state of meditation. The repetitive nature of the 'empty pause of the breath' meditation is ideal to induce theta wave activity.

Asanas For The Finer Body

The following meditation exercises were designed to exercise and open the so-called finer body or energetic body that resides within the physical body, as well as make us understand and work with the dynamics of awareness and attention. Furthermore the exercises have a positive impact on work on consciousness and self-study, as well as strengthening the different brains, once applied according to the right instructions.

To get an idea and understanding regarding what the finer body is and how it feels, rub the palms of your hands together for a couple of minutes until you feel a lot of heat in your hands. Then place your hands, palms facing each other, two to three centimetres apart and you will detect an electrical charge like stream or an electromagnetic field between the palms of your hands.

Another method is to place your hands two centimetres above the shoulders of a person and you will be able to palpate an electrical charge like heat radiating from the person's body. This is the energetic body you can feel, that penetrates throughout the whole physical body and beyond.

Like acupuncture works with the different meridians and impacts on the whole nervous system, as well as on the whole body and emotions, Asanas for the finer body work on psychosomatic patterns, as well as helping bring all of what we no longer need up into the field of our awareness.

Hence once we are aware of certain matters that were hidden within the unknown, we can acknowledge them and consequently can do something about them. It is these kind of exercises and even more so the gamma-brainwave' Meditation, that is really doing the work on consciousness for us, which we then utilise through self-study and self-observation, that consequently can be executed through a stronger sense of 'Self', hence through the power of the Great Ideas and help that enters.

The following graphic shows the main stations we are working with during the Asanas for the finer body.

1. Instinctual/Movement Brain.
2. Emotional Brain.
3. Intellectual Brain.
4. Twelve Finger Point.
5. Bindu.
6. Screen/Field of Consciousness.
7. Ida/Awareness.
8. Pingala/Attention.
9. Shushumna/Concentration/Neutral.
10. Moon/Feminine/Passive.
11. Sun/Masculine/Active.

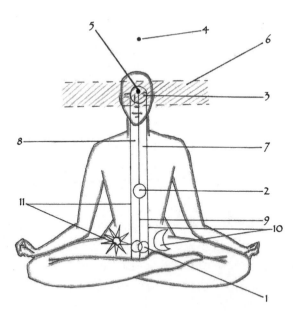

Graphic 1 (Illustrations: Annabelle Hartley)

Rooting Meditation:

- *To enable consciousness to expand, we need to be firmly rooted within the physical body. Work on consciousness as well as work with the finer body requires a firm grounding in the physical, otherwise we are faced with the risk of falling too much into awareness and as a result start imagining all sorts of states during meditation.*

- *The Rooting Meditation always should be practiced before we start with our actual meditation.*

- *The inhalation and the exhalation should be as gentle as possible. The breath is only a help to facilitate awareness and attention to move along the energetic pathways with ease.*

- *Asanas for the finer body are regarded as a mental practice, and are not considered to be a breathing exercise.*

- *The eyes have to be kept disengaged and at ease, softening further back into the skull.*

 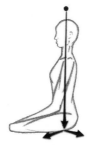 

Step 1. Take your attention towards the tip of the nose. **Inhale** – Up to the twelve-finger point.

Step 2. Exhale – Down along the spine through the tailbone, and let the energy spread below your sitting bones.

Take your attention back to the tip of the nose and repeat Step 1&2 until you feel firmly anchored.

According to the ancient teachings, the rooting meditation is linked to the Sanskrit sound Hu or Hum, which has a descending quality. To enable the scattered energies of the five senses and the mind to gather and withdraw via

219

an ascending motion, a counter weight has to be established via a descending motion that is composed of traces of 'Substance of Gravitas', to simply keep the balance.

Containment Meditation:

- *To be able to contain the energy of our five senses within ourselves, as well as in times we can't afford to lose too much energy or are struggling with identification, this meditation supports us to keep our natural equilibrium and helps building a stronger connection to ones real sense of 'Self'.*

- *Soften your eyes while sitting still and remember to only use your most gentle and subtle breath.*

- *Keep your awareness and attention synchronised with the flow of the gentle breath throughout the whole exercise.*

Step 1. Take your attention towards the tip of your nose.
Inhale – Up to the twelve-finger point.
Exhale – Down to the tailbone.

Step 2. Inhale – Up to the Bindu along the back of the spine or body.
Exhale – Down the front of the spine or body.

Keep inhaling up the back through the Bindu & down the front through the tailbone until you find a balanced momentum within that cycle.
Allow the breath to become more and more subtle.

You might reach a point in this meditation in which you experience the energy actually circling within that cycle by itself. Once those qualia is reached by means of regular practice, that occurrence is an indication to let go of all breathing to simply spending some time to assimilate the flow of the contained energy to let it settle.

Not everybody will experience that independent flow of circling energy. Most people tend to feel after having done five to ten minutes of gentle breathing, that their attention naturally wants to rest, and that one wants to spend some time assimilating the feeling of containment.

Awareness And Attention Meditation:

The awareness and attention Asana for the finer body exercise relates directly to the content of the chapter 'Stage VI – Consciousness'. It will put the theory into practice and will give one the possibility to explore and experience the energies of the passive and active forces and their difference in quality, as well as the way they manifest within us.

The awareness & attention exercise will facilitate harmonising those two opposing forces known as the feminine and masculine energy, as well as helping to open and clear the Nadis or sympathetic ganglions 'Ida' and 'Pingala', along the left and right side of the spine.

- *Soften your eyes while sitting still and become aware if there is any difference in the way you perceive or feel your left and right side of your body.*

- *Than visualise or sense the quality of the passive force within the left side of the body and then the quality of the active force in the right side of the body.*

- *Imagine the quality of the light of the moon appearing next to the left side of the spine at the lowest part of the spine.*

- *Then imagine the quality of the light of the moon on the right side of the spine at the lowest part of the spine.*

- *Apply only the subtlest kind of breathing during the exercise.*

STEP 1. Very gently Inhale – The quality of the light of the moon up & down along the left side of the spine,
Up to the height of the Bindu & back down to the level of the coccyx.
Keep repeating 7 to 10 times

Then, very gently Inhale – The quality of the light of the sun up & down along the right side of the spine,
Up to the height of the Bindu & back down to the level of the coccyx.
Keep repeating 7 to 10 times

Assimilate the energy for five minutes just by simply sitting still and relaxed.

- **Practice the above exercise in Graphic 4, everyday for seven days.**

- *After having practised* **Step 1** *for seven days, add* **Step 2 in Graphic 5** *to* **Step 1.**

Graphic 5

STEP 2. Inhale – The quality of the moon up to the height of the Bindu.
Keep it there on the left.

Contain your breath for a moment while resting in the centre of the Bindu.

Exhale – Down along the right side of the spine and connect with the quality of the sun.

Inhale- The quality of the sun up to the height of the Bindu on the right. **Keep it there on the right.**

Contain your breath for a moment while resting in the centre of the Bindu.

Exhale – Down along the left side of the spine and connect with the quality of the moon.

Then alternate up on the left, down on the right, up on the right…Relax & assimilate the exercise!

- **After having practiced the fusion of Step 1&2 for seven days, add Step 3 in graphic 6 to finalize and make the awareness and attention exercise complete.**

Inhale & exhale the quality of the sun and moon up and down simultaneously.

Then simply rest behind the Bindu to assimilate the whole exercise.

Initially we want to keep the two qualities of awareness and attention separate. The gradual merging of the two qualities takes place by means of regular practice that ultimately will result in concentration. Once the emergence of concentration is neutralizing both active and passive forces, they transform into a new proposition in form of an altered state of

223

consciousness, i.e. the complete withdrawal of awareness and attention towards one point behind the eyes.

This is the moment the exercise has fulfilled its purpose and one should shift to rest behind one's eyes and abide there for five more minutes.

Charging The Different Brains Meditation:

This Asana exercise for the finer body facilitates and awakens the deeper understanding of the nature of the four different brains and the way they actually function, as well as it creates a strong energetic connection with each single one of them within us. It links to the chapter 'Stage II: Understanding the Internal World'.

- *We disengage and soften our eyes, while we take our attention towards the tip of our nose.*

- *Each time we connect with the twelve-finger point after an inhalation during this meditation, we want to contain our breath for a couple of seconds, during which we want to connect with the quality of energy continued within the twelve finger point.*

- *We gather the energy contained in the twelve-finger point and bring it down into the physical via the help of the exhalation.*

STEP 1. Inhale – Up to the 12-finger point.
Contain your breath.
Exhale down along the spine into the
Instinctual/Movement brain.

Inhale – Feel the brain expanding.
Exhale – Relax & undo.

Take your attention back to the tip of the nose and repeat the whole breath cycle five to seven times.

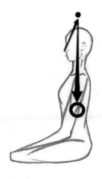  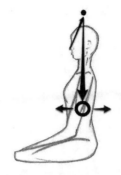

STEP 2. Inhale – Up to the 12-finger point. **Contain** your breath. **Exhale** down along the spine into the **Emotional brain.**

Inhale – Feel the brain expanding.
Exhale – Relax & undo.

Take your attention back to the tip of the nose and repeat the whole breath cycle five to seven times.

STEP 3. Inhale – Up to the 12-finger point. **Contain** your breath. **Exhale** down through the crown into the **Intellectual brain.**

Inhale – Feel the brain expanding.
Exhale – Relax & undo.

Take your attention back to the tip of the nose and repeat the whole breath cycle five to seven times.

Then let go of all breathing and rest behind your eyes for five more minutes.

In time, and by means of regular practice, you will refine your sense of perception regarding the different brains to such an extent that you will sense the difference in their quality and dynamics, as well as you will get a strong sense of connectedness to the way they function.

This will benefit and feed into one's study of the different brains and the way they function and don't function in our regular life. The deeper we dive into this Meditation the more our brains will come into balance and ultimately in perfect alignment. But it is important to know that one has to consciously challenge and work with each brain in our everyday life, by feeding them with the right stimulus they require to grow, while simultaneously practising the meditation described above.

Gamma-brainwave Meditation – Objectless Meditation

The ideal way to go into Objectless Meditation, which is the advanced form of meditation, is by either sitting in meditation early in the morning when the mind had a rest and could assimilate the previous day via the formations of dreams during sleep, or by practising any intelligent form of physical exercises followed by five minutes of deep relaxation.

Gamma-brainwave Meditation works best when our mind is in a state of compassion for the 'Isness' of all there is and how things are. That kind of compassion can be acquired by assimilating Great Ideas and concepts that are full of life and meaning, as well as that the effort we apply to our meditation has transformed into inspirational effort, i.e. meditation has become full of meaning to us and has turned into an inseparable part of our life.

The Objectless Meditation described below covers two aspects: One is, to generate theta-brainwave activity first that induces the process to detach us from the world around us, while it simultaneously still gives our mind something to do before it willingly surrenders to the prospect of sitting in communion with the objectless nature of the ever expanding consciousness, into which it ultimately will disappear once gamma wave activity has impacted on it.

Spanda Meditation – inducing consciousness to expand

- *The duration of this meditation should be a minimum of thirty minutes and ideally, should be slowly extended to forty-five minutes or even an hour once our life circumstances allow it.*

- *We already know by now, having practised all the other meditations before, how to disengage our eyes, as well as that our breath has become very subtle in meditation and our body has become at ease sitting still.*

- *So, always when we take our attention back towards the tip of our nose in this meditation, and with each inhalation we want to feel the coolness that*

228

is generated by the subtle flow of the incoming breath, at the tip of our nose.

- *Each time when we reach the twelve-finger point after the inhalation in this meditation, we want to surrender and be drawn into the third breath that arises out of the diminishing force at the end of the actual inhalation.*

- *There we want to abide for a couple of seconds before we are taken back into the physical by the falling away of the exhalation.*

- *Each time when we inhale up to the Bindu between the eyes in this meditation, we contain our breath and hold our attention there, to become absorbed by the third breath, as well as we want to allow our awareness to expand laterally (sideways), while feeling the screen of consciousness widening into infinity.*

- *In STEP 2 in this meditation, while we rest our awareness and attention within the field of consciousness, we want to apply the most gentle and subtle breath possible. With the inhalation we feel the screen of consciousness together with our awareness expanding, and with the exhalation we surrender into the spaciousness and undo. After a while we want to extend and sense this expanding feeling during the inhalation along both sides of our body. Our whole sense of being wants to expand with the inhalation and undo with the exhalation.*

- *Then we give up all conscious breathing and stay absorbed in deep Objectless Meditation, filled with an all-pervading sense of compassion.*

STEP 1. Inhale – Up to the 12-finger point.
Contain during third breath.
Exhale – Down to coccyx.

Inhale – Up to Bindu.
Contain during third breath.
Exhale – Expand awareness laterally & let go.

Go back to tip of the nose and very slowly repeat 9 to 15 times.

229

 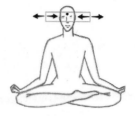

STEP 2. Keep awareness &
attention on the field of
consciousness.
Inhale – Expand laterally.
Exhale – Let go & relax.

**Keep In- & exhaling 9 to 15 times.
Then rest behind the bindu within
this objectless spaciousness for as
long as you intended to sit 30 min
to an hour.**

As it was said before, and always has to be remembered, we only will reach the level of deep meditation once we practice on a regular basis.

We should start with alpha meditation that can be considered as beginners meditation, and explore different deep-relaxation techniques. After having practised deep-relaxation for a while, it is wise to implement the different Asanas for the finer Body before practising theta meditation, which is considered as the intermediate level. Objectless or 'Gamma-brainwave' meditation, which is the advanced form of meditation should be implemented once the body is stilled and at ease to sit motionless for up to an hour.

Gamma waves can reach a frequency of up to 100 Hz, which is more than double to the beta brainwave frequency that is usually active while we are awake. The scientists associate and relate finer functions like perception and consciousness to gamma wave activity as well as that they can lead to relevant permanent changes in brain function by means of regular meditation, that govern and induce sensations like peace, contentment, detachment, centeredness, containment and objectivity.

**'Meditation is our daily appointment with the Management Upstairs,
thence a meeting with the Absolute or God. Who possibly wants
to ever miss that?**

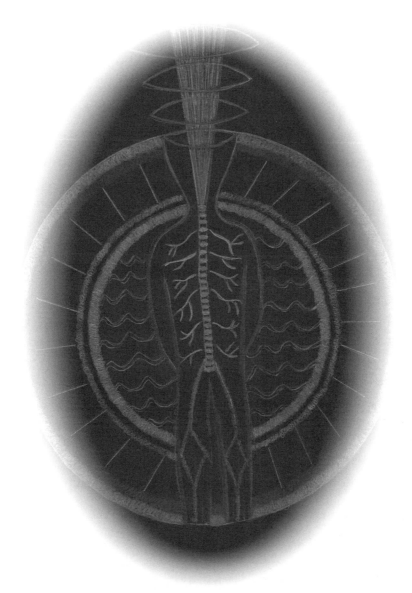

16. The Process - Stage IX: The Art of Self-Study

The idea of self-study goes all the way back to the Yoga Sutras of Patanjali, which explain in chapter two of the Sutras, 'the path to realisation', that three components are required in yogic disciplines that are comprised of discipline, self-study, as well as the orientation toward the ideal of pure awareness or the highest objective.

The following teachings had a huge impact on me during the times of my studies with my teachers long ago, and stayed with me to this day. They were inspired by the 'Yoga Sutras', as well as ideas derived from the 'Fourth Way Teaching', Assagioli's Psychosynthesis, as well as from my teacher's very own sources of knowledge. Explaining Great Ideas by means of the language and comparison of different systems and philosophies, the student gains a better understanding of the universal nature of the teachings, as well as that their underlying message is the same.

Like most of the teachings in this book, I have worked with and applied so many different ideas from so many different sources throughout the last three decades. I have drawn from my own sources of experience and having taught them in so many different teaching environments and implemented the teachings in hundreds of different lectures, they carry my own personal signature and have transformed into a more contemporary teaching method that suits our modern times and modern ways of thinking.

This is unavoidable, yet is not watering down or blurring the timeless teachings, due to the fact that the neutrality in language is not compromised and none of the different subjects in this book are based on my personal interpretation, or are explained by old knowledge.

Self-study is performed by means of self-observation, and self-observation requires the help of different approaches and perspectives that are linked to liberating ideas, as well as some support and inspiration, without which self-observation can't be sustained for very long. This is due to the divided nature of our mind, which we have observed within ourselves and understand so well by now.

The aim of self-study is to deepen self-observation, accumulate as much information about the way we function internally, and become a more conscious being. To be able to deepen self-observation we have to further remove ourselves from the object of our observation and establish a new and different standpoint from which we can self-enquire and observe ourselves from a more neutral perspective.

'Self-observation is to step out of oneself to be able to observe oneself'.

This will lead to a profound increase of awareness and consciousness of oneself in relation to the 'Isness' of things. So, similarly to what was explained in the chapter The Art of Meditation, we have to soften further back into ourselves, to be able to see what actually lies right in front of oneself. That is, that what one initially took and understood as oneself.

The more we keep enquiring along this direction of deeper self-observation, the more it will lead us towards higher faculties, via the more evolved parts of our different brains.

'Self-study gradually leads us to an increase in consciousness of what one had been and to what one is right now'.

The more knowledge and facts we gain over our actual inner conditions and non-conscious states, the more this will lead to the realization that the only option and possibility we have is to 'Change'. This process, of seeing things from a new standpoint and becoming more deeply conscious, as well as seeing things from a new light, is called *awakening*. The moment we start diving into ourselves and find the right entry into ourselves, we start waking up.

According to the 'Yoga Sutras', factors that compose this path to awakening are a strong faith in the new knowledge we have received that sees us through the initial stages, as well as the energy we gain out of our faith that leads to conscious effort that enables us to apply the theory of the new knowledge in life to transform it into actual experience. Then we have to apply mindfulness, which is rooted in a neutral state of mind, as well as a non-judgemental view on things that ultimately will lead to integration and internalisation, which will gradually form into wisdom.

It is obvious that we are not able to wake up by what mind created life has on offer. To be able to awaken from our non-conscious states we are desperate for ideas from another source. It is like we can't cure a drug addiction by means of taking more drugs. We need another source that functions as an antidote to become free of the addiction. We cannot wake up from mind created life by means of mind created life. We require different and new ideas, as well as new concepts or methods that are not created and don't belong to mind created life.

So this gives rise to the question of what can possibly awaken us in the real sense?

The answer is simple, we need a new out-look and method, as well as the influence of Great Ideas to awaken.

Furthermore, we can awaken by the help of people who have put all their effort and energy into work on themselves and have freed themselves from the powerful hold mind created life had over them. Also it is applied conscious effort that can help us to awaken.

If we are at the right place at the right time, we might meet some people along the way that know the way out of our ordinary conditions and help us to gradually awaken. Regardless of all the help we might receive from others, as well as no matter how much inspiration we receive, in the end of the day, the work is down to us and the amount of input we are willing to invest is down to us as well.

The Gateway to Liberation by Means of Great Ideas

The concept or idea of liberation is as old as mankind itself and has led to pioneering ways of thinking and action, as well as it has manifested the timeless knowledge that can be found in ancient scriptures and the teachings of old and new philosophers and mystics.

The idea of liberation came into manifestation based on the realisation that we are not free and that there possibly is a way out of our ordinary condition that lead us to a greater freedom. The ideas of liberation that always surround us outside our ordinary condition, only refer to ourselves, as well as to our internal conditions and not to any external conditions.

We are surrounded by these liberating ideas whether we believe in them or not and regardless of whether we can feel them or not. Often when we are faced with scenery of outstanding nature or contemplate on the infinity of the outer space, we might feel that there is something else. Something that can show us a freedom we don't possess. Mainly people who are attracted to and are inspired by Alpha-Influences and have accumulated 'Substance of Gravitas', usually can feel that liberating ideas truly exist.

This is the very reason that makes people start searching and come across different forms of philosophical teachings, that makes them believe that the answers can be found in secret societies and hidden mystic schools somewhere far away.

This is what I believed when I was in my early twenties, as well as the authors of a number of influential books. Nothing can create a stronger pull than the mystery of the unknown. So people usually embark on a journey and some of them find a mystic school. There they soon find out that liberating ideas don't belong to the school, or are the possessions of a school, but that they are universal, which soon leads to the realisation that it is an illusion to think that something like higher education actually exists. Neither can we simply go to a school and be told about, different levels of consciousness, to reach a new state of consciousness.

The teacher of the school only can help us realise that the action and the impact of the Great Idea lies in the effect they have on ourselves, as well as the response we have to them and the amount of effort we are willing to put into them.

Different systems and philosophies, as well as a variety of different teachers are teaching liberating ideas, but they will only have an effect and impact on us as long as we contemplate them and think about them from all different angles, and we must truly feel from the depth of our heart that we must actively apply them to ourselves.

Now, the question might arise of what actually is a Great Idea that is not created by mind created life?

The answer is not that simple, due to the fact that there is hardly anything available to us in our ordinary state of consciousness, that could be compared with or comes close to the concept of Great Ideas.

These ideas can be compared with very precious and delicate instruments that can easily be misused and wrongly handled. That is one of the reasons why they are disguised and transmitted in a specific language that can't be that easily understood or attract interest. It would require a lot of effort to come to terms with them. So even when people do meet them in life, and as we said before we are always surrounded by them, they would not be able to make the right connections to place them, due to a disbalance within the function of their different brains.

Another reason why they are not seen and recognised is that out of our usual mechanicalness and habitual responses, as well as our deeply engrained 'I-believes' and personal philosophy, we would immediately try to explain them with our old knowledge or our familiar ideas that come from mind created life.

So what kind of new ideas can safeguard us through that narrow pathway into liberation?

One very powerful liberating idea, which can be found in most philosophical teachings, is the understanding that we are not one but a dived self that is split up into many contradictory little 'I's'. The idea that we are not one stands, far outside the ordinary ideas mind created life has implanted within us, as well as that only very few people will even consider assimilating this idea, since they cling to their belief that they are one and always the same.

Beyond the confinements of ourselves there are other Great Ideas we can possibly meet that can liberate us, provided that they are thoroughly understood on all levels as well as having penetrated through all our different brains.

Another very delicate liberating idea, which stands outside our mind created life, is the revelation that 'we cannot do'. This idea has to be considered and looked at very carefully, to not be misunderstood, in which case it could lead to consequences that are not conducive to our inner development and might become counterproductive to our inner growth.

A lot of people who come across this idea interpret it's meaning incorrectly, and think that it is not worth trying anything at all anymore, which can become very serious and destructive.

If we look at this idea from the teachings point of view, it becomes very obvious that everybody is always doing the only possible thing they can do in response to the events of life, as well as that all that is happening at this present moment in time is going in the only direction it possibly can go and we have hardly any say in it.

We might say something, but that usually does not change a thing. So the liberating idea that 'we cannot do' clearly relates to our habitual and mechanical behaviour, and as long as we are under the control of the non-conscious states, that is we are not awake, things will simply go the only way they can go, which can be along a countless number of directions of cause and effect.

By actively applying the liberating idea that 'we cannot do' to ourselves in our everyday life, and experience the fact of how often we contradict ourselves and how little we can change and do in life, we arrive at the understanding that the only possible way to deepen our self-observation, is that we have to self-study by means of the liberating ideas.

Regarding the Great Idea of 'we cannot do', we might realize that what we consider or understand as doing, is in actual fact not doing but responding mechanically, that is 'It' does, that our habits and conditionings make us do, all the little 'ME's' make us do, and that we have almost no control over that, and even more so we have absolutely no say in it.

After a long period of regular meditation practice we finally acknowledge how little we can do to stop our mind and thought activity, as well as how random and very often inconcise our thought patterns are. This is a profound process of disillusionment, without which liberation is not possible.

The moment we have arrived at this realisation and can feel it on all levels and understand it from the depth of our being, we have become more liberated, we have become more humble and appreciate the depth of knowledge of liberating ideas, as well as we have become more receptive and ready to receive the help from liberating ideas. This experience will take off the edge of our desperation, it will make us less driven by mind created life, as well as opening new possibilities and ways of understanding.

Ultimately we come to the conclusion that everybody cannot do, hence we can finally start shifting from theory into practise.

So to reduce all that was mentioned before into one simple statement, we can say that '**the gateway to liberation is based on the realisation and <u>true</u> understanding that in our ordinary state of mind 'our 'Self' is not one but many' and that 'we cannot do'.**

This realisation is the foundation on which the work on consciousness by means of meditation and self-study really can begin. Everything that happened and took place before this realisation, all the little insights, encouragement and glimpses of higher levels of consciousness we were given, was part of the preparation work and an incentive that led to this first objective. In return it will open up the possibility that we can shift away from the laws of mind created life, and can come under new laws.

By means of these new laws we can reach a much higher state within ourselves as beings, and may even reach a stage at which we can do and have real will. To gain real will, we have to develop something within us that is not subject to change. So we have to search for and work hard, to finally evolve into the unchanging nature within.

The Force of Meaning

Each Great Idea as well as every universal teaching that makes us think differently and carries the idea of liberation, is reaching us from beyond mind created life and is mainly comprised of the force of meaning.

This force is infinite in its power. It transforms non-conscious effort into conscious effort and conscious effort into inspirational effort. It is the underlying force that initially meets us by means of Alpha-Influences that are attractive enough to gather a workforce of supporting 'I's' that help accumulating 'Substance of Gravitas'.

The force of meaning is active in all beliefs we hold that have not become mechanical. It sees us through the dry times in our meditation practice, as well as through times of sadness and despair, hence the feeling of hopelessness never arises.

'The power of mind created life divides the force of meaning unites'.

It is the force of meaning that awakens our higher emotions that shift us onto a higher level of consciousness, as well as it helps break down our contradictions, to direct us towards true conscience. It manifests the neutralising force that transcends the force of opposition, because it stands above this law. There is no opposing force that can oppose the force of meaning. Friction simply dissipates, the moment something has become truly meaningful to us, hence opposing force ceases to exist. The scale of meaning is multi-dimensional and next to limitless.

Beta-Influences are on the lower end of the scale, while the influence of Nature and Gamma-Influence range at the upper end of the scale. Finding meaning in certain situations brought up by life's events, as well as by ideas and people, can change our life forever. A talk to a stranger on a long train ride can lead to a complete turning point in life. The stranger might turn out to be in contact with different liberating ideas, or even with Gamma-Influence. In addition, accidentally coming across a certain book that belongs to a higher category of books can be life changing, due to the book transmitting Alpha-Influences.

So the moment we acknowledge that we cannot change life, yet that the only possibility is change, we will arrive at the understanding of another liberating idea that 'mind created life cannot be an end in itself' for us. As a consequence of that, we gradually stop being very much life orientated, as well as we transcend the belief that we can improve mind created life to such an extent that it will lead and take us somewhere and is worth becoming an end in itself.

The teaching of liberating ideas does not consider mind created life to be an end in itself, due to the fact that it is under far too many mechanical laws, that will keep it always under the same conditions. So we have to make use of life, by simply taking it as an opportunity and means that will take us under different conditions. This only can take place when we allow the objective of liberating ideas to awaken, which is uniquely connected to something we solely can do to ourselves.

This is the reason why all timeless teachings say, that we all carry the potential to evolve within, and are in essence born with the ability to self-develop. All the teachings are solely about oneself, as well as a certain possible development in relation to life and some specific accidental events that can transform our whole being, which changes us into a truly compassionate person.

Liberating ideas state that as long as we can keep our integrity towards the teaching, as long as we don't undermine the teaching and ourselves, and that we understand the meaning and the instructions of the teaching, then whatever life is going to throw at us and puts in front of us, will not put us off balance and destroy us.

There are no surprises by mind created life that can overwhelm us, because we understand and know from the depth of our being that life simply is like it is. By being firmly rooted in the knowledge and understanding that we cannot do, the meaning of achievement, failure, wealth and success will diminish more and more, and will mean less and less to us. It ultimately will be replaced by the force of meaning of the timeless teachings that are always surrounding us. At this stage we will be able to perceive them and feel them, as well as knowing that life can't give us what the meaning of the liberating ideas or the teachings can give us.

By remembering to remember the teaching and what it means to us in all situations in life, as well as in all internal situations, in due course and by means of conscious effort, the process of the work on consciousness and its force of meaning will become increasingly active in our life.

To summarise:

- We can say that initially the only thing we really can do is to try to remember to remember to self-observe, and apply in our everyday life what Great Ideas are teaching us.
- Then we can say that once we have realised how little we can do and how helpless we are towards life and the way our mind has control over ourselves, we are starting to awaken.
- Furthermore we can say that seeing change as the only option by means of liberating ideas as well as meditation, the teaching is slowly taking our interests away from mind created life and starts becoming a counter weight to life and its events.
- Finally we can say that once life has stopped becoming the means to an end, the force of meaning has started to work through us and within us.
- Ultimately we can say that the moment mind created life has lost its impact and control over us, all we meet in life will become full of meaning, due to the fact that it is perceived through the eyes of the universal teaching and its liberating ideas.
- And last but not least we can say that by gradually being transformed by the power of the meaning Great Ideas contain, we not only have come to peace with ourselves and the truth of what we are, but we have come to peace with life as well as with everybody and everything in it.

Transformation or The Art of Dying

In organic life transformation can be observed everywhere. This process is known to us as metamorphosis in which the organism alters its general form, condition or state, as well as its mode of life. This is seen in changes by means of development from cell into embryo, or from larva into an insect as well as from egg into an animal.

Different forms of transformation are constantly taking place in our physical body in the form of the change of one type of material into another that often takes place by the process of assimilation by means of our metabolism. Every seven years the body completely renews itself via the process of constant cell division. So almost nothing is left of the original body after a period of seven years. Alchemy transforms one metal into another, and theology sees transformation as a change in disposition.

Most of the ancient scriptures and philosophies contain a form of teaching of applied psychology that ignites the process of transformation. The teachings based on Great Ideas tell us how to transform knowledge into experience and personality into essence, as well as how we transform non-conscious emotions into higher emotions, and the divided 'Self' into 'permanent self'.

The practice of the science of meditation will transform thought into non-thought as well as awareness and attention into concentration and the non-consciousness into consciousness. Furthermore it will transform the energetic body into third body and the 'Self' into 'Non-Self' as well as it transforms all that is subject to change within us into the unchanging nature within us.

Irrespective of that, every kind of process of transformation, which leads to lasting change, has three common pre-dominators, that is that we first of all have to awaken to the truth of a state or inner condition, which usually takes a long time, and once we have woken up to the truth we have to die again to be born again, like the Phoenix arises out of the ashes.

Each time we go through a process of transformation, we first have to wake up and then die again to be newly born. This is another law we come across that is called the Law of Transformation, which usually takes place via an unexpected conscious shock, that wakes us up to the truth of a state or condition. Because of that the truth of a certain state has come up into our field of consciousness, being illuminated by the light of our awareness. That is, it can't be denied or ignored anymore.

Then for a long time we struggle with the actuality of the truth and condition that generates constant friction, which in return is manifesting the Law of Opposition. By staying firmly rooted and connected within the universal teachings, the liberating ideas that contain the force of meaning will enter as the neutralising force, transcend the law of opposition and manifest a new proposition in the form of a new truth and new condition.

Once the universal teachings have become alive within us by means of the force of meaning, as well as the process of our inner evolution has become active in life, with the guidance of an experienced teacher, we will gradually be able to implement positive shocks out of our own conscious effort to consciously ignite a process of transformation.

This is how we start transforming our non-conscious states and habits that keep us in deep sleep and in the ordinary state of consciousness into a new proposition that is nourished and sustained by the power of the universal teachings.

For example, if we want to transform the condition of being a smoker into the condition of being a non-smoker, by simply just stopping smoking we create a massive shock to the system that will manifest an unsustainable void in which we will not be able to stay for very long.

So to be able to get out of the shock, we have to implement a counter shock or positive shock that neutralizes the vacuum and has got enough power to transform the old habit into a new habit that is more conducive to our wellbeing. The positive shock can be in the form of a detox and exercise programme, accompanied by a stop smoking program and a support group, which might generate an amount of energy in form of will action that is larger than the amount of energy of the smoking habit. Hence we will be able to quit due to sufficient energy resources that see us through the struggle.

Positive shocks are a means to develop a different kind of will action. That is the will to remember to remember the teaching, as well as the will to not compromise with one's meditation. Positive shocks can be a powerful tool to become more conscious and evolve in our state of being. Yet they never should be implemented without the guidance of an experienced teacher, otherwise they could lead to great harm and can become counterproductive to our work on consciousness.

To summarise:

- We can say that liberating ideas carry the methods and tools that ignite a process of inner transformation.
- Then we can say that we can't transform life but under the right circumstances, and with the right support, we can transform ourselves. Transforming ourselves implies that we are transforming lower frequencies into higher frequencies by means of meditation.
- Furthermore we can say that higher frequencies transform cross substances into finer substances. That is lower vibrations of consciousness into higher vibrations of consciousness.
- Finally we can say that meditation is nothing more than the process of dying, in which we die to the world of matter to awaken to the world of the formless, as well as we die to the concept and the idea of self or 'I', to awaken to state of non-self or 'I am', a state of being that is manifest within all of us in form of the unchanging nature within.

A brief Outline of Process of Self-Enquiry

The process of self-study or self-enquiry is a verified, definite and entirely practical process of applied Eastern psychology that leads to a complete transformation of our state of being. So what we have to consider is that everything that grows, has to grow at a certain speed as well as in a certain time frame. When things grow too fast in too little time, they might have areas of weaknesses that don't support and sustain the whole organism.

Once the organism has reached its final size, the areas of weakness will be an integral part of it for the rest of its life and can't be replaced by something stronger anymore. That is, it always will have a disadvantage regarding its survival and health compared to organisms that grow at a balanced speed. The same idea can be applied to our inner growth or evolution. The more we try to speed up the process, the more weaknesses and gaps we will have manifested once the universal teachings are assimilated and have become active within, hence we haven't fully transformed and got stuck in the chrysalis.

Now from the moment we are under the direct impact of Gamma-Influences, and are committed to putting our effort into our Self-Study and inner development, on the one side we are freed from the law of accident regarding everything in relation to the Great Ideas and universal teachings. On the other side we will stay under the law of accident in regards to our personal private life and our work life, which has to unfold in the way it is supposed to unfold, hence we will be kept in the unknown.

So the moment when we remember to remember liberating ideas and perceive life's events from a universal teaching point of view, every event will make sense to us and will become conducive to our inner development, because we will utilise the event of life by applying liberating ideas by means of conscious effort, which in return will support and feed into our inner growth. Hence from a universal teaching point of view nothing is down to accident anymore as long as we remember the teaching, that is respond to life from a higher level of consciousness.

This is the teaching of Transformation:

Once one has gained sufficient life experience, and one has gone through different phases of disillusionment regarding life and the way we initially envisioned it to be, and also one has become tired about Beta-Influences that are generated by mind created life, one will be drawn increasingly towards Alpha-Influences, that inspire us and contain knowledge that make us think differently.

Being exposed to the impact of these influences during a long period of time will accumulate a significant amount of 'Substance of Gravitas', that will keep our heart's interest more continuously along those lines of thought, without becoming seriously distracted. A sufficient number of little 'ME's' will stay attracted to the Alpha-Influences and gradually form a union. This union of supporting 'I's' will have a major impact on our heart's desire, that is, it will be filled with more Inner longing. That is the inner longing to know and find an answer to the rising questions the Alpha-Influences have brought up, as well as the nagging realisation that the only option for us is change.

Due to the magnetic quality of Inner longing we will be attracted to Gamma-Influence that will meet us in form of an environment of studies or in the form of a teacher, which is specialised in this field of expertise, that will teach and show us how to put the knowledge we already have acquired from all the Alpha-Influences into action.

One of the first things we learn about at the beginning of our studies is that we have to exercise our 'Finer Body' and as a result we are taught how to practice the 'Rooting Meditation'. Under these powerful facilitating influences we will soon be introduced to the Great Idea of Self-study, as well as what and how we have to Self-study. By understanding the importance of the concept of self-study, we soon realize that we only can change when we know how we tick and internally function on a daily basis, as well as from where and how we generally react to the external world, the events of life and most important to all the people in it.

So while we hear about and study more liberating ideas, it is the Containment Meditation that facilitates us through this process. Soon we discover the actuality of the different brains and their functions within us, and we learn how to apply the 'charging the different brains' meditation that ignites the work process on this important subject. The more our different brains start working to their full potential, the more 'Unchanging Gravitas' will be established.

While we study the theory of the non-conscious states we regularly practice the theta-brainwave meditation. With the support of the universal teaching and via the practice of meditation, in due course we will develop a so-called 'Neutral Observer', that once established, will be a powerful companion while we start to actively work with all the non-conscious states.

For a long period of time we only observe them, but the more permanent 'Unchanging Gravitas' becomes, the more we will start resisting them to transform them into a new proposition. More and more the knowledge of the universal ideas will actively work within us and by practising the 'Awareness and Attention' Meditation, as well as with the help of conscious effort, much more help will enter and we will slowly acquire a so-called 'Permanent Sense of Self'.

Here at this stage, we are regularly practising the Gamma brainwave Meditation, and after a long time of continuous practice by means of inspirational effort, the 'Gamma' Meditation will induce the gradual realisation of the state of Self-consciousness, in which we experience the knowledge of the full truth of what we actually are in essence.

From now onwards this state will increasingly manifest more and more during our meditations as well as during the day. On this level of our evolution we have reached a point at which we have come to peace with ourselves as well as with mind created life. More refined inner abilities are active within us and by diminishing the presence of the non-conscious states significantly, we become increasingly free of the suffering that is caused by them.

The next stages along the path of our inner development are hypothetical to a lot of people and might only lead to too much imagination, due to the fact that they have to be experienced to gain a true understanding about the simplicity and unspectacular nature of their manifestations. Only that much can be said that by having arrived at this stage we will be taught and instructed from within by the wisdom of 'Sentrum', with which we are 'in-tuition' that will lead to the manifestation of the unchanging nature within.

To summarise:

- We can say that regardless of all the good intentions we have, the whole process of our inner transformation, as well as our regular meditation practice, has to be seen and approached from the point of view of being an amazingly exciting and refreshing adventure.
- Then we can say that a lot of people in our modern world tend to take the depth of a process like this far too seriously, which without question has to be avoided.
- Furthermore we can say that in reality and from the very beginning, the whole experience of inner growth should be an awe inspiring and exhilarating process.

Conclusion

Meditation is as much about life as it is about death – or is as much about dying as it is about living, henceforward you die to your mind and thoughts that are subject to change, hence not permanent, and become alive to what is permanent within, hence not subject to change.

Finally, all that we have explored in this book is in regards to the first direction of the universal teachings only, that include meditation and the Asanas for the finer body, as well as aspects of Self-study that can be easily practised and applied in one's own life.

There are a multitude of other aspects in respect to the science of meditation and self-study that can't be addressed within the confinement of a book that functions as a means to transmit knowledge, as well as a medium to teach. All the other forms of knowledge that still belong to the process of meditation require a different medium in form of other kinds of Alpha-Influences, as well as in form of people that know from experience.

Many new ideas as well as some of the meditations that can be found in different sections of this teaching, without any doubt will give rise to a number of questions. Please refrain from trying to explain them with what you already know. It usually means that it is simply not the right time to assimilate this particular kind of knowledge or Great Idea and one should come back to it at a much later point. That is, one simply should move on and work with the liberating ideas and meditations that ignite a Aha-moment and some meaning within yourself, which is an indication that one is ready to work with them and apply them, to slowly assimilate them.

The ideas of the other directions of the universal teachings, as well as the science of meditation, will have to wait to be explained, and might reach you in form of another book.

Now - just to conclude this teaching, I honestly can say from the depth of my being that regularly sitting in meditation as well as studying and practising the work on consciousness is worth every bit of effort.

In gratitude to all the many people that have taught me, as well as to the timeless teachings, I could not wish for my life being more meaningful, inspiring and fulfilling as it already is, and I am very much looking forward to every moment in the future that is filled and inspired by the universal teachings, regardless of how much effort it will demand.

So please promise to your 'Self' the moment your heart is internally pulled by the universal teachings, to <u>always remember</u> that – meditation and the work have no beginning and no end, and they are an ever evolving experiment within one's own laboratory inside our physical body. It undoubtedly can gradually take you, and that is solely based on my very own personal experience, beyond mind and thought right into the heart of the unchanging nature within.

The true state of Meditation arises – when live and death have ceased to oppose each other

17. My Own Journey

To write about my own past has been a very interesting experience. In spite of that fact, the purpose of this book is to shed light on the *science* of meditation and not on my personal story, bearing in mind that by the time I had met my teachers, the past, or let's put it in a different way; the parts of the past which trigger 'the little me singing its story', had lost their charge and became increasingly irrelevant with regards to everyday life. During the last two decades there has barely been time to revisit the past.

So it took me some time to consider the pros and cons of the relevance to the reader of this section as compared to the previous ones.

It was striking to see how often one has to use the word **me** and **I** when writing in the first person: two simple words, me and I, occupying such an important place in our lives.

The autobiography could have been written in first person, but I chose to write it in the third person, simply because this body, mind and being has gone through many transformative changes along the way, as well as it has prevented me to place my sense of 'I' into it.

The past was fantastic and I loved every bit of it - but that was then and now is now regardless off.

Nevertheless, whilst writing this section I remembered how inspiring and encouraging it is to read about other people's journeys and experiences and how often I could find parts of my own life reflected in theirs; having asked the same questions, looked for the same answers and realising that we all go through our ups and downs and that we are not alone on this journey.

But most importantly, that these events happened to real people. People who are still alive and that it is not simply fiction. People's life journeys and experiences are what add so much meaning to my own life. If one is unbiased and listens carefully, one can learn so much from others. The art is in the way one listens to our surroundings and companions.

Birth and Early Childhood

Conceived seven weeks later than his twin, and stuck for hours in the birth canal during birth, was probably not the best way to life in 1963, and it didn't stop there. Having been born prematurely, the doctors kept him in hospital during the first few weeks of his life without the support of an incubator. His mother was convinced that he would never leave the hospital alive and so took him home after signing the paperwork confirming that it was her risk and responsibility if anything should go wrong.

Unfortunately his premature body couldn't retain any food, so his mother cooked liquid meals and fed her little boy four drops at a time, slowly increasing the amounts. It took nine months before Lex was able to eat properly.

By that time his bones had turned soft and his feet and legs had started to deform beautifully (a medical disorder known as rickets).

Thank God they did! The deformation served him very well later in life as a professional dancer. It prevented him from having to serve in the army and turned out to be a great advantage to being able to sit cross-legged with ease during prolonged periods of meditation. These are only some examples of seemingly incidental happenings in life, which are in actual fact indications that nothing happens without any reason.

The family doctor, who closely supervised his mother during that difficult time, had become part of their family by then.

One day he said, "If your son survives all of this physical suffering, he will become a fighter and survivor and nothing in life will be able to throw him." And he was right.

It has to be mentioned that there are three things Lex was born with, which have stayed with him throughout. One was his positive attitude towards life and people; the second was a deeply engrained sense of discipline, harmony and almost naive fearlessness towards life and third, an openness to all sorts of ideas, influences and a natural connection to his intuition, creativity and sense of beauty.

He was a genuinely happy person and it took an awful lot to wipe that big smile off his face. Even later in more difficult times, his positive approach to situations and people was unshakable.

Just a few months later, Lex went through a period in which he contracted every childhood illness you can imagine. Shortly after, a very severe bout of croup attacks caused the boy's parents endless sleepless nights. His mother took to parking the convertible Mercedes directly in front of the house, ready to take him to hospital when required, which happened quite frequently.

This explains his deeply engrained dislike of posh cars, which he developed later in life and which has stayed with him up to the present.

The next big shock came when a tonsil operation didn't go according to plan and caused severe haemorrhage in his throat, keeping him in hospital for six weeks. This was followed by chronic sinus problems, which necessitated the doctors to stick thick needles through the nose into his sinuses to drain the mucus, which had started to cause unbearable pressure in his head - a procedure, which was repeated up to fifteen times every summer. He can still remember the crackling noise when the needle went through the nasal passage into the sinus cavity.

Around the age of three something quite strange started happening during the night. Initially it manifested as flashes of images containing different scenes, which did not relate back to the safe and caring life he was born into. These initial flashes soon turned into specific scenarios of terrible wars, frightening rituals and scenes of slavery or other types of suffering one could possibly imagine. It always ended with his death; whether he was buried alive, drowned in the ocean or suffocated in a mass grave. This was combined with a strong sensation of falling backwards from somewhere high above his bed. After the fall he usually found himself curled up under his duvet bathed in sweat and full of fear, not understanding what had happened.

It reached a point that Lex was unable to sleep on his own and the boy's grandparents, who lived just a little way up the hill, took him overnight where he was allowed to sleep in the space between both of them. But that didn't stop him going somewhere else every night.

His grandpa was the only person who completely understood and could relate to his experiences since he had gone through the same terrors at night as a child himself.

One day he said, "You know Lex, there are some things in this world which can't be explained, but I promise you that at one point this will stop."

At the age of six Lex managed to sleep in his own bed again and he can still remember the day, aged around eleven, when he awoke in the morning without having to be covered by his duvet from head to toe with only his nose sticking out for air. When the nightly happenings stopped it felt like pure freedom.

Before registering at school, each future pupil had to participate in a special programme, which tested their abilities, talents and potential. It was a sort of IQ test for children. Lex's results turned out to indicate overdevelopment of sense perception, hypersensitivity to external influences and according to the psychologist an ability to grasp concepts and ideas, which were exceptionally unusual for a boy of his age. As a result, his parents decided to give him another year of freedom and play, which Lex spent in the outstanding nature surrounding his family's home.

He never understood the result of the test because he was not particularly smart at school. Literature, foreign language, geometry, technical drawings, arts and sports were the exception, these subjects seemed to come naturally to him, resulting in top grades. However, physics and chemistry, as well as maths and geography were something completely foreign to him.

Up to the age of ten, Lex and his siblings grew up in a very privileged environment. But then recession hit and unfortunately his parents lost a lot of their wealth and their life took a different turn. Before this life changing turning point his mother was a designer and his father owned a factory. Both of them were art collectors and there was that one unforgettable day when they received a collection of ancient sculptures and statues, which had been shipped from India. Lex must have been seven or eight years old, but the impact on his being from that day was so profound, that it predetermined the course of his future life.

Part of the shipment was a beautiful bronze sculpture, Gautama Buddha, approximately 50cm in height, which radiated a sense of calm, peace and contentment that can't be described in words. It caught his attention and drew him in.

During the following months, Lex must have sat in front of that Buddha for hours; cross-legged and motionless, mimicking the sculpture's posture. He clearly remembers that it felt like the most natural thing to do and the posture itself seemed to bring up a subconscious memory of something he had done many times before. He secretly sneaked into the living room during the day just to sit still and be in that presence of peaceful nothingness, which the Buddha seemed to evoke within him, followed by the pleasant experience of the world disappearing around him.

Those precious moments of sitting in front of the Buddha awakened a sense of sweet but almost painful longing and a strong magnetic pull within Lex. It became an underlying drive and motivation that increased in intensity the more he matured, to hopefully ultimately find an answer, somewhere out there in this beautiful world, to all these burning questions.

Mastering the Body

No words can describe his excitement when his parents encouraged him to join a nearby sports club to train as a gymnast. He loved working with his body and the prospect of challenging it to its limits. At that time Lex was convinced that he could fly and couldn't wait to do backflips and spin around the high bar finishing with a double loop in the air before landing safely on his feet.

Four years later his family had to move to Munich and his career, as a gymnast was doomed. The only thing the Bavarians were interested in at that time was football. Gymnastic clubs were next to non-existent in beautiful Bavaria. So the only alternative for Lex was to take up tap dancing.

His teacher was surprised by the way his body was built; with its long legs, strangely turned out feet and a wiry spring like quality that in actual fact was an ideal prerequisite for classical dance.

She soon convinced his parents that ballet would be the right thing for their son to be trained in and as a consequence he was taken to ballet school.

Within two years he was recognized as one of the great dance talents in Germany, which opened up the possibility to become a dance student at the Bavarian Opera in the centre of Munich, an opportunity that could not be turned down.

A year later, around the age of fourteen, Lex was offered a grant to the John Cranko Ballet Academy in Stuttgart, which, at that time, was the most renowned ballet school in the world. After three years of six to seven hours of training six days a week, in addition to working in the evenings to earn some money to pay for food, he graduated with a degree in dance and as a state approved dancer.

At seventeen he started work as a professional dancer at the German Opera in Dusseldorf, dancing in up to two hundred performances a year.

He never really felt at ease or comfortable within himself being on stage and performing, it did not make a lot of sense to him, being watched by hundreds of people.

However he loved rehearsing and training his body in the studio. Lex was fascinated by the variety of training techniques, and all the different ways one could refine the body's ability to expand beyond its physical limits, and to move with such speed without losing the connection to a silent motionless space within. So he started observing how one's state of mind influences the ability to move without limitations, which led to more questions such as:

"What animates this body?"

"How does gravity impact on one's momentum in movement?"

He soon became an outsider within the dance company. His colleagues didn't share the same interests. All they talked about was their alignment and their posture or analysing someone else's dance technique on stage. Everybody around him seemed to be obsessed with their own bodies, as well as their career or simply gossiping about others. The competition was relentless with some going to great lengths to get what they wanted.

He couldn't relate to that kind of attitude and always thought, 'but guys there is so much more out there'.

Around the age of twenty, Lex was vaccinated against flu to which his body reacted badly, leaving him very ill. He struggled with fever for weeks and the only thing he knew was that he had to go home, to be with his family.

Shortly after arriving home, Lex was taken to hospital where he almost died. The vaccination had affected his organs and his liver function was about to collapse. It took him almost a whole year to recover after which his spark for dance had gone and a couple of years later, around the age of twenty-two, he walked away from his life as a professional dancer.

A Thousand Books

His dancer's salary financed his passion for literature. Most of his spare time during his years in Dusseldorf was spent hibernating at home reading or meditating. His self-esteem and belief in himself as an artist and professional dancer, his whole sense of self, which was based on the identification with his profession and others, was deeply shaken during the time of his illness.

He went through phases where he was hardly able to leave his home. The outside world caused an anxiety within, which was too much to cope with and his apartment and meditation practice were the only places in which he felt safe and protected.

That inner tension and self-doubt followed him everywhere and stayed with him for another whole decade.

So he almost swallowed books, desperately looking for answers. Every book relating to philosophy and mysticism or meditation, as well as literature about India, yoga and pranayama or psychology - you name it, ended up in his apartment. He was especially drawn to books which described other people's journey in the hope that they would mention the source and origin of their knowledge and the teacher instructing them. Examples of these books included, Irina Tweedy's, *My Way Through the Fire*, Lama Anagarika Govinda's *The Way of the White Clouds* or Paul Brunton's *A Search in Secret India*, appeared to have found what they had been looking for - a true teacher. Other books that influenced him most during that time were; *Talks With Ramana Maharshi*, J.G. Bennett's *Transformation*, Shree Aurobindo's complex work of the *Integral Yoga* and *Auroville*, C.G. Jung's work on archetypes, Kuebler Ross' books about dying, *The Tibetan Book About Death*, *The Bhagavad Gitta and Upanishads*, *The Life of Buddha*, any books by Hermann Hesse and *The Yoga Sutras of Patanjali*.

It soon dawned on him that without the guidance of a teacher who facilitates one's personal progress, and introduces one to specific techniques, which are only transmitted through word of mouth, one can't progress very far on one's inner journey. That realisation - that A-ha, led Lex to the conclusion that he would never find the complete answer in a book and that it was time to become active and take on the challenge of finding a teacher whom he strongly believed was out there somewhere just waiting for him.

The phrase, 'When the disciple is ready, the teacher appears', encouraged him and strengthened his conviction.

By that time he had given up his career as a dancer and so he took on any work he could find in order to finance his first trip to India, which was planned to be at least a one-year journey, but hopefully longer if there was enough money left over.

In Search of an Answer

What a shock it was for Lex and his friend, Shika, to be driven in a taxi through the slums of Bombay to reach the coach station from where they planned to travel to Puna. The slums were endless and the scenes along the way were terrifying and heart breaking. Seeing the poverty combined with the smell of rotten garbage, as well as the sheer level of noise was too much for them to absorb, and the first reaction Lex had to those surroundings was that this couldn't be real and could only be a nightmare, while his heart beat rapidly.

But the greatest paradox within all that mass was seeing in people's eyes, the humble surrender to all this suffering in the presence of death at every corner. People still had a smile on their faces and they walked along with so much grace and beauty, enhanced by the colourful saris and kurtas they wore. Kids played and laughed next to the dying on the streets seemingly unaffected by that reality.

The shock caused by the devastating reality surrounding him was the moment when he 'self-remembered', as he had done all those years ago whilst sitting in front of the Buddha as a little boy. His mind emptied and it failed to grasp what it perceived. That was his first experience of a so-called conscious shock by which one is thrown back into one's 'self' and self-remembers.

Puna was a paradise compared to Bombay. They were there to visit the ashram of Bhagavan and they planned to travel from there to visit other masters if necessary.

Bhagavan was supposed to be an enlightened master and Lex couldn't wait to meet him. It was the beginning of the Shri Rashneesh movement, which started attracting thousands of westerners.

The ashram was a luxurious complex with beautiful gardens and outstanding facilities. Lots of marble everywhere and the compound was filled with people dressed in red cloth.

The first week was about settling into the routine of the ashram and practising different meditations. There was an extensive selection of workshops and therapies on offer, which were supposed to support one's personal meditation practice.

There was a clear structure of hierarchy within the Ashram. Starting with the sevadars who took care of the whole place and kept it meticulously clean and then the lower management who structured the events and times of discourses, up to the so called VIP's who were closest to Bhagavan and created an un-penetrable circle around him. Everybody was driven to move up the ladder in the hope of getting closer to Bhagavan.

Then there were the people who made sure that everybody was free of any scent, because his followers were only allowed to attend Bhagavan's discourses when they were literally scent-free due to his allergic reaction to artificial smells.

So after being sniffed by a row of specifically selected sniffers you were allowed to sit in a massive Satsang hall, which could accommodate up to 2,000 people. Near the front, rising out of a marble floor, was a raised level with a beautiful throne placed right in the centre.

It went absolutely silent whenever Bhagavan made his entrance, his hands in Namaste, wearing a beautiful long garment and a massive hat.

Everybody bowed down to the floor once he took his seat on the throne, everybody that is, except Lex. A voice deep within himself prevented him from bowing down. He felt as though he didn't belong; couldn't understand the fuss about Bhagavan and questioned the sheer luxury of the place while so many people surrounding the ashram lived in such poverty.

Still, Bhagavan's lectures were outstandingly beautiful and full of humour. Without doubt he was very knowledgeable person who was able to answer every question his disciples asked him in a practical and humorous way. But he didn't seem to have the qualities and signs of a true teacher, which Lex had found so beautifully described in his books. This moment gave rise to the realisation that Bhagavan was not the right teacher for him.

His companion, Shika, loved the whole place and Bhagavan's teachings and convinced him to stay for another three months. So he half-heartedly gave in and after spending a fortune on workshops and treatments, he ended up contracting pneumonia during the third month of his stay and dragged himself to the airport to be taken back home where he could receive proper treatment. His dream to find a teacher was completely shattered and all his imaginations of how his life will have changed after spending a year in India went down the drain in an instant.

The only thing he took back with him was the memory of the name 'Gyan Anusandan' meaning *the one who seeks knowledge*, which was offered to him by Bhagavan to replace his family name by which one is being accepted as his disciple, which Lex declined, and that was it.

When the Disciple is Ready the Teacher Appears

After his return from India Lex hit rock bottom. All his hopes, expectations of life and his money were gone and with them went his sense of purpose and meaning of existence itself.

But what upset him most was, that the longing and pull in his heart had increased tenfold and there was nothing he could do to stop it. It reached a point where it became unbearable and his closest friends, who couldn't understand his obsession and self-absorption, found it difficult to place and thought that he has lost his mind. 'Get your act together', and 'enough of this drama', was all they could say. He still feels embarrassed and deeply sorry for the way he behaved. He was almost like a little child who throws tantrums when it does not get what it wants. But during that period of his life he simply didn't know any other way.

One day someone gave him a telephone number to call, but unfortunately by that time Lex had convinced himself that there was nothing and no one out there able to answer what his heart was longing for. He had accepted the Isness of his life and within that the conviction that these things are only meant to happen to those very special people in the books he had read.

He kept the phone number, which had a Swiss dialling code, in his wallet. It stayed there for almost another year until things in his life turned counterproductive, increasing his anxiety and self-doubt to the point that it almost got out of control. So Lex picked up the phone and called.

Life as a Yogi

The deep voice, which answered the phone, impacted every part of Lex's being and he knew within seconds that this person was sent to him for a reason.

Ishwar Ananda, that's what his students called him in India, gave Lex some very helpful advice over the phone.

He pointed out that Lex was at a very critical and vulnerable stage in his life and he gave him a specific exercise he was advised to do for fifteen minutes every day. This exercise would keep him together until he could come and visit him in person, which was to be in three weeks for a two-hour one-to-one session. Ishwar explained that he usually worked with people on a one-to-one basis and that his approach was based on principles of Far Eastern psychology and self-study, as well as meditation exercises, homeopathy, radionics and other practical tools that are imparted when certain situations in life requires them.

That was all Lex needed to hear and the next three weeks seemed to pass in slow motion.

The train that headed for Zurich in Switzerland left Stuttgart main station early in the morning. He had never been so excited and nervous at the same time, except the days before Christmas or his birthdays as a child.

The house where Ishwar saw his clients, when he was not in India, was built on a hill overlooking the city of Zurich.

The door was usually open and there was a small reception room leading into his treatment room where people usually waited before the start of their session.

As usual, Lex was far too early and sat down on one of the chairs with his heart racing. His nerves got hold of him while he contemplated what to say, yet there was nothing he could think of to say or talk about. The whole atmosphere of the house was one of tranquillity and peace. He just sat there feeling very small and insignificant, until a door opened.

Standing there was a slim man with very defined features, dark long hair and deep brown eyes that looked straight into the most hidden part of him.

Lex got a sense that there was nothing this man couldn't see and there was nowhere to hide.

Ishwar invited him to come through and have a seat on one of the two armchairs facing each other. The room was furnished in a very minimalist way. There was nothing to distract one's attention and the three massive windows invited the sky and the garden into the room.

Lex sat down and could not stop sobbing; the pain that had accumulated in his heart could no longer be held back. Years of held tension released from his body and Ishwar did not stop looking into his soul. He could literally feel how every part of his being was being screened and assessed by Ishwar's radiant gaze. There was no judgement in Ishwar's eyes, only understanding and silence and Lex knew at that very moment that he had found what he was searching for, ever since that day as a young boy when he sat in front of the Buddha.

Initially Ishwar gave Lex the impression that he was working as a therapist, using entirely practical methods and techniques, which had to be put into action in everyday life. His daily meditation exercises and breathing techniques, which represented only one aspect of Ishwar's approach, altered regularly depending on the ever-changing events and situations of life.

Half way through the first year of his regular visits, Ishwar informed Lex that he was accepted as a student of the 'work' and that he would be his teacher for a very long time. One year later Ishwar revealed that he was a Sufi teacher, that a lot of his work was rooted in Kashmiri Shaivism Yoga: an ancient tradition which has originated in Varanasi, India and that he taught Spanda techniques which are used to work on consciousness. Another major aspect of his work addressed the practice and study of Far Eastern psychology, which is an important part of every ancient philosophy. According to the mystics, every philosophy contains the teaching of psychology.

Ishwar used elements of the language on which the Fourth Way Teaching[104] is based, which is much easier to grasp for our Western mind than the terminology of Sanskrit based translations of ancient psychology teachings. The Fourth Ways underlying message and the content of its psychology teaching, is the same as any of the other ancient systems, but its origin goes back much further than Gurdjieff, who had put it into a more modern language. Ultimately all mystic teachings lead back to the same source and their inherent message is the same.

It was very clear that Ishwar's teaching was not a traditional Fourth Way school teaching. His whole approach to working on consciousness derived its vitality from the universal pulse of Spanda and meditation, as well as other viable sources that help to be working on all levels at the same time.

Ishwar's school was a Sufi school and like any real Sufi teacher he transformed and included any useful external or internal influence, which were conducive to his student's inner evolution and to the work itself.

This is the conclusion Lex arrived at a decade later, because little was explained or put into perspective during the years of his studies with Ishwar. For a long time he was left with the unknown. No one really knew what the work and its teaching truly was about.

To be left on your own, faced with the unknown, was part of the teaching and fuelled the immense pressure of the workforce to create enough friction, unanswered questions and the required intensity to keep one awake, thus preventing acquired mechanical habits and patterns from taking over.

Throughout this first year Lex was introduced to techniques of self-enquiry and self-study, which were part of the first direction of the work. Then he became part of a small group of students, which met regularly to learn about the second direction of the work: work with other people. Years later he started with the third direction of the work: work for the school, while he simultaneously kept working on the first and second direction and his one-to-one sessions with his teacher. It was a fulltime job, which was intended to take place in the middle of his life, and his profession earned him just enough money to cover his cost of living in addition to financing countless trips to Zurich and India during all those years.

The work had a profound impact on Lex's life. Every minute of the day was about the teaching and the work. Every phase and event in his life could increasingly be put into a greater context. The teaching became a powerful counter balance to life's events and every event or happening in life could be put in relation to the work and because of that, everything in his life became full of meaning.

During that first year someone, somehow, left him a book.

The picture of a portrait showing an old man with a turban and a long white beard on the second page of that book made Lex's heart jump. He could not think of anything else for days to come.

Looking through the book, he soon realized that this man was a living mystic in India who taught a scientific approach to meditation. On one of the last pages of the book, not obviously positioned, he found a contact address. This book was not on sale in any public or specialised bookstore anywhere.

The pull to find out what that man was about, made him write a letter.

Two months later he received a reply from the mystic himself, with the advice to read more about this approach to meditation and that there was no rush to come to India to meet him in person. He advised spending as much time as possible studying the teaching and to meet up with a small group of people who were practising this path of meditation. The teaching required a strong commitment and sacrifice, which only a sincere seeker would be willing and able to take on. There were only a few people in the West who followed this particular mystic's teaching at that time.

The mystic did not allow his work to be publicly advertised and his students were strictly instructed to refrain from trying to talk other people into this teaching. He had his own ways to pull in the students who were meant to receive his teaching from within and there was no need for external activities to make that happen. *When the disciple is ready the Master appears.*

The mystic's teaching was not based on any religion or belief; yet didn't expect anybody to abandon his or her religious background. Its ethical code was simple and neutral, emphasising equality of every person from whichever background they come from, living an honest life, earning one's own living, not being financially dependent on others or owing anything to anybody and to take full responsibility for one's own life.

Students were supposed to commit to a pure vegetarian diet and refrain from any use of alcohol or drugs.

Another important message of the teaching was not to become dependent on the physical form of the teacher, because the real teacher had to be found within during the process of meditation.

It was not acceptable to run away from life or use the teaching as an escape from one's personal problems or responsibilities. It was advised to use one's common sense and become very practical; weighing up the pros and cons when it came to making decisions in life and that one had to practice the teaching in the middle of life and the surroundings and background one was born into.

The practice was based on committing to sit two and a half to three hours in meditation every day and applying another technique throughout the day, mainly during the times when the mind was not required to concentrate on one's responsibilities at work or private life.

Aged only twenty-six, Lex was accepted by the mystic on his path of meditation and became his student.

That's when his life as a yogi started.

The one thing Lex could rely on and was really good at, was his deeply engrained discipline and ability to focus, especially when it was about something meaningful to him. He put all his energy and effort into his practice and studies with the hope that he would not disappoint his teachers. He literally surrendered himself to his wonderful teachers; their work and the practice of daily meditation via sheer 'will-action' and the longing in his heart to go home. His trust in their teaching was unshakable.

So for the next twelve years and with the help of his relentless discipline, he got up most mornings to sit in meditation for two and a half to three hours. Then, after a cup of tea, he went about his work all day as a freelancer, running a little business in the centre of his hometown. In the evenings he usually practiced yoga or another exercise regime and if not too late, he would follow this with another hour of meditation before he went to bed. If he could not manage to do his sitting in one stretch, he caught up with it later in the day or evenings to complete the time he had promised to commit to daily.

These years were interspersed with many trips to India to visit the mystic and journeys to Switzerland to meet his Sufi teacher and fellow students of the work.

Years later Lex discovered that his Sufi teacher's master was the very same master who accepted him on the path of meditation, although Ishwar never mentioned it himself.

Nothing more can be told about the details of the process Lex experienced. This has to stay within the confinement of his student-teacher relationship with Ishwar and his master and disciple relationship with Babaji.

The Final Shock

Many years later, Ishwar's students were called to India to receive a special teaching. Ishwar and his students were invited by Katya Baba, a Sadhu who only leaves his cave in the Himalayas every twelve years to come down from the mountains to share his knowledge with other mystic schools at the Kumbha Mela. It is the biggest spiritual gathering in Allahabad, India. Up to eleven million people gather.

Once they arrived at the compound where the Mela took place, the sight that unfolded in front of them blew them away. Hundreds of thousands of tents covered an area that reached far into the horizon. It was a scene, which could almost not be comprehended. They were guided through a labyrinth of passages between the tents, which were set up like little villages, each surrounded by a linen fence. Every little village represented a school of thought of ancient teachings. All the different sects of Sadhus were represented and the most respected holy men and mystic teachers lived in special, beautiful tents provided by the government. Most of them had their own servants and cooks at their disposal to show special respect and appreciation for their presence at the Mela.

Lex and his fellow students' own massive and utterly beautiful tent was erected right in the middle of the gathering next to Ishwar's private tent, which was comprised of two rooms and a large reception room beautifully furnished with rugs and pillows. Right next to it was Katya Baba's dais on which he slept, ate and sat during their entire stay. A high fence protected them from any outside visitors and the gate was guarded twenty-four hours a day.

They were surrounded by thousands of tents, each burning their own log fire and playing their rhythmic music twenty-four hours a day. After the second night, about a third of the students left because they were unable to deal with the unbearable heat combined with the noise level and the overwhelming smell of smoke plus the stench of excrement that was accumulating along the alleyways.

Many old and sick people, some suffering from leprosy, had begun their

269

pilgrimage from distant parts of India weeks before the Mela took place, in order to take their last holy bath in the Ganges during the processions and ceremonies at the end of the Mela. Many of them died right there, being carried away and supported during the process of their departure by the increasing energy of devotion that filled the air and which was palpable everywhere. To them, it meant that their journey on earth had come to completion and being ultimately freed from the cycle of birth and death.

So, only the hard core of the group stayed put and one of them was Lex.

Because of the amount of mosquitos, massive tanks filled with DDT were driven around. On one of their walks back from the Ganges, they were hit by a huge cloud of DDT, which had been sprayed to get rid of the flies. Within hours Lex's immune system broke down and he was struck by fever and tiny spots in his face began to swell. Most days and nights he spent sitting in meditation, listening to his teacher's lectures or sat in front of Katya Baba absorbing his presence. The increasing pressure generated by a constant stream of external influences did not stop impacting on him and started to affect his system on all levels.

After five days of sleep deprivation and a body that was in constant agony, his mind and 'little me' gave up and crumbled into insignificance. This was followed by a sense of expansion and clarity, with which he had become familiar in his daily meditations, but not whilst he was walking around and about. That was his first experience of the *arising unchanging nature within*.

The unbearable noise level around him turned into the sweetest silent music in the state of absence of thought. All the colours around him became vibrant and full of life. Lex felt connected with everything that is.

That experience lasted one day and one night and then he left the Mela.

He followed his teacher to Varanasi to spend another couple of weeks with him and a few of his students.

During the Kumbha Mela his Sufi teacher showed signs of extremely strange behaviour. He almost encouraged people to worship him and all his humbleness had gone. Ishwar's behaviour and teaching techniques, and especially what he expected from some students, became inhuman and humiliating. It felt like all his powers had gotten out of control and all his beautiful qualities seemed to have disappeared.

Lex separated from the group and sat down on the riverbanks of the

Ganges, looking at the beautiful city of Varanasi on the other side. His heart was in pain and his mind couldn't grasp what was happening. He asked himself, "What is going on here and how can that be?" He had given his heart and soul to this man and his teachings, which without any doubt had transformed his life and self forever. He started praying, "Please Babaji don't take this away from me, I won't be able to cope without his support and influence. Besides your meditation and teachings, this school is my life, how will I ever be able to live without it. Please don't take this away from me."

So he went back and confronted his teacher and challenged him in front of the other obedient students. They had chosen to keep their eyes closed to what was happening and all of them seemed to be under a spell.

Ishwar only looked at Lex with energy of superiority in his eyes and ordered him to leave. So he turned away and started walking. Whilst Lex was crossing the river Ganges in a small boat, something within him died and his heart went numb and froze and with it froze the pain. He knew that things would never be the same again.

When the teaching has fulfilled its purpose, the physical presence of the teacher disappears – well, that is what is supposed to happen according to mystic teachings.

The Friction Stops

In an almost trance like state Lex went to see his Master Babaji. He somehow managed to fly back to Delhi and take a train to his master's compound near Agra, in the north of India. He had visited this simple but beautiful place many times before and it had always lifted his heart knowing that he will be sitting in the presence of Babaji again. The sense of peace and tranquillity radiating from his physical presence during his Darshan, lectures and question and answer sessions to his Western students was un-worldly. But this time everything seemed to be different. The place felt hectic and the worship reflected in the faces of all the disciples around him felt strange and unreal; something he could not relate to or feel part of in the way he had done before.

Lex's only hope was that all of that hollow emptiness in his heart, as well as the sense of being completely lost and alone, would be taken away in the presence of his master.

After a sleepless night in which his restless mind repeated the events of the time in Varanasi over and over again, he went to the Satsang ground to await Babaji.

The moment the master arrived a massive wave of devotion radiated from the crowd to welcome him. Babaji took his seat on a simple cushion that was placed in the middle of the dais. Sitting there in half lotus, his body became motionless in an instant and only his head moved slowly from left to right and back again, screening the crowd during Darshan.

But Lex did not feel a thing. No sense of love and devotion, no uplift in his heart; absolutely nothing, and even when the master's gaze pierced into his eyes for a couple of seconds, the only thing he could feel was that devastating emptiness in his heart. No emotion, no anger, no pain or relatedness; just frozen emptiness.

All Lex saw sitting on that dais was a human, a very knowledgeable man looking very much like a professor with a white turban, long beard and very understanding eyes. No matter how much Lex tried to find that God-like radiance and aura of light in and around him, the way he had seen it in the past, he could not find it.

After Satsang, Lex went back to his room to meditate. There, in that small simple room, he started remembering things his teacher Ishwar had spoken of in the past. Many of these things he did not consider as being relevant at that time.

He remembered him saying:

"Never put anybody lower or higher than yourself."

"You should not derive your sense of self via identification with other people or one person."

"Please never forget that everybody is struggling along the path as well as in life."

But the most striking thing he remembered him saying in one of the group meetings was, that there will *be a time of great shock and that from then onwards the student will be on his own.*

According to the teaching, that final shock is required to ignite a process within which the teaching slowly starts internalising and to ultimately crystallize and become permanent at a given moment in time; yet it is entirely dependent on how each individual student keeps actively applying all they have studied, experienced and learned from the teaching.

That revelation made him contemplate the way he had conducted himself in the teaching and with his teachers and the way he projected his hopes, ideals and the ultimate goal with all their God like qualities and powers onto them.

He suddenly realised that he always perceived his teachers through his own lenses. Lenses that he never questioned. So that whatever he projected on them is what he perceived, and it dawned on him that all his fellow students were doing exactly the same in their own individual way, and that this veil of self-imposed illusion was ripped off him by this horrible shock; forcing him into a more objective and neutral state of mind in which he could see things the way they simply were.

That revelation made him realise how powerful the mind can be and what kind of wonderful illusions it is able to create. Lex thought about how often teachers and masters misuse this tendency of projection in people and that the disciples, often through their very blind devotion and belief, empower the teacher.

On reflection he knew that this wasn't the case with his teachers at all.

He had received so many hints on how not to fall into the traps and imaginations of his own mind. The moment he surrendered to the fact that there is no need to work himself into the ground anymore, the penny dropped and something changed.

Ultimately, Lex was able to feel that the ideal end-all described in the books and explained in different teachings, is too far away and beyond that which is realistically achievable. *The realisation that he did not have to thrive to become holy* anymore put everything into a completely new perspective and he started laughing out loud. After the fits of laughter had calmed down, all friction within him came to an end.

The intensity of the work pressure created by his teachers during the last decade was ultimately taking its toll and started bearing fruits.

Lex had reached a stage in which he was so endlessly tired of himself and his mind. The work pressure had slowly penetrated through all the solid layers and manifestations of what he believed and imagined himself to be and all of what he desired to become in his imaginations. The uninterrupted process of disillusionment and his willingness to face up to it had dismantled and tired his mind out.

What was left was Lex being at peace with himself and a lasting connection to what the teaching calls 'Unchanging Gravitas', which is something very simple and unspectacular, yet so much more than his mind could ever possibly imagine.

Seven Years of Assimilation

Lex had reached a point in his development in which the work and daily meditation practice became an inseparable part of his life. Lots of things had changed, were less disciplined and more spacious. He didn't live the secluded and withdrawn life of a yogi anymore and was involved in many creative projects.

During his times of study with his teachers he was running a little business in the south of Germany and taught countless classes in different health and fitness centres. But after that chapter of his life had slowly come to an end, he was ready for a change and moved to work in Spain. From there to Cornwall, then to Brighton and finally to London where he felt truly at home.

He started training as a Cranio-Sacral and Somato-Emotional Release therapist specialising in posttraumatic stress disorders and earned his living through teaching yoga, pilates, meditation, different movement based workshops and one-to-one Gyrotonic sessions. To start with, he worked in different clinics in Brighton, then London and later, in his own little clinic in the south of London.

Lex observed how the cosmological side of the teaching acted on people and how the ideas of different laws influenced and determined their way of life.

But the most influential and revealing part of that time was how much he learned from his clients; their difficulties, insecurities and the way their history impacted on them, while facilitating them through their process of change in which they faced their traumas and dealt with the emotional aftermath and implications the trauma had caused.

In hindsight, there is hardly anything he hadn't witnessed in these countless sessions with so many different and wonderful people. It was the greatest lesson in compassion Lex could possibly receive and the most wonderful apprenticeship in practising the second direction of the teaching: 'work with others', outside the confinement of a Sufi school and right in the middle of his own environment.

He came to realise that he had never lost and never is without a teacher, they were right there in front of him in the form of his clients and yoga students, as well as his family or colleagues and his amazing friends.

That's how the teaching started internalising over these years; becoming more and more active and alive within him. Knowledge transformed into experience and experience transformed into becoming.

Discovering the Unchanging Nature Within

As a therapist it is vital to be on the table and receive regular treatment oneself. It is impossible to facilitate others if one hasn't processed and dealt with one's own stuff, and applies what one has studied or what was given in one's own practice and life.

How can one ever possibly become neutral and non-judgemental towards others if there is any kind of trauma or unresolved stuff active within oneself?

Lex usually travelled to Brighton to see his cranio-sacral therapist Maggie Gil for regular sessions. He had been on her table many times and trusted her implicitly. It was always a real treat to receive, especially after he had treated many clients during the month and his own energy levels were at times a bit low.

One day something very significant and totally unexpected unfolded during his treatment. The moment Lex was on the table and Maggie had put her hands on the dorsum of his feet to evaluate the body, his cranio-sacral rhythm stopped. He started shifting into a particular state of consciousness and in an instant his whole former life appeared right in front of him in one single massive display. Everything was in there in minute detail within one single instant of perception.

It showed him how his time as a baby with all his illnesses had taught him to detach from the physical body and to become more resilient to physical pain. It explained to him how the experiences he went through at night as a little boy related to out-of-body experiences that took him back into the genetic memory of evolution. It revealed to him how his time as a gymnast and dancer taught him how to explore and master his movement brain. It indicated how the time as a young man studying all those books, helped him to develop and further evolve his intellectual brain. It made him aware that the period with his teachers was a time of initiation; learning a new language – a profound teaching in flexibility and how to function under extreme pressure and to experience working on all levels at the same time, awakening higher emotions and utilising them through meditation. It showed him that the work with his clients and students helped him understand and allowed him to explore the emotional brain and that it was a teaching in neutrality and relatedness to people and to be compassionate without identification. It made him understand that all this time in meditation allowed him to experience more subtle levels of consciousness and develop more refined faculties of perception and to be able to grasp concepts and ideas that lay beyond the understanding of the mind and intellect.

All of that had happened in a glimpse of a moment and then it stopped and vanished. One moment later Lex lost all sense of his physical body and through an impulse of mystic transport he remembered.

His thoughts, his mind and sense of 'I' or 'Me' had disappeared and Lex was gone. What had appeared instead was the simplest peaceful state of perception possible. It only can be described as a sort of frequency, a very subtle, almost motionless pulsation, which could rise out of nothingness in the state of absence of thought in which nothing is subject to change.

This pure state of the unchanging nature lasted for almost one and a half hours before he regained his body awareness again.

Much more insight about scale, higher faculties and the workings of consciousness was given to him while he was absorbed in that state. But it would be a poor attempt to try putting it into words.

How do you possibly explain non-self? It is like trying to describe the taste of a mango to someone who has never tasted or seen a mango. If you choose to do so, they only learn about the theory and concept of a mango, which usually only triggers their imagination and creates preconceived ideas. Go and buy them a mango and let them taste it themselves, then they will know and that experience will be theirs forever.

It was more difficult for him to think than to not think after the session. It was the most simple and natural state he had ever experienced. There were no spectacular flashes of light or amazing colours. It was just silent peaceful simplicity combined with a deep sense of oneness with the 'Isness' of what is.

He had experienced this kind of state once long ago at the Kumbha Mela but at that time it was evoked by external overload, unbearable friction and pressure. This time it did not require any external influence and it felt much deeper and real.

It must have left a very strong imprint somewhere within. From that day onwards it appeared in most of his meditations out of nowhere. Sometimes it suddenly manifested on a walk and increasingly during sessions with his clients. Lex could not produce it out of his own will.

It just appeared and that's it. When it was present – great, and when it was absent also great. It did not make any difference to him nor did it really matter and it definitely did not turn him into a different person.

Sharing Knowledge

The idea of designing a yoga teacher-training course grew more and more in him. He had studied, practiced, taught and applied so many different methods and approaches to body work, movement and yoga during the last three decades and thought that it would be a challenging experience to create a modern yoga teacher training course.

One of his teachers had given him a hint decades ago that he would be involved in a venture relating to yoga. Inspired by the memory, he called his friend and colleague Joanne Sarah Avison and invited her to become part of this venture and to teach on the course. She was living and breathing Fascia and always was at the forefront of new developments in that field of scientific research. Together they would be able to cover all the subjects required in a yoga teacher-training programme.

Already at their first meeting they were flooded with inspiration and started creating their curriculum to cover a 200-hour, and a more advanced 300-hour course. After two years of intensive work they received accreditation by the Yoga Alliance US and two other accreditation bodies in the UK. A year later they found themselves sitting in front of a group of students who had signed up for the course in a yoga centre in central London and a month later they sat in front of another group of students in the south of Germany.

Their students became increasingly drawn towards the philosophical aspect of yoga during the first couple of months of their training. While holding the philosophy lectures, which usually took place in the evenings, Lex found himself gradually implementing aspects of the teaching he had received as a student by his own teachers.

It was never planned and definitely not his intention to do so. But what started to happen was the manifestation of a field of resonance he was so familiar with during the times of studying with his teachers. This new field, which contained similar qualities, was palpable in the air and Lex could not help but follow its impulse. At the beginning he used some revised notes he had written down during the times of his studies, but increasingly the state of the unchanging nature appeared during these lectures and at one point in 2008 he just surrendered to it and left the notes untouched.

That was the beginning of the fourth direction of the teaching called Work For The Greater Good.

Work on the fourth direction of the universal teachings, as well as work on consciousness and the science of meditation has been my main focus and objective ever since.

Alexander Filmer-Lorch

Helmsdale, England May 2012

18. Frequently Asked Questions

Is it OK to only self-study and not to meditate?

Meditation is Self-Study. There is no better way to find out more about your 'Self' than by means of meditation. To facilitate change we have to work on many levels at the same time. So you study yourself in external life by means of self-observation and you simultaneously study your internal life by means of meditation. You only would gain a fraction of the knowledge of the truth about yourself by only applying self-study.

I have come across Systems and teachings that only apply self-study and self-observation, how does that work?

Every non-mechanical teaching is valid and conducive to our inner growth. Some of them just might not have come across the liberating idea of meditation, or simply have specialised in the psychological nature of the work on consciousness. Usually one meets a teaching that is just perfect for one's inner growth right now and years later meets another teaching that implements the idea of meditation. Whichever way round does not matter. But if you meet one that offers both and inspires you, why not give meditation a chance too?

What happens if I miss my Meditation?

If you miss your meditation, than you have only missed an opportunity to meet the Absolute. The universal teachings are not working with guilt. The idea of guilt does not even exist within them. They are based on true love and compassion, as well leaving all the responsibility to you as to how much you are willing to invest or commit to. It's all down to you and there will not be such a thing as judgment. The teachings only inspire, facilitate and offer true meaning, but they are not doing the work for you.

one and a half hours every day, but only when it is not based on a hard and challenging discipline. It has to come out of inspirational effort. For most people fifteen minutes to half an hour on a regular basis will work wonders and will have a profound impact on life.

How do I know that I am doing it right?

By deleting the thought of doing it right or wrong, and concentrating on the field of consciousness in front of you instead.

Where and when should I practise?

Practice meditation in a quiet place where you feel relaxed and safe. Any time is good as long as you keep sitting in meditation on a regular basis. The most beneficial time is very early in the morning, when the world is still asleep and mind activity around you is at its minimum.

When should I seek out a meditation teacher?

When you start having questions about meditation, as well as when you feel you need some inspiration, or want to deepen your knowledge and understanding of meditation, as well as when you want to start working on all levels at the same time as well as you want to work on consciousness.

What should I pay attention to when practising?

The only thing in meditation that requires your attention, is the field of consciousness, never lose your awareness of the screen of consciousness. Most noticeable changes during meditation are described in the chapter The Art of Meditation.

Does it help to sit in a group?

A meditation group can be extremely beneficial in regards to establishing a firm meditation practice, as well as meeting like-minded people and during the dry times of our meditation practice.

Should I always exercise before meditation?

Any form of exercise helps to channel the energies of the body and the mind towards meditation. There are no strict rules. Your body requires regular exercise; why not combine it with meditation to get the most out of it?

Why would I want to meditate and what does it do to me?

What impact your meditation will have on you and what you can gain out of it, you will find described in the 'The Benefits of Meditation' chapter. Why you would want to meditate can be due to having to deal with too much stress and you consider meditation to be a solution, as well as by having come across liberating ideas and by being inspired by them consider meditation as something beneficial to one's own inner progress.

What is the purpose of being present?

That which is permanent and not part of the veil of illusion only can be found within the present moment. Vertical scale, along which we shift onto another level of consciousness, only can be accessed in the present moment, as well as the 'Isness' of things only can be perceived in the now.

What does it mean to open one's heart, what is the purpose of it?

Opening one's heart means to be unbiased and to be open to new or Great Ideas that make one think differently, and its deeper meaning relates to developing the higher parts of the emotional brain, so that the heart starts radiating higher emotions, that transcend into universal love and compassion. That is, our heart evolves in its capacity to assimilate liberating ideas.

How will I meditate when I cannot control my mind?

By realising that we cannot control our mind, as well as experiencing that in reality we cannot do so. It is the sheer regularity of simply sitting in meditation that ultimately will tire the mind out. The more we resist the mind the stronger the friction will become and the more we will become a Ping-Pong ball of the opposing forces.

Most people consider the mind to be something negative and as something egoistic that stands in the way of meditation. As long as you keep this attitude of mind, the mind fights against itself. The moment you see the mind as something very valuable, which helps you to interact and put things into greater perspective it will be on your side. So to tame the mind, just put it under the influences of liberating ideas, and the moment your intellect is satisfied that there is a great amount of meaning to be found in meditation, the mind will love to sit in meditation.

What if there is not enough time to sit?

There always will be enough time to sit the moment one finds real meaning in meditation. We find so much meaning and importance in so many meaningless things and allocate a lot of time to them. So initially it requires conscious effort to free up fifteen minutes a day for meditation, but by means of regular practice our meditation will become more meaningful than lots of things we have considered as meaningful. Put your meditation practice into your diary and consider it as an important meeting that can't be postponed.

What if your family or partner does not support you in your desire to meditate?

This is due to preconceived ideas. Show them articles about the latest scientific research that proves the benefits of meditation, also you don't need to use the word meditation. Tell them that you are doing your stress-management exercises you have learned at work, or that you are advised to do deep relaxation techniques to balance your stress levels. No one should have anything against these kinds of approaches.

Is it better to sit before or after eating?

A full stomach is not conducive to meditation because the process of digestion requires too much energy. It is best to keep a couple of hours between your food intake and your meditation.

I go through phases of meditating. How can I be more consistent in my practice?

Inconsistency in meditation means that you are probably inconsistent with a lot of things you start doing. This is down to lack of 'substance of gravitas' or a so-called non-conscious state called 'laciness'. Another reason could be that you have fallen too much into awareness, which is described in the chapter 'Consciousness'. Conscious effort is the solution to the problem of inconsistency.

Can I meditate if I am depressed?

Yes, but only under the guidance of a therapist who is trained to teach meditation. From a universal teaching point of view what people usually consider as depression is nothing more than a low that is based on identification with negative emotions, or that we don't agree with a situation in life. This so called type of depression has nothing to do with real depression or clinical depression and can be usually dealt with by dis-identifying with one's internal and external condition, as well as with an intense workout programme or a plan of action.

What happens if I fall asleep during meditation?

Initially most people start falling asleep during meditation, which is due to Alpha and Theta-brainwave activity, in which our nervous system starts shutting down, which reduces the influx of adrenaline. With regular practice this will disappear and instead of falling asleep our consciousness will start expanding and take us into an altered state of consciousness, in which we are highly alert.

Will people think I am a new age freak or a tree hugger?

Thanks to the popularity of yoga people think very highly of meditation or are at least familiar with its meaning and don't associate it with the new age idea anymore.

Can I meditate lying down?

In times of illness yes absolutely. Otherwise we should always sit with our spine erect. Lying down is usually associated with sleep and is not the best solution for meditation.

Can anyone meditate?

If you are not mentally ill or under mind-altering drugs, then everybody is able to meditate. Some might initially have to put more conscious effort into it than others, but with a little bit of dedication and the power of meaning everybody will ultimately find stillness in meditation.

What is the definition of meditation?

The definition of meditation is to die while we are alive. We die to everything that is subject to change within us during the process in meditation. That is we die to our mind and thoughts until nothing is left that thinks, and together with that all concepts of 'I', 'Me' and 'Them' die as well.

How hard is meditation?

It is as hard as you want it to be and can imagine it to be. If you eradicate the idea of it being hard and its imagination, then meditation becomes as easy as breathing.

What is it for?

It is designed to wake you up from your state of sleep caused by habits and conditionings.

How do you do it?

By willingly undoing, not doing.

Other people are much better in meditation and much more evolved, what do I have to do?

How do you know that they are not just better in disguising? No one can judge the state of being of someone else. From a universal teaching point of view meditation is not about others, all work on consciousness as well as self-study is not about others. It is solely about our own inner development and we are not interested in what others do. If we are judged or criticised by others, then they simply don't know better. All the Great Ideas are about and aim for is, us becoming of benefit for the greater good. Becoming of service to others in whichever form this takes place. What greater meaning could there be in life? Nothing else comes to my mind.

What if I see colours or light in meditation?

As long as colours and light just come and go randomly, as well as vibrational sounds, one should not give them any attention due to the fact that they appear out of our control.

The power of the mind should not be underestimated, because all those sounds, lights and colours can be produced by the mind itself. Even higher states of consciousness can be replicated by the mind but only for a limited amount of time. As a rule all that stays and is experienced in the same way again and again in meditation, and can be reached out of one's own effort, can be considered as a real inner experience. All that just comes and goes randomly does not deserve our attention because it might only appear to distract us.

What is meant with the term 'my essence'?

Essence is what we are born with and don't have to learn or acquire. It consists of everything, which comes natural to us, all that we don't have to struggle towards to, that is all our talents.

How can I find a real teacher?

By being inspired by as many Alpha-Influences as possible. In time this will create 'inner longing' that has magnetic qualities and will pull you into the right directions.

What does coming in peace with myself mean?

It means that all frictions you have with all the different aspects and different sides of yourself, the ones you like as well as the ones you dislike have ceased to exist. This happens when you realize that all you observe within, all your habits and contradictions are acquired and learned and have nothing to do with the truth of what you are.

What about using a mantra?

The use of mantras can be very conducive to meditation, because they can be applied during the day as well. You want to come across the right mantra before you start practising it, due to the fact that once it becomes active in you it is difficult to get rid of it again. Traditionally, mantras always are given by a mystic or a true master, that is when they work best.

Will I be able to remember past lives when I meditate?

What use do you get from remembering past lives? What benefits are there for the present life in remembering past lives? Why waste time with past lives when we only have a certain amount of time at our disposal to become a different being. The Mind is usually interested in these kinds of things, but not the Self.

Can one be in a state of absence of thought during the day as well?

Absolutely. Once one has practised meditation for a long time 'Gamma brainwave' activity will take place during the day as well and is not only active in deep meditation. So the altered state of consciousness can keep us in a thoughtless state while we go about our things sometimes for hours or even days. In some people after lifelong practice it will have become permanent.

What can I learn from philosophical books?

Philosophical books can contain profound knowledge that can make us think in a different way and help us to find a different outlook on life. They can inspire us and can help keep our interest along a certain direction that might lead to transformation. What books can't do is to answer the questions they might give rise to.

19. Contacts

Alexander Filmer-Lorch can be contacted via email at:
  alex@insidemeditation.co.uk

To find out about private sessions, workshops, meditation & philosophy teacher trainings, treatments or telephone & Skype sessions with Alexander please visit:
  www.insidemeditation.co.uk

For yoga teacher trainings with Alexander Filmer-Lorch & Joanne Avison please visit:
  www.aocy.org

More drawings of the Mandalas of Erika Shapiro can be found on:
  www.yogiyoga.co.uk

More book cover designs & illustrations by Victoria Dokas can be found on:
  www.victoriadokas.com

20. Universal Language Dictionary

Active –Is an element of three that represents the driving quality that is part of every form of manifestation within the domain of creation.

Aether – In this school of thought 'Aether' is regarded as pure essence, seen as the fifth element of nature or as the quintessence that unlike all the other elements is not subject to change, is penetrative and non-material.

AHAM – A universal mantra that represents all levels of consciousness along the vertical scale. Its action is based on a descending emanation that carries the will of the Absolute in form of its manifestation, as well as an ascending power that withdraws all that is created back to its original source.

Akasha – Is what gives space to all manifestations of the existence. It is also seen as the Centre as well as the Bindu or the void in the centre around which all levels of consciousness emanate from and withdraw.

Alpha-Influence – Consists of impressions that reach us in form of the creative and touch us on a deeper level, to awaken our interest for new ideas.

Alpha Wave – A brainwave that ranges in frequency from 8 to 13 cycles a second. It represents the state of calmness and non-arousal.

Attention – The masculine part of three qualities within the faculty of perception, that is always ready to act.

Awareness – The feminine part of three qualities within the faculty of perception, that is receptive and motionless.

Beta-Influence – Consists of impressions that are generated by mind created life and reach us in form of all attractions that give us intense but short-lived satisfaction that creates the desire to needing more.

Beta Wave – A brainwave that ranges in frequency from 13 to 30 cycles a second. They represent the state when we are engaged in mental activity.

Bindu – Sanskrit term that means point or dot, a physical location between the eyebrows. All life energy withdraws to and accumulates at this point behind the eyes in the process of meditation.

Bitter Flavour – It comes up when we have compromised our integrity in form of lying as well as acting in a non-ethical manner.

Blissful Denial – Relates to a state in which we have no awareness of our divided nature as well as of all our contradictions.

Clear/True Conscience – Is what is buried beneath all our contradictions and fluctuating nature of our personality.

Conscious Effort – One of three forms of effort that requires dedicated energy with which it has to be reinforced again and again by an act of will.

Creative Centre – Manifests once all the four brains (intellectual, emotional, movement and instinctual) are working to their full potential.

Current of Consciousness – That is connected to infinity, and meets us within the field of consciousness that appears the moment we close our eyes and become aware of a screen in front of us.

Day Dreaming – One of the non-conscious states that are mechanical in nature and we identify with.

Daytime State (Ordinary) – One of the four levels of consciousness. The daytime state is what we spend most time in, from a different level of consciousness point of view.

Delta Wave – A brainwave that ranges in frequency from 1.5 to 4 cycles a second. Appears when we are in deep dreamless sleep.

Divided Attention – A state in which we are aware of the subject as well as the object simultaneously.

Divided Self – Defines the condition of ourselves. That is there is nothing in us developed, that is not subject to fluctuations or change.

Emotional Brain – A form of brain or intelligence that can be located in the solar plexus area of our body and is physically represented by the Entric nervous system.

Empty Pause – The gap between exhalation and inhalation that is utilised in meditation to still the mind.

Force of Meaning – It is a force that is permanently surrounding us and is reaching us in form of new ideas.

Full Pause – The gap between the inhalation and the exhalation that is utilised in certain specific forms of meditation to balance awareness and attention.

Gamma-Influence – An impression that carries the ability to impart knowledge. It meets us in form of a study environment, as well as in the form of a teacher that is specialized in a specific field of expertise.

Gamma Wave – A brainwave that ranges in frequency from 40 to 100 cycles a second. It relates to consciousness and different forms of perceptions.

Great Ideas – They reach us in form of universal teachings as well as through different forms of Alpha-Influences, and through people who have practised and experienced the knowledge of universal teachings. They carry the force of meaning and can evoke higher emotions within us.

Higher Emotions – Higher emotions are awakened when we are in a state of awe or experience certain Aha-moments.

I-Thought – The sense of I that is stripped of all connotations and does not require an opposite.

Ida – One of the Nadis that can be located along the left side of the spine, representing the passive energy.

Identification – One of the non-conscious states that reinforces our mechanicalness.

Imagination – One of the non-conscious states that reinforces our mechanicalness.

Inner Longing – Pulls us towards Gamma-Influence.

Inner Stories – One of the non-conscious states we become identified with, as well as feed into our mechanical behaviour.

Inspirational Effort – A form of effort that does not require any energy because it is inspired by the force of meaning.

Instant Considering – One of the non-conscious states we identify with and that manifests as a mechanical response.

Instinctual Brain – A form of brain or intelligence that can be located in our physical body at the bottom of the spine within the spinal cord in form of the autonomic nervous system.

Intellectual Brain – A form of brain or intelligence that can be located in our physical body in the skull in form of the central nervous system.

Intuition – A higher faculty within that lies dormant in everybody and has to be developed.

Isness – Relates to the truth and most essential state of being of all that is manifested and not manifested.

Little I or Little Me – Form part of our personality and mind and usually have no knowledge of each other. They are acquired by means of imitation and respond mechanically to influences of life.

Lower Emotions – Are emotions we have acquired by imitations. They are not real and can be worked with and transformed.

Lying – One of the non-conscious states we identify with, and which has become habitual.

Mechanical Talking - One of the non-conscious states we identify with and has become habitual.

Mind – A great instrument that is comprised of multiple facets and can be seen as a hard drive that imprints all that it receives via external impressions that once utilised, can become a powerful agent to support our inner evolution as well as meditation.

Mind Created Life – It is a world that mankind has superimposed on organic life and has penetrated more and more into the hidden parts of organic life and nature.

Movement Brain - A form of brain or intelligence that can be located together with the instinctual brain in our physical body at the bottom of the spine within the spinal cord in form of the autonomic nervous system.

Neutral Observer – A state of awareness that is developed by means of conscious effort to facilitate self-observation and plays a vital part during the initial stages of the process of meditation.

Neutralising Force -Is an element of three that represents the uniting quality that is part of every form of manifestation within the domain of creation.

Non-conscience Effort – Is an entirely habitual or mechanical kind of effort that keeps sustaining our non-conscious states.

Objective Consciousness – One of the highest forms of consciousness that we have to evolve into by means of self-study and meditation. It is a state that has to be experienced and can't be described in words.

Organic Life – Human beings still form part of organic life that is under specific laws of evolution.

Padding – A form of psychological substance that separates our different Me's and contradictions in form of denial and ignorance.

Passive – Is an element of three that represents the motionless quality that is part of every form of manifestation within the domain of creation.

Path of the Objective Man – A universal teaching that is designed to be applied in our modern world. Other paths are the path of Karma or the path of a Yogi etc.

Pingala - One of the Nadis that can be located along the right side of the spine, representing the active energy.

Positive shock – A course of conscious action that has the power to break down certain mechanical habits.

Prana – Life force or vitality that sustains every living being.

Pre-ceive – An altered state of perception in which one receives knowledge of truth that has not manifested as a new proposition yet.

Qualia – Pointers that everybody meets and experiences during the process of meditation.

Real Emotions – Are evoked through life circumstances and manifest in countless forms like feelings of friendship, love, grief, sadness, peace, contentment, happiness etc.

Scale – Everything has scale to it. Like the scale of a tree or the scale of our potential. Some forms of scale are two-dimensional, some are three-dimensional, some are four-dimensional.

Scale of meaning – Is an infinite scale that manifests in all liberating ideas or Great Ideas.

Screen of Consciousness/Field of Consciousness – Appears in front of us the moment we close our eyes to sit in meditation. It is this empty screen that one's mind is active reflects all manifestations of thoughts, feelings and emotions, to be perceived by awareness.

Self-Consciousness – One of the different levels of consciousness in which we will know the truth of what we are in essence.

Self-Observation – A technique that is applied in self-study, in which we soften deeper into ourselves to be able to observe our different states of mind and actions.

Self-study – A technique that is applied to facilitate our inner development to become more conscious.

Selling & Shopping Negative Feelings – One of the non-conscious states we identify with and has become totally habitual in us.

Sentrum – A higher faculty that awakens once the universal teachings have been internalised.

Shushumna – One of the main nadis that is located within the spine through which the energy can be channelled towards the Bindu.

Sleep – One of the different levels of consciousness in which we have no knowledge about the truth of ourselves.

Solar Plexus – The location of our emotional brain in the form of the Entric nervous system.

Spanda —Pulse of consciousness that induces consciousness to expand.

Strong Sounding Intent – Filled with the power of the active force that by means of conscious effort can manifest our objective. This form of intent is utterly flexible and not as rigid as the form of will we usually apply to reach our objective.

Substance of Gravitas – Knowledge that has turned into practical experience that adds gravitas to our self-study and meditation.

Subtle Body/Invisible Body – The energetic body that is invisible to our physical eyes yet can be perceived by a higher ability within. It can be palpated as an electromagnetic field by the palms of our hands a few centimetres off the body.

The Law of Transformation – Relates to the fact that change is only possible when we; first have become aware of what needs to change, second that we have to transcend it, and third we have to include what we have transcended into the whole.

The Unchanging Nature Within –Is what is not subject to change within us, as well as what is permanent within us.

Theta-Influence – One of the strongest external influences to which we can be exposed.

Theta Wave – The range of theta wave frequency is between 7 to 14 cycles per second. We are in a state of theta-brainwave activity when we are daydreaming.

Third Body – Is a formless body within the invisible body that lies dormant and is activated by work on consciousness.

Third Breath – Third breath can be experienced in specific meditation exercises within the breath cycles.

Triad – Is a universal law that is comprised of the active, passive and neutralising forces that take part in manifestation.

True Intelligence – Requires a certain condition within the different functions of the four brains to be able to manifest.

True/Permanent Sense of Self – appears in a higher state of consciousness usually when we have acquired a different kind of will.

Twelve-finger point – A point approximately twelve fingers above the top of the head that is used as a reference point in meditation.

Unchanging Gravitas – Manifests once the Great Ideas have become active within

Undivided Self – See permanent self.

Universal Language – Is a language that defines the universal teachings. Each system or teaching has developed its universal language in which each term is very clearly defined and it's meaning is agreed, to avoid any misunderstanding.

Universal Teaching –Teaching that reaches us from beyond mind created life and carry liberating ideas that are timeless and true, as they make us think differently and induce a process of transformation.

Vertical Ray/Ray of Eternity – Can be accessed within the presence, and contains the scale of consciousness as well as the scale of infinity.

Appendix A – Anatomy of the Brain

A) *The Forebrain*

The forebrain is divided into Telencephalon and Diencephalon.

1) Telencephalon:

The telencephalon consists of two cerebral hemispheres of the cerebrum and their inter connections.

The cerebrum is the largest part of our brain and is divided into two hemispheres by the medial longitudinal fissure. A fibrous band of nerves called the corpus collosum connects the two hemispheres with each other. The cortex of each hemisphere is divided into four lobes: the frontal lobe, the parietal lobe, the temporal lobe and the occipital lobe. The ridges one can see on the surface of the cortex are the gyri and the deep groves separating them are the "sulci", which help to divide the cerebrum into its four lobes.

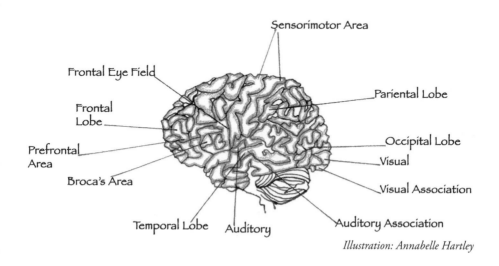

Illustration: Annabelle Hartley

a) The Frontal Lobe

The frontal lobe is responsible for the main functions of the brain. Its function allows us to recognize future consequences resulting from our actions and enables us to judge them. Memory, cognition, analytical and critical reasoning are functions of the frontal lobe. Our emotional traits and language skills are stored there and the premotor cortex is responsible for voluntary activities and motor patterns.

b) The Parietal Lobe

The parietal lobe functions deal with sensations such as pain, pressure, touch, joint movements and temperature. It also deals with discrimination of the intensity of stimuli such as hot from warm and cold from chilly. It stores data and helps to recognise familiar objects, which are placed into our hands without necessarily looking at them, as well as it helps us to recognise spatial relationships.

c) The Temporal Lobe

The temporal lobe relates to auditory sensations and is our language centre (Wernicke's Area). The left part of the lobe is mainly involved in speech. The temporal lobe is responsible for connecting to our emotions, speech, memory, as well as sensations of smell are registered there.

d) The Occipital Lobe

The occipital lobe is the smallest lobe and is mainly responsible for interpreting visual impulses via the visual pathway. Rays reaching the eye stimulate the retinal sensors and this stimuli is conveyed to the cuneus. From there, it goes through the optic tracts and the lateral geniculate bodies of the thalamus from where it continues to the visual cortex. Each visual cortex receives sensory information from the external half of the eye present of the same side and from the inside half of the eye present on the other side of the head and the image is finally projected in the cortex.

Visual Cortex

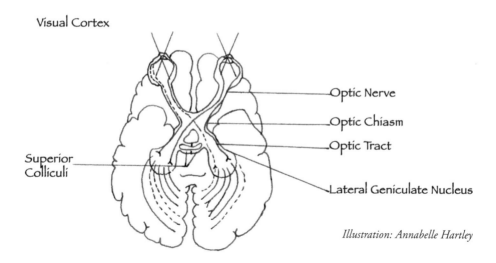

Optic Nerve

Optic Chiasm

Optic Tract

Superior Colliculi

Lateral Geniculate Nucleus

Illustration: Annabelle Hartley

2) The Diencephalon:

The diencephalon contains two well-known structures called thalamus and hypothalamus.

a) The Thalamus

The thalamus is a paired structure and forms part of the diencephalon. Each egg shaped thalamus consists of nuclei or grey matter and these are joined by a mass of grey matter called massa intermiedia. This centre can be seen as a relay station for incoming nerve impulses, which sends them to the appropriate parts of the brain for further processing. These are sensory signals, auditory signals, visual signals and somato-sensory signals, which go through this structure before they are further processed in the brain. This centre also controls our motor control and is responsible for controlling muscular movements. In short, it enables the brain to receive information on what is happening outside the body.

b) The Hypothalamus

The hypothalamus is mainly responsible for maintaining homeostasis in the body. It keeps the conditions in the body constant and prevents the occurrence of sudden changes. It regulates sensations like hunger, thirst, temperature etc. It takes care of our circadian rhythm (sleep and awake cycle) and plays a part in emotions, autonomic functions, motor functions and exerts control on the pituitary gland.

c) The Pituitary Gland

The pituitary or hypophysis gland is a small endocrine gland, which is secreting different hormones to maintain hormonal balance in the body.

Vertical Section of The Brain

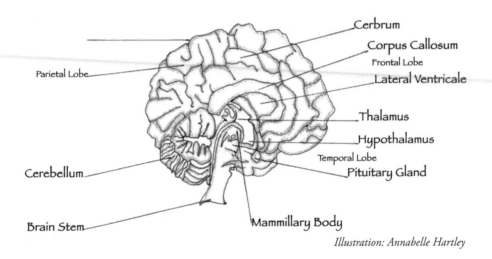

Illustration: Annabelle Hartley

B) The Mid-Brain

The mid brain is divided into two parts by the Aqueduct of Sylvius, which is called the cerebral peduncle, made of white matter and the tectum. Its functions are to act like a relay centre, getting sensory information from the ear to the cerebrum. It controls our reflex movements of the muscles of the head, neck and eyes. It's like a passage for different neurons, which are coming out or going into the cerebrum.

C) The Hindbrain (Rhomb Encephalon)

This part of the brain, which contains the ponds and the medulla oblongata are also known as the brain stem. All cranial nerves in the brain stem are found here.

1) The Pons:

The Pons play a part in the level of arousal or consciousness and sleep as well as sending impulses to and from the brain. It also plays a part in controlling our autonomic body functions

2) The Medulla Oblongata:

The Medulla Oblongata forms the lower part of the brain stem. It is responsible for all the basic and vital activities of the body. It contains respiratory, cardiac and vasomotor centres. It is responsible for our breathing to maintain a regular heart rate and blood pressure, swallowing, urination and lifesaving reflexes. It executes the most important functions of the brain hence regulating our life processes.

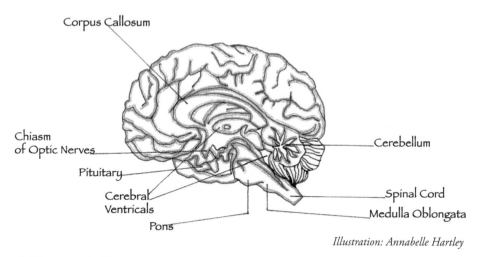

Illustration: Annabelle Hartley

3) The Cerebellum:

Cerebellum means, 'little brain'. It contains an outer grey cortex and an inner white medulla. It coordinates our muscular movement, maintains our balance while walking, swimming or cycling etc. and is involved in learning new movement and regulating our coordination.

From the medulla oblongata the central nervous system extends down through the foramen magnum and continues in the spinal column. From the spinal cord, nerves spread out to form the peripheral nervous system.

D) The Cerebrospinal Fluid CSF

The cerebrospinal fluid **(CSF)** is produced from arterial blood by the choroid plexuses[105] of the lateral and fourth ventricles by a combined process of diffusion, pinocytosis[106] and active transfer. Ependymal cells also produce a small amount[107].

The **choroid plexus** consists of tufts of capillaries with thin fenestrated cells. Modified ependymal cells cover these. The total volume of CSF in the adult ranges from 140 to 270 ml. The volume of the ventricles is about 25 ml. CSF is produced at a rate of 0.2 - 0.7 ml per minute or 600-700 ml per day. The circulation of CSF is aided by the pulsations of the choroid plexus and by the motion of the cilia[108] of ependymal cells.

CSF is absorbed across the arachnoid villi[109] into the venous circulation and a significant amount probably also drains into lymphatic vessels around the cranial cavity and spinal canal. The arachnoid villi act as one-way valves between the subarachnoid space and the dural sinuses[110]. The rate of absorption correlates with the CSF pressure. CSF acts as a cushion that protects the brain from shocks and supports the venous sinuses (primarily the superior sagittal sinus, opening when CSF pressure exceeds venous pressure). It also plays an important role in the homeostasis and metabolism of the central nervous system.

The cranio sacral rhythm, which is induced by pressure changes in this refined semi hydraulic system, can be palpated on every part of the body. Besides the respiratory pulse, circulatory pulse and the heart rate, the cranio sacral rhythm is the slowest and most subtle rhythm in the body.

Appendix B – Meditation Research Paper Abstract

RESEARCH PAPER:[111]

Long-term meditators self-induce high-amplitude gamma synchrony during mental practice.

Abstract

Practitioners understand meditation, or mental training, to be a process of familiarization with one's own mental life leading to long-lasting changes in cognition and emotion. Little is known about this process and its impact on the brain. Here we find that long-term Buddhist practitioners self-induce sustained electroencephalographic high-amplitude gamma-band oscillations and phase-synchrony during meditation.

In addition, the ratio of gamma-band activity (25-42 Hz) to slow oscillatory activity (4-13 Hz) is initially higher in the resting baseline before meditation for the practitioners than the controls (healthy student volunteers) over medial frontoparietal electrodes. This difference increases sharply during meditation over most of the scalp electrodes and remains higher than the initial baseline in the post-meditation baseline. **This data suggest that mental training involves temporal integrative mechanisms and may induce short-term and long-term neural changes.**

Little is known about the process of meditation and its impact on the brain.[112] Previous studies show the general role of neural synchrony, in particular in the gamma-band frequencies (25-70Hz), in mental processes such as attention, working-memory, learning, or conscious perception.[113] **Such synchronizations of oscillatory neural discharges are thought to play a crucial role in the constitution of transient networks that integrate distributed neural processes into highly ordered cognitive and affective functions)[114] and could induce synaptic changes.[115]** *Neural synchrony thus appears as a promising mechanism for the study of brain processes underlining mental training.*

Discussion

We found robust gamma-band oscillation and long-distance phase-synchrony during the generation of the non-referential compassion meditative state. It is likely to be based on descriptions of various meditation practices and mental strategies that are reported by practitioners that there will be differences in brain function associated with different types of meditation. In light of our initial observations concerning robust gamma oscillations during this compassion meditation state, we focused our initial attention on this state. Future research is required to characterize the nature of the differences among types of meditation.

Our resulting data differ from several studies that found an increase in slow alpha or theta rhythms during meditation.[116] The comparison is limited by the fact that these studies typically did not analyse fast rhythms. More importantly, these studies mainly investigated different forms of voluntary concentrative meditation on an object (such as a meditation on a mantra or the breath).

These concentration techniques can be seen as a particular form of top-down control that may exhibit an important slow oscillatory component.[117] **First-person descriptions of objectless meditations, however, differ radically from those of concentration meditation.** Objectless meditation does not directly attend to a specific object but rather cultivates a state of being. Objectless meditation does so in such a way that, according to reports given after meditation, the intentional or object-oriented aspect of experience appears to dissipate in meditation.

This dissipation of focus on a particular object is achieved by letting the very essence of the meditation that is practiced (on compassion in this case) become the sole content of the experience, without focusing on particular objects. By using similar techniques during the practice, the practitioner lets his feeling of loving-kindness and compassion permeate his mind without directing his attention toward a particular object. These phenomenological differences suggest that these various meditative states (those that involve focus on an object and those that are objectless) may be associated with different EEG oscillatory signatures.

The high-amplitude gamma activity found in some of these practitioners are, to our knowledge, the highest reported in the literature in a non-pathological context.[118]

Assuming that the amplitude of the gamma oscillation is related to the size of the oscillating neural population and the degree of precision with which cells oscillate, **these data suggest that massive distributed neural assemblies are synchronized with a high temporal precision in the fast frequencies during this state.**

The gradual increase of gamma activity during meditation is in agreement with the view that neural synchronization, as a network phenomenon, requires time to develop,[119] proportional to the size of the synchronized neural assembly.[120] But this increase could also reflect an increase in the temporal precision of the thalamo-cortical and corticocortical interactions rather than a change in the size of the assemblies.[121]

This gradual increase also corroborates the Buddhist subjects' verbal report of the chronometry of their practice. Typically, the transition from the neutral state to this meditative state is not immediate and requires 5-15 s, depending on the subject. The endogenous gamma-band synchrony found here could reflect a change in the quality of moment-to-moment awareness, as claimed by the Buddhist practitioners and as postulated by many models of consciousness.[122]

In addition to the meditation-induced effects, we found a difference in the normative EEG spectral profile between the two populations during the resting state before meditation. It is not unexpected that such differences would be detected during a resting baseline, because the goal of meditation practice is to transform the baseline state and to diminish the distinction between formal meditation practice and everyday life. Moreover, Gusnard and Raichle[123] have highlighted the importance of characteristic patterns of brain activity during the resting state and argue that such patterns affect the nature of task-induced changes.

The differences in baseline activity reported here suggest that the resting state of the brain may be altered by long-term meditative practice and imply that such alterations may affect task-related changes. Our practitioners and control subjects differed in many respects, including age, culture of origin, and first language, and they likely differed in many more respects, including diet and sleep. We examined whether age was an important factor in producing the baseline differences. We observed by comparing the three youngest practitioners with the controls and found that the mean age difference between groups is unlikely to be the sole factor responsible for this baseline difference.

Moreover, hours of practice but not age significantly predicted relative gamma activity during the initial baseline period. Whether other demographic factors are important in producing these effects will necessarily require further research, particularly longitudinal research that follows individuals over time in response to mental training.

Our study is consistent with the idea that attention and affective processes, which gamma-band EEG synchronization may reflect, **are flexible skills that can be trained.**[124] It remains for future studies to show that these EEG signatures are caused by long-term training itself, and not by individual differences before the training, **although the positive correlation that we found with hours of training and other randomised controlled trials suggest that these are training-related effects.**[125] The functional consequences of sustained gamma-activity during mental practice are not currently known but need to be studied in the future. The study of experts in mental training may offer a promising research strategy to investigate high-order cognitive and affective processes.[126]

Acknowledgements

From a Far Eastern Psychology view point, the idea or concept that one individual possesses, or has developed, all the skills, talents and knowledge to achieve one's objective is non-existent. Every person is lacking something and without any input and help of others, the outcome of our objective would lack in substance and quality.

This book would never have been written without the help of others. I want to thank all my students and clients for all that they have taught me, and are still teaching me. Furthermore, I want to thank the Upledger Institute UK where I trained to become a therapist. Their trainings and teaching methods changed my life forever.

My gratitude goes to my teachers Ishwar Ananda, Babaji and Rin-pen who taught and initiated me into the science of meditation and applied Eastern psychology and philosophy.

I want to thank my friends Linda and Anji, as well as all my other friends for their patience and encouragement.

All of the complex graphics in this book were carefully hand drawn by Annabelle Hartley, who is a gifted designer and continues to amaze me with the sheer scale and wide range of her artistic skills.

The delicate Mandalas that symbolise and reflect a gateway into the main sections of the book, were painted by Erika Shapiro and add a specific influence to the written words. I wish to thank them both for the effort and love they have put into their work.

No words can describe my love and gratitude for my partner Robie, whose support and help, on so many levels, from the beginning to the end of this whole writing venture, has been unbelievable.

Furthermore, I want to thank my great friend Julia Bond who kick-started the process of writing this book and pre-proofread the different chapters. I can't thank her enough for all her work.

Many thanks to Angela Filmer my wonderful mother-in-law, who carefully proof-read the book and insisted on buying the first five copies of the finished article.

Many heartfelt and special thanks go to my Family. Mom, Dad and my sister Janine, her husband Heiko and my nephew Jonas who support and believe in whatever I explore, work on, study and put into action.

Special thanks to Victoria Dokas, who is an amazingly gifted illustrator and book cover designer, which I can highly recommend to every publisher and Author.

I want to thank Amy Cooke and the whole team of Troubador Publishing Ltd, who were involved in the publishing process of *Inside Meditation*. They made the whole publishing experience accessible and transparent. They truly stick to what they say, propose and commit to, in the most professional way possible. One could not wish for a better publishing house.

Very special thanks go to Valerie James. I feel honoured that someone with her expertise, took the time to read the whole manuscript before writing the forward to the book.

I want to thank the author Joanne Sarah Avison my great colleague, friend and well-respected expert in the science of fascia and applied anatomy in yoga, sports and movement practice for reviewing and endorsing the book.

A special thank you to my friend and colleague Maggie Gill, who is one of the most gifted cranio social therapists. I am very fortunate to see her for treatments once a month.

Many thanks to the author Carmel Greenwood for her advice and reading the unedited manuscript, as well as the endorsement she sent regarding the book.

And last but not least I thank our dog Lottie for giving me the excuse to walk in nature every day. These walks have been a great help in allowing me to clear my head after hours of writing.

References

[1] The Mind and Life Institute brings together many specialists across the globe including: psychiatrists, experimental psychologists, cognitive scientists, epistemologists, theologians, Buddhist monks, affective neuropsychologists, neurobiologists, etc. See for example, *Destructive Emotions and how we can overcome them, A dialogue with the Dalai Lama narrated by Daniel Goleman*. Bloomsbury, London, 2003 and *Healing Emotions: conversations with the Dalai Lama on Mindfulness, Emotions, and Health* (ed) Daniel Goleman, Shambala, Boston 1997

[2] Dr Karen Armstrong was awarded the TED prize for her International Charter of Compassion. *Twelve Steps to a Compassionate Life*, Bodley Head, London 2011

[3] Professor Martin Levine, *The Positive Psychology of Buddhism and Yoga: Paths to a Mature Happiness,* Lawrence Erlbaum Associates, Publishers, London 2000

[4] In Search of the Miraculous – P.D. Ouspensky (1838–1947)

[5] Possehl (2003), pp. 144–145

[6] Jonathan Mark Kenoyer describes one figure as "seated in yogic position." "Around the Indus in 90 Slides" by Jonathan Mark Kenoyer

[7] Chapple, Christopher.(1993), pp.6–9

[8] Oystein Vorland 2008-09.

[9] *An universal etymological English dictionary* 1773, London, by Nathan Bailey

[10] *Christian spirituality: themes from the tradition* by Lawrence S. Cunningham, Keith J. Egan 1996 ISBN 0809136600 page 88

[11] *The Oblate Life* by Gervase Holdaway, 2008 ISBN 0814631762 page 115

[12] abcFeuerstein, Georg. "Yoga and Meditation (Dhyana)." Moksha Journal. Issue 1. 2006. ISSN 1051-127X, OCLC 21878732 The verb root "dhyai" is listed as referring to "contemplate, meditate on" and "dhyāna" is listed as referring to "meditation; religious contemplation" on page 134 of MacDonnell, Arthur Anthony (1929 (1971 reprint)). *A practical Sanskrit dictionary with transliteration, accentuation and etymological analysis throughout.* London: Oxford University Press

[13] Mirahmadi, Sayyid Nurjan; Muhammad Nazim Adil al-Haqqani Naqshbandi, Muhammad Hisham Kabbani & Hedieh Mirahmadi (2005). *The healing power of sufi meditation*. Fenton, MI: Naqshbandi Haqqani Sufi Order of America. ISBN 1930409265.

[14] Goleman, Daniel (1988). *The meditative mind: The varieties of meditative experience*. New York: Tarcher. ISBN 0-87477-833-6.

[15] Jean L. Kristeller (2010). Ruth A. Baer & Kelly G. Wilson. ed. "Spiritual engagement as a mechanism of change in mindfulness- and acceptance-based therapies". *Assessing mindfulness and acceptance processes in clients: Illuminating*

the theory and practice of change (Oakland, CA: New Harbinger): 152–184. ISBN 9781572246942.. Page 161 states "In Christianity, the term 'contemplation' is parallel to the term 'meditation' as it has entered contemporary usage"

[16]Joseph, M. 1998, *The effect of strong religious beliefs on coping with stress* Stress Medicine. Vol 14(4), Oct 1998, 219-224

[17]Buddhist scholar B. Alan Wallace has argued that focused attention is a basis for the practice of mindfulness. He writes that "Truly effective meditation is impossible without focused attention... the cultivation of attentional stability has been a core element of the meditative traditions throughout the centuries" (p. xi) in Wallace, B. Alan (2006). *The attention revolution: Unlocking the power of the focused mind.* Boston: Wisdom. ISBN 0861712765.

[18]Matt J. Rossano (2007). "Did meditating make us human?". *Cambridge Archaeological Journal* (Cambridge University Press) 17 (1): 47–58. doi:10.1017/S0959774307000054. This paper draws on various lines of evidence to argue that "Campfire rituals of focused attention created Baldwinian selection for enhanced working memory among our Homo sapiens ancestors.... this emergence was [in part] caused by a fortuitous genetic mutation that enhanced working memory capacity [and] a Baldwinian process where genetic adaptation follows somatic adaptation was the mechanism for this emergence" (p. 47).

[19]P.C. Roychoudhury (1956) *Jainism in Bihar*, Patna p.7

^ **ab** Ahimsa - The Science Of Peace: *by Surendra Bothra 1987*

[20]A clinical guide to the treatment of human stress response by George S. Everly, Jeffrey M. Lating 2002 ISBN 0306466201 page 199

[21]Hadot, Pierre; Arnold I. Davidson (1995) *Philosophy as a way of life*ISBN 0631180338 pages 83-84

[22]]*Zen Buddhism : a History: India and China* by Heinrich Dumoulin, James W. Heisig, Paul F. Knitter 2005 ISBN 0941532895 pages 15

[23]*Zen Buddhism : a History: India and China* by Heinrich Dumoulin, James W. Heisig, Paul F. Knitter 2005 ISBN 0941532895 pages 50

[24]]*Zen Buddhism : a History: Japan* by Heinrich Dumoulin, James W. Heisig, Paul F. Knitter 2005 ISBN 0941532909 page 5

[25]*Soto Zen in Medieval Japan* by William Bodiford 2008 ISBN 0824833031 page 39*The Cambridge History of Japan: Medieval Japan* by Kōzō Yamamura, John Whitney Hall 1990 ISBN 0521223547 646

[26]*Prayer: a history* by Philip Zaleski, Carol Zaleski 2005 ISBN 0618152881 page 147-149

Global Encyclopaedia of Education by Rama Sankar Yadav & B.N. Mandal 2007 ISBN 9788182202276 page 63

[27]*Spiritual Psychology* by Akbar Husain 2006 ISBN 8182200954 page 109

[28]*An introduction to the Christian Orthodox churches* by John Binns 2002 ISBN 0521667380 page 128

^"Hesychasm". *OrthodoxWiki*. Retrieved 12 May 2010.

[29]"Mount Athos: History". *Macedonian Heritage*. Retrieved 12 May 2010.

[30]*Christian Spirituality: A Historical Sketch* by George Lane 2005 ISBN 0829420819 page 20

^*Christian spirituality: themes from the tradition* by Lawrence S. Cunningham, Keith J. Egan 1996 ISBN 0809136600 page 38

references

^ *The Oblate Life* by Gervase Holdaway, 2008 ISBN 0814631762 page 109

^ *After Augustine: the meditative reader and the text* by Brian Stock 2001 ISBN 0812236025 page 105

[31] Abelson, Peter (April 1993) Schopenhauer and Buddhism. *Philosophy East and West Volume 43, Number 2,* pp. 255-278. University of Hawaii Press. Retrieved on: 12 April 2008.

[32] *Enlightenment and reform in 18th-century Europe* by Derek Edward Dawson Beales 2005 ISBN 1860649491 page 13.

[33] Shakya, Tsering "Review of *Prisoners of Shangri-la* by Donald Lopez". online

[34] *A clinical guide to the treatment of human stress response* by George S. Everly, Jeffrey M. Lating 2002 ISBN 0306466201 page 200

^ *Encyclopedia of Psychology and Religion* by David A. Leeming, Kathryn Madden, Stanton Marlan 2009 ISBN page 559

[35] Murphy, Michael. "1". *The Physical and Psychological Effects of Meditation: Scientific Studies of Contemplative Experience: An Overview.*

[36] *By Marc Kaufman,* Washington Post Staff Writer Monday, January 3, 2005; Page A05

[37] Inspired by Jill Bolte Taylor PH.D. – My stroke of insight page 20 – 23.

[38] Second College edition (Boston: Houghton Mufflin Company, 1985)

[39] Jill Bolte Taylor Ph.D. 2008, My Stroke of Insight page 13

[40] **Electroencephalography (EEG)** is the recording of electrical activity along the scalp. EEG measures voltage fluctuations resulting from ionic current flows within the neurons of the brain. *Niedermeyer E. and da Silva F.L. (2004). *Electroencephalography: Basic Principles, Clinical Applications, and Related Fields.* Lippincot Williams & Wilkins. ISBN 0781751268. In clinical contexts, EEG refers to the recording of the brain's spontaneous electrical activity over a short period of time, usually 20–40 minutes, as recorded from multiple electrodes placed on the scalp.

[41] A neuroscientist at the university's new $10 million W.M. Keck Laboratory for Functional Brain Imaging and Behavior.

[42] Published in the Proceedings of the National Academy of Sciences November 2004

[43] Richard Davidson, the lead researcher, professor of psychiatry and psychology and director of the HeathEmotions Research Institute

[44] Based on February 13 publication, 2010 by Ray Williams in Wired for Success

[45] Research study by the Emory University's center for Collaborative and Contemplative Studies

[46] Scientist at UC Davis's Center for Mind and Brain

[47] scheduled for publication in the journal *Emotion*

[48] Abstracts from article by Wray Herbert – November 18th 2010Author, 'On Second Thought: Outsmarting Your Mind's Hard-Wired Habits'

[49] Kiecolt-Glaser JK, Garner W, Speicher CE, Penn GM, Holiday J, GlaserR. Psychosocial modifiers of immunocompetence in medical students. Psychosom Med 1984;46:7–14.

Glaser R, Kiecolt-Glaser JK, Malarkey WB, Sheridan JF. The influenceof psychological stress on the immune response to vaccines. Ann NY

Acad Sci 1998;47:113–142.

Cohen S, Herbert TB. Health psychology: Psychological factors andphysical disease from the perspective of human psychoneuroimmunology. Ann Rev Psychol 1996;47:113–42.

[50]Antoni MH. Cognitive-based stress management intervention effects onanxiety, 24-hr urinary norepinephrine output, and T-cytotoxic/suppressor cells over time among symptomatic HIV infected gay men. J Consult Clin Psychol 2000;68:31–45.

[51]Psychosomatic Medicine 65:564–570 (2003)

[52]Cambridge Dictionary Online

[53]Wikipedia

[54]Free Merriam-Webster Dictionary

[55]YourDictionary.com

[56]Businessdictionary.com

[57]A psychological term, which stands for our intrinsic inclination towards selfhood.

[58]A psychological term, describing a state of being which does not depend on the identification with "I belief's".

[59]A psychological term in this school of thought, which will be explained a bit further down the line.

[60]A philosophical term used in this school of thought, which will be explained at a later stage in this book.

[61]Pyotr Demianovich Ouspenskii

[62]"Padding" - a psychological term which will be explained at a later stage in this book

[63]Philosophical term forming part of the universal language

[64]A philosophical term which belongs to the universal language

[65]Thomas Hobbes 'The Leviathan', *Civil peace and social unity through perfect government*. Oregon State University: Phl 302, Great Voyages: the History of Western Philosophy from 1492-1776, Winter 1997.

[66]Alexander Pope, essay on Man Epistle II - http://www.harpers.org/archive/2008/03/hbc-90002748

[67] <http://books.google.com/books?id=MYkTAQAAMAAJ&dq=Autobiography%2C%20Say

[68]Ralph Waldo Emerson – 'Gnothi Seauton', poem 1831

[69]J.S.Avison www.aocy.org

[70]The Power of Now by Eckard Tolle

[71]The Fourth Way Teaching calls the four brains the "four different centres". The terminology brain used here points directly to its connection to an existing nervous system in the body and attributes intelligence to it as well as it indicates that it is a living & energetic organism which can grow and evolve.

[72]Page 21 Psychosynthesis Assagioli

[73]Self-Consciousness a term used in The Fourth Way Teaching& Psychoanalysis & Counseling

[74]An expression my friend an colleague Joanne Avison uses in her lectures

[75]Warm blooded vertebrates including humans

[76]Guenter Albrecht-Buehler, Ph.D.Fellow, European Academy of Sciences, BrusselsFellow, Institute for Advanced

references

Studies, BerlinRobert Laughlin Rea Professor of Cell BiologyNorthwestern University Medical School, Chicago

[77] Sounds True – many voices, one journey, Sounds True Inc. at soundstrue.com

[78] Author of Molecules of Emotion – why you feel the way you feel

[79] Neuropeptides are small protein-like molecules used by neurons to communicate with each other. They are neuronal signaling molecules, influence the activity of the brain in specific ways and are thus involved in particular brain functions, like analgesia, reward, food intake, learning and memory. See..ww.neuropeptides.nl

[80] San Francisco Medical Society, sfms.org article by Leslie A. Takeuchi, BA, PTA

[81] The Bible

[82] Harper, Douglas. *Online Etymology Dictionary*. Retrieved 2009-05-22.

[83] Martin Heidegger, *What is called Thinking?*

[84] The different Meditation techniques will be explained in detail in Chapter 15 (The Art of Meditation)

[85] Dictionary.reference.com

[86] Robert van Gulick (2004), Stanford Encyclopedia of Philosophy

[87] Answers.com

[88] *Sigmund Freud, 'New Introductory Lectures on Psychoanalysis', 1933*

[89] *R.J. Joynt, 'Are Two Heads better than One?' Behavioral Brain Sciences, 1981*

[90] William James, Essay 1904 'Does consciousness exist?'

[91] James W. (1890). The principles of psychology. New York: Henry Holt, Vol. 1, pp. 403-404

[92] Etymonline

[93] Merriam-Webster

[94] *"A Late Period Hieratic Wisdom Text: P. Brooklyn 47.218.135"*, Richard Jasnow, p. 95, University of Chicago Press, 1992

[95] Analects XV.24 (tr. David Hinton)

[96] - Leviticus 19:18 the 'Great Commandment'

[97] Plato's Socrates (Crito, 49c) (c. 469 BC–399 BCE)

[98] The Stanzas on Vibration

[99] Unseen Rain, Quatrains of Rumi by John Moyne and Coleman Barks page 40, ISBN 0-939660-16-4

[100] Ouspensky quoting Gurdjieff 'In search of the Miraculous' & 'The fourth Way'

[101] Yoga practise – Asana means posture

[102] Savasana is a yoga posture in which we lie on our back, with legs slightly apart and palms facing up.

[103] Dhyan or Dhyana means Meditation

[104] P D Ouspensky

[105] Choroid plexus: It produces the cerebrospinal fluid (CSF) which is found within the ventricles of the brain and in the subarachnoid space around the brain.

[106] Introduction of fluids into a cell by invagination of the cell membrane, followed by formation of vesicles within the cells.

[107] The ependymal cells line the walls of the ventricles and form the specialized choroid plexus epithelium, which

secretes the cerebrospinal fluid (CSF).

[108]Small hair-like organs on the surface of some cells.

[109]Arachnoid villi are small protrusions of the arachnoid (the thin second layer covering the brain).

[110]The dural venous sinuses (also called dural sinuses, cerebral sinuses, or cranial sinuses) are venous channels found between layers of dura mater in the brain. They receive blood from internal and external veins of the brain, receive cerebrospinal fluid (CSF) from the subarachnoid space, and ultimately empty into the internal jugular vein.

[111]Antoine Lutz[*,†], Lawrence L. Greischar[*], Nancy B. Rawlings[*], Matthieu Ricard[‡], and Richard J. Davidson[*,†]

Author Affiliations

[*]W. M. Keck Laboratory for Functional Brain Imaging and Behavior, Waisman Center, and Laboratory for Affective Neuroscience, Department of Psychology, University of Wisconsin, 1500 Highland Avenue, Madison, WI 53705; and [‡]Shechen Monastery, P.O. Box 136, Kathmandu, Nepal.

Communicated by Burton H. Singer, Princeton University, Princeton, NJ, October 6, 2004 (received for review August 26, 2004).

[112]Austin, J. H. (1998) Zen and the Brain: Toward an Understanding of Meditation and Consciousness (MIT Press, Cambridge, MA).

Davidson, R. J., Kabat-Zinn, J., Schumacher, J., Rosenkranz, M., Muller, D., Santorelli, S. F., Urbanowski, F., Harrington, A., Bonus, K. & Sheridan, J. F. (2003) Psychosom. Med. 65 , 564-570. **Abstract/FREE Full Text.**

[113]Fries, P., Reynolds, J. H., Rorie, A. E. & Desimone, R. (2001) Science 291 , 1560-1563. **Abstract/FREE Full Text.**

Miltner, W. H., Braun, C., Arnold, M., Witte, H. & Taub, E. (1999) Nature 397 , 434-436. **CrossRefMedline**.

Srinivasan, R., Russell, D. P., Edelman, G. M. & Tononi, G. (1999) J. Neurosci. 19 , 5435-5448. **Abstract/FREE Full Text**.

Tallon-Baudry, C., Bertrand, O., Peronnet, F. & Pernier, J. (1998) J. Neurosci. 18 , 4244-4254. **Abstract/FREE Full Text.**

Rodriguez, E., George, N., Lachaux, J. P., Martinerie, J., Renault, B. & Varela, F. J. (1999) Nature 397 , 430-433. **CrossRefMedline**

[114]Singer, W. (1999) Neuron 24 , 49-65. **CrossRefMedlineWeb of Science.**

Varela, F., Lachaux, J. P., Rodriguez, E. & Martinerie, J. (2001) Nat. Rev. Neurosci. 2 , 229-239. **CrossRefMedlineWeb of Science.**

[115]Hebb, D. O. (1949) The Organization of Behavior: A Neuropsychological Theory (Wiley, New York).

Paulsen, O., Sejnowski, T. J. (2000) Curr. Opin. Neurobiol. 10 , 172-179. **CrossRefMedlineWeb of Science.**

[116]Shapiro, D. H. (1980) Meditation: Self-Regulation Strategy and Altered State of Consciousness (Aldine, New York).

[117]von Stein, A., Chiang, C. & Konig, P. (2000) Proc. Natl. Acad. Sci. USA 97 , 14748-14753. **Abstract/FREE Full Text.**

references

[118] Baldeweg, T., Spence, S., Hirsch, S. R. & Gruzelier, J. (1998) Lancet 352, 620-621. **MedlineWeb of Science.**

[119] Kuramato, Y. (1975) in International Symposium on Mathematical Problems in Theoretical Physics, ed. Araki, H. (Springer, New York), Vol. 39, pp. 420.

[120] Campbell, S. R., Wang, D. L. & Jayaprakash, C. (1999) Neural Comput. 11, 1595-1619. **CrossRefMedlineWeb of Science.**

[121] Singer, W. (1999) Neuron 24, 49-65. **CrossRefMedlineWeb of Science.**

[122] Tononi, G. & Edelman, G. M. (1998) Science 282, 1846-1851. **Abstract/FREE Full Text.**

Engel, A. K., Fries, P., Konig, P., Brecht, M. & Singer, W. (1999) Conscious. Cognit. 8, 128-151. **CrossRefMedlineWeb of Science.**

[123] Gusnard, D. A. & Raichle, M. E. (2001) Nat. Rev. Neurosci. 2, 685-694. **CrossRefMedlineWeb of Science.**

[124] Posner, M. I., DiGirolamo, G. J. & Fernandez-Duque, D. (1997) Conscious. Cognit. 6, 267-290. **CrossRefMedlineWeb of Science.**

[125] Davidson, R. J., Kabat-Zinn, J., Schumacher, J., Rosenkranz, M., Muller, D., Santorelli, S. F., Urbanowski, F., Harrington, A., Bonus, K. & Sheridan, J. F. (2003) Psychosom. Med. 65, 564-570. **Abstract/FREE Full Text.**

[126] Lutz, A. & Thompson, E. (2003) J. Conscious. Stud. 10, 31-52.

↵ † To whom correspondence may be addressed. E-mail: alutz@wisc.edu or rjdavids@wisc.edu.

Author contributions: A.L., M.R., and R.J.D. designed research; A.L. and N.B.R. performed research; A.L. and L.L.G. analyzed data; and A.L. and R.J.D. wrote the paper.

Abbreviations: ROI, region of interest; EEG, electroencephalogram.

Freely available online through the PNAS open access option.